Multicultural Consciousness in the Novels of Kamala Markandaya

Multicultural Consciousness in the Novels of Kamala Markandaya

Sudhir K. Arora

AUTHORSPRESS
Publishers of Scholarly Books

Worldwide Circulation through Authorspress Global Network
First Published 2012
by
Authorspress

Marketing
E-35/103, Jawahar Park
Laxmi Nagar, Delhi-110 092
e-mail: authorspress@rediffmail.com

Editorial
Q-2A Hauz Khas Enclave,
New Delhi-110 016
e-mail: authorspress@rediffmail.com

Multicultural Consciousness in the Novels of Kamala Markandaya
ISBN 978-81-7273-601-9

Printed in India at Srikrishna Offset Printers, Delhi.

Preface

Indian Writing in English is rich and varied in every form—be it poetry, novel, drama, prose or criticism. Indian Novel in English is at its pinnacle, and the credit goes to the trio—R.K. Narayan, Mulk Raj Anand and Raja Rao—in making it popular. In the post-Independence era, women novelists who are substantial voices have enriched the field by introducing the freshness in themes and techniques. Among the Indian women novelists of post-independence era, the name of Kamala Markandaya comes first, as she has pioneered the field and paved the way for the women novelists like Anita Desai, Nayantara Sahgal, Ruth Prawar Jhabvala, Shashi Deshpande, etc. She entered the domain of Novel with *Nectar in a Sieve* in 1954 and became popular by virtue of her talent. She is sometimes praised for the depiction of rural India, and sometimes criticized for presentation of obscenity in her novels like *Two Virgins*. She is a diasporic novelist who has penned eleven novels: *Nectar in a Sieve, Some Inner Fury, A Silence of Desire, Possession, A Handful of Rice, The Coffer Dams, The Nowhere Man, Two Virgins, The Golden Honeycomb, Pleasure City* and *Bombay Tiger* (posthumous).

Tagging a novelist in a particular image damages the author's creativity. To study a novelist from one perspective reflects the myopic vision of a critic. A novelist has also to be studied from other angles, which may equally claim for validity. Plurality of approaches is the right tool to assess a novelist. I strong feel that Kamala Markandaya's novels have to be studied for getting the new hidden dimensions. She is a novelist who can be studied from different angles. Hence, I have attempted to deconstruct her novels to trace out the fresh interpretations and the layers present in her novels.

Besides her traditional narrative techniques like 'First Person Narration', 'Third Person Narration', 'Third Person Non-Omniscient Narration', I have chosen 'Male Narration' and 'Bed-Narration' to prove my stance that her novels possess the fresh appeal for the reader who can carve out the image of her women through these innovative techniques. From the point of view of deciphering her mind and her art of narration, re-critiquing her novels is indispensable. Hence, I have taken this study to search out the numerous possibilities that her characters offer.

Shakespeare had to keep the audience in his mind and, hence, introduced the supernatural element in his plays. Kamala Markandaya had to introduce some of the touches, though not Indian in spirit, for the sake of the Western reader for whom, it is alleged, she wrote. But, notwithstanding, she has given a voice to her women and new vista for further explorations. Though she is not alive, her place in Indian Novel in English is secure.

Sudhir K. Arora

Indebtedness

Some papers included in *Multicultural Consciousness in the Novels of Kamala Markandaya* were published earlier in different journals and anthologies of repute. I acknowledge the graciousness of the editors and publishers of the concerned journals and books. I also acknowledge the stimulation given to me by well-wishers and scholars interested in Indian Novel in English.

University Grants Commission, New Delhi for providing financial help.

Dr. D.C. Chambial, editor, *Poetcrit* for his appreciable assistance.

Prof. P.K. Mukhopadhyaya for publishing the research paper.

Dr. C.L. Khatri, editor, *Cyber Literature*, Patna, for his promoting spirit.

Prof. K.V. Dominic, Editor, *IJPCL*, Thodupuza, Kerala for his appreciation.

Dr. Jaydeep Sarangi for his friendly suggestions.

Dr. Binod Mishra, IIT Roorki, for his encouragement.

Dr. A.N. Prasad, editor, *Unheard Melodies* for his friendly cooperation.

Prof. R.K. Bhushan for his literary assistance.

Dr. R.C. Shukla for his affectionate cooperation.

Dr. Shaleen K. Singh for his help in collecting material.

Dr. Sushma Sharma, Former Dean, for her love and blessings.

Prof. S.Z.H. Abidi for his guidance.

Sudhir K. Arora

Contents

1

Kamala Markandaya: A Snapshot

Kamala Purnaiya, whose pen name is 'Markandaya', came on this planet in Chimakurti, Mysore State, in 1924 in an affluent aristocratic Hindu Brahmin family. She enrolled for B.A. Degree in History at Madras University but could not complete her graduation (which she completed much later) because of her interest in writing and journalism. She took up the job of an army liaison officer for a brief period but left it for her career as a freelance journalist. During the years 1940-47, she worked as a journalist and social worker in villages. In 1948, she bade farewell to her native country and left for England where she married an Englishman, Bertrand Taylor. Besides novel writing, she also participated in other intellectual activities. In August 1973, she presented her important paper "On Image" in a seminar on "Socio-literature" at the East-West Centre Cultural Exchange, Honolulu. In April 1975, she was a plenary speaker on Commonwealth Writer Overseas at ACLALS Conference, Sterling, Scotland. She visited India from time to time but, alas, on Sunday May 18, 2004, she passed away leaving her daughter Kim Oliver and numerous lovers of literature behind her.

Kamala Markandaya, the first outstanding novelist of the post-independence era, registered her presence with *Nectar in a Sieve* (1954), a novel of 'Rural India', that proved to be the bestseller in the United States and, hence, became the Book-of-the-Month Club Main Selection. Since then, she has established herself as a class of her own by depicting patriotic and sacrificing feelings in *Some Inner Fury* (1955), husband-wife space in *A Silence of Desire* (1960), colonial cultural form of exploitation in *Possession* (1963), hunger and human relations in *A Handful of Rice* (1966), racial conflicts and forces of nature in *The Coffer Dams* (1969), crisis of identity in an alien land in *The Nowhere Man* (1972), sexual exploitation in *Two Virgins* (1973), British self-interest and reaction of Indian youths in *The Golden Honeycomb* (1977) and the possible harmonious relations of the East and West in *Pleasure City* (1982). A cursory glance over her career of 28 years spanning from 1954 to 1982 clearly exhibits her deep-rooted love for rural India, her keen and realistic observation, her female heart that feels for women, her perception of isolation and rootlessness in an alien land, her quest for self-realisation and her understanding of shifting landscapes from outer to inner reality as a result of change. Dr. A.V. Krishna Rao observes: "Kamala Markandaya's novels, in comparison with those of her contemporary women writers, seem to be more fully reflective of the awakened feminine sensibility in modern India as she attempts to project the image of the changing traditional society" (55).

Kamala Markandaya attempts to do justice to her female characters who explore themselves in the male-oriented society, which often creates hindrances on the path of their journey, that leads them to the world of 'Person'. Kit's points of view, "Certain domains belong to men alone, and Indian women learn early not to encroach" (*Some Inner Fury* 117) is counteracted by Usha in her reply, "Who ever heard of a revolution for man only? No, it's everyone. Men and women. They do belong to the same species" (*The Golden Honeycomb* 432). There is a certain kind of growth in her female protagonists who begin their journey from the traditional set-up to a modern one. What they do is done while living in the system. Arora writes in this connection: "Her feministic approach is of co-operation, not of confrontation, as she knows that there is no replacement model and ultimately a woman has to merge herself in this male world" (6). Her women are passing through the transitional phase which is neither too traditional nor too ultra modern. The journey from Rukmani who holds the flag for women taking initiative by coming out of the four-wall boundaries first to get provision from the village, and, then, to go to the city where she earns by writing letters for others, comes to an end in Valli who comes out from a traditional set-up to work as a sales assistant in the Shalimar Gift Shop and Emporium. Her women protagonists are not inferior to their male counterparts who realise their presence and their contribution not only in running the family but also in taking important decisions.

Some of her female characters are: Rukmani (*Nectar in a Sieve*), a determined lady who struggles against odds, Mira (*Some Inner Fury*) who is bold enough to take decision for her, Sarojini(*A Silence of Desire*) who makes her husband feel that he is wrong in doubting her integrity, Nalini (*A Handful of Rice*) who brings her husband to the right path with her love and care, Helen (*The Coffer Dams*) who makes him realise that he is wrong in his treatment to the tribal people, Vasantha (*The Nowhere Man*) who cooperates with her husband in moments of alienation and displacement, Saroja (*Two Virgins*) who in spite of being younger wins the favour resisting all the temptations and remaining a virgin, Usha (*The Golden Honeycomb*) who proves to be a fit companion and boosting force to Rabi in his fight against the British rule and Valli (*Pleasure City*) who has a will to do. Sudhir K. Arora traces out Markandaya's personality in her women characters. He states: "Kamala Markandaya uses novel as a befitting medium to reveal different facets of the image of woman and has shown her own self-definition and her emphatic identification with her characters. It is true to some extent that she, despite her strongest pretension to objectivity and high imaginativeness, is subjective and autobiographical, as she has derived nourishment for her novels from life as observed and experienced by her. Her women characters like Rukmani, Mirabai, Sarojini, Anasuya, Helen, Vasantha, Saroja seem to have been fashioned after the various facets of her crystal-clear personality" (5-6).

Kamala Markandaya's narrative techniques, with which she always makes experiments in order to have a desired effect, are worth mentioning for her concern for art and its expression. Her statement, "I do write and rewrite and polish endlessly.... I cannot tell you how I know, when to stop, having achieved the effect I wanted. I simply know that that is just right; and then I stop being haunted" (in a letter to Joseph 216), is the clear instance of her being conscious of her narrative techniques. Very honestly, Sunaina Kumar observes: "Kamala Markandaya's work, which is unfortunately uneven in quality, attempts a palatable blend of theme and technique. She is interested in both, the 'what' and the 'how' of narrative" (54). She has employed the forceful narrative designs for the fabric of her novels. The major narrative designs include: 'First Person Technique', 'Third Person Omniscient Technique', and 'Third Person Non-Omniscient Technique'. She has also used 'Stream of Consciousness', 'Interior Monologues', 'Dreams', 'Flashback', 'Recollection', 'Bed-narration' etc., which throw light on the different facets of her characters.

Kamala Markandaya has employed 'First Person Narrative Technique' in her two novels *Nectar in a Sieve* and *Some Inner Fury*. Rukmani in *Nectar in a Sieve* is the female protagonist who narrates the story with some nostalgic touches. Her story-telling through 'First Person Narrative Technique' impresses the reader who goes through the novel with the undivided attention. The narration is formed in circular pattern as the story ends where it began. In *Some Inner Fury*, the protagonist Mira narrates the story but with a difference as in *Nectar in a Sieve*, Rukmani is semi-literate and, here, the narrator Mira is a highly educated urban girl. Kamala Markandaya experiments in her next novel *A Silence of Desire* where she uses 'Third Person Omniscient Narration'. For the first time, the narration is through a male character Dandekar who succeeds in depicting the clash between faith and reason. Autobiographical mode is absent.

'Third Person Non-Omniscient Technique' is used in *Possession*. Here, the narrator is a minor character, Anasuya, who narrates the story of her friend Caroline. The technique is non-omniscient and, hence, the narrator's presence is not felt everywhere. The narrator Anasuya narrates the story very objectively like a reporter. *A Handful of Rice* is again in 'Third Person Narration' and the story is narrated through a male character Ravi, who tells the story of his life effectively. 'Third

Person Narration' is repeated in *The Coffer Dams*. But, now the novelist has moved towards the use of stream of consciousness. Regarding the technique of *The Coffer Dams*, Sunaina Kumar writes: "There is an attempt to experiment with a new narrative technique. With the gradual withdrawal of the omniscient narrator the experiencing characters take over. A preponderance of dialogue and scene are the result and yet the author's manipulating presence is still felt" (57).

The novel is mature on account of its narration and style. The language has become picturesque and symbolic. Uma Parameswaran calls the novel "a landmark in prose style" and speaks highly of *The Coffer Dams* stating: "Gone is the distance of third person narrative in favour of stream of consciousness technique which plumbs the emotional working of characters in a language that cuts clean and sure as a surgeon's knife" (165).

Markandaya has used 'Third Person Narrative Technique' in *The Nowhere Man* and the story is narrated through Srinivas's points of view. She has explored all the possibilities of narration through the touches of flashback. In *Two Virgins*, the narration is through Saroja who tells the story of her sister Lalitha and her experiences. The story is meandering and the plot is not well-knit. The village life is the focus of narration which has become a rather boring one. Sunaina Kumar, who is highly critical of the narrative technique of *Two Virgins*, writes:

> Markandaya's progress from *The Nowhere Man*'s elevated style and serious philosophy to *Two Virgins* is disastrous. There is neither social significance nor technical excellence in this collection of vignettes of village life. The narrative experiment of *Coffer Dams* is not repeated in *Two Virgins*. The setting here is a village in South India and the theme the loss of innocence and the approaching maturity of two sisters Lalitha and Saroja. Saroja is the medium through whose eyes events are filtered though she does not occupy the centre-stage in the story. (61-62)

The Nowhere Man is a successful attempt of Kamala Markandaya who has done a lot of homework before writing. To go through the novel is a new experience, and it succeeds well partly because of story and partly because of its gripping narration.

In *Pleasure City*, the narration is not absorbing; rather the reader is lost in the labyrinth of words. The sentences are incomplete. Verbs are missing. Connectives are not connected. The story part is missing and the main focus is on the Tully-Rikki friendship. M. K. Naik does not appreciate Markandaya's new style. He states: "The new style with its primacy of oblique and convoluted expression, tortured syntax and jerky sentence structure, however, does not make for easy reading" (238).

As Kamala Markandaya believes in the literature of social concern, her novels are sociological in nature. In her novels, she makes her characters, particularly her women, socially conscious. Social consciousness is woven in the texture of her novels. For this, she takes:

> the wheat of story and puts it into the machine of social set-up to get the flour of conflict. The conflict in the mind of her characters particularly women results in the dramatic element in her novel. It provides an outlet to the characters for the flowing of their inner feelings. Their person or identity comes to the fore through dialogues and conflicts in their mind. The male characters that speak of female ones show their attitude of possessiveness over them while it is the woman who unfurls a woman—the inner woman through her narration. (Arora 121)

The charge that she has neither vision nor depth against Kamala Markandaya is not wholly true. The difference is of approach. A thing if studied from one angle will not make a right evaluation. It may have other angles which may equally be valid. She recommends compromise, mutual understanding, and love for making an everlasting relationship. Through her women characters, she has infused stamina in women for struggling against odds and making themselves conscious of their identity. She is in-between the two cultures—the East and the West. She imbibes the best out of the two extremes. She is Western with Indian heart. She is the Vasantha (*The Nowhere Man*) who has the water of the river Ganga in the foreign land. She has covered almost the essential themes of life, viz., rootlessness, displacement, alienation, social reality, human relationship, East-West encounter, hunger, degradation, etc., in her novels. Hence, one can view the panorama of life in them. Human life depends on three fundamental hungers: hunger of stomach, hunger of sex and hunger of fame, and all these hungers are portrayed on her fictional canvas.

Kamala Markandaya is definitely "one of the most productive, popular and skilled Indo-Anglian novelists and a superb representative of the growing number of Indian women writing serious literature in English" (Hemenway 52). In her narrative techniques, she has introduced innovations which have made her an artist of high order. Her prose style is forceful with poetic touches. It seems that she is a poet in prose. When she describes a landscape, she becomes quite poetic. Sample the narration for smooth flow of the passage which has poetic impressions:

> Mangoes were ripening. Flocks of parrots settled in the trees and feasted. Amma congratulated herself. She had taken the first crop in for pickling before their arrival. The mangoes floated in brine. They were small and green, hard as marbles; saliva ran just looking at them, such was the power of salt and sour. The fruit on the trees were larger than fists, and softened by touches of gold. Sun–kissed, said Amma. She pressed her fingers to her lips...
>
> (*Two Virgins* 152)

The graph of Kamala Markandaya's career from *Nectar in a Sieve* (1954) to *Pleasure City* (1982) displays the ascending order in contents and techniques. Her narrative techniques have the different facets that highlight the characters particularly female ones focusing not only their outward personality but also the inner one. Through her male narration, she reveals some feminine characteristics which form the image of a woman from a man's viewpoint. The bed-narration is on the verge of pornography as it takes shots of the bed-scene particularly of the first night. Here she crosses the threshold of Indianness for the sake of the Western reader who takes much pleasure in seeing the nakedness of the Indian beauty. But, on the whole, she is a major woman novelist who has tried her best to imbibe the best from the East and the West. Her place as a serious novelist is secure, as she has given a new orientation to Indian Fiction in English.

Works Cited

Arora, Sudhir K. *A Study of Kamala Markandaya's Women*. New Delhi: Atlantic, 2006. Print.

Hemenway. *The Novel of India Vol. II. The Indo-Anglian Novel*. Calcutta: Writers Workshop, 1975: 52. Print.

Kumar, Sunaina. "Technique and Theme in the Novels of Kamala Markandaya." *Indian Women Novelists* Set II, Vol. II. Ed. R.K. Dhawan. New Delhi: Prestige Books: 53-69. Print.

Markandaya, Kamala. *Two Virgins*, 1973. Vikas Publishing House, 1975. Print.

____ *The Golden Honeycomb*, New Delhi: B. I. Publication, 1977. Print.

Markandaya in a letter to Margaret Joseph dated 9 Oct. 1976 quoted by Joseph in *Kamala Markandaya*. New Delhi: Arnold Henemann, 1980: 216. Print.

Naik, M. K. *A History of Indian English Literature*. New Delhi: Sahitaya Akademi, 1982: 238. Print.

Parameswaran, Uma. *Kamala Markandaya*. Jaipur: Rawat Publication, 2000. Print.

Rao, A.V. Krishna. *The Indo-Anglian Novel and the Changing Tradition*. Mysore: Rao and Raghvan, 1972: 55. Print.

2

First Person: Story Narration with Personal Touch

Techniques are the means which a novelist employs to make his or her work interesting and gripping. Kamala Markandaya has successfully used the narrative paradigms in her novels to give an outlet to her impressions and first-hand experiences that she got during different phases of her life. The very first narrative paradigm, 'First Person Narration' is often followed by all the novelists who feel quite comfortable in expressions and, thus, associate with the characters. It can be traced in Kamala Markandaya's two novels: *Nectar in a Sieve* and *Some Inner Fury*.

Nectar in a Sieve

The very first novel *Nectar in a Sieve* clearly displays Kamala Markandaya's knack in using 'First Person Narrative Design'. In this novel, the narrator is a village woman —Rukmani, who, being the protagonist, gives a vent to the feminine sensibility. The great advantage of this technique is that not only the novelist but the reader also associates himself with the character and, to some extent, is familiar with the character. In spite of being objective and impartial, the novelist becomes one with the protagonist Rukmani and makes her representative for expressing her point of view. She is at her best when she presents Rukmani's determination and will to fight against the odds. It seems that she is expressing her own struggle in England where in the beginning she faced odd circumstances and had to perform various jobs in order to earn her livelihood. The setting of the novel is the rural background, and Rukmani narrates the story with the rural touches.

But the novel does not remain untouched with the Western impressions that enwrap her language without her knowledge. She has attempted her best to present the Indian flavour but its practical effect is missing. Theoretically she succeeds in giving details of rural life but the reader's attention is diverted as, sometimes, he feels quite intimate with the native soil and, sometimes, he feels an alien like the novelist. Nevertheless, the novel presents a pathetic tale of a rural simple Indian woman who "never lost her faith in life or her love for her husband and children—despite her endless battle against relentless nature, changing times, and dire poverty" (quoted on the cover). In the words of *Christian Science Monitor*, she has done "a superb job in telling her story" (cover page) which "will wring your heart." (Associated Press, cover)

Before analysing the novel from narrative viewpoint, it is mandatory to know the story which runs thus: The protagonist Rukmani is the youngest of all the daughters—Shanta, Padmini and Thangam—of a village head man, who after losing his power and influence, gets her married to a tenant farmer Nathan. She has a poor impression on seeing her new home but when Kali tells her that Nathan himself has built it, she feels grateful. She befriends Kali, the wife of a tenant farmer like Nathan, Janaki, the wife of a village shopkeeper Perumal, Kunthi, and Old Granny who sells fruit and vegetables. She learns planting seeds, milking the goat and churning milk for butter. She plants beans, potatoes, brinjals and chillies and, in this way, contributes in adding income to the family. Despite her pregnancy, she helps Kunthi in her labour pain without caring for her mysterious attitude. Janaki admires her for her reading and writing while Kali mocks at it and also frightens her when her husband kills a snake.

A daughter is born to Rukmani. She names her Irawaddy. Nathan who longed for a son becomes indifferent but when Irawaddy calls him Appa at the age of ten, he starts loving her. When seven years pass, she becomes quite worried, and for having a son, she prays daily without any effect. She visits her mother who is under the treatment of Dr. Kennigton for T. B. Her mother introduces her daughter to Kenny whose treatment results in her pregnancy. Soon, a son is born to her and the birth makes Nathan happy. Both name the child Arjun and in quick succession, she gives birth to Thambi, Murugan, Raja, Selvam and Kuti. Ira now becomes a helping hand to her. As the family now needs more food, she sells her vegetables to Old Granny, a good old woman though Biswas, the moneylender offers her more.

The advent of Tannery proves to be a fatal one to the family. Rukmani smells a danger out of it but to Nathan and Kunthi, the tannery is good, as it will provide more opportunities. Ira who is growing up is not allowed to move where she likes. This control surprises her but she keeps mum. Old Granny finds a suitable match for Ira who is married according to the Indian custom. The monsoon results in rain and storm, which cause suffering and pain, as Rukmani and Nathan see their paddy crop being destroyed. Now they will have to live on salted fish, roots and leaves.

The tannery attracts the farmers who are ready to become labourers, as they have no other choice. Kunthi lures men and sells her body. Her two sons join the tannery and later Rukmani's sons Arjun and Thambi follow suit. Rukmani and Nathan who celebrate the festival of Dipawali with the children feel excited at bonfire and return happily to home, where they make love and enjoy sex after a long interval.

Rukmani feels anxious over the fate of her daughter Ira whose husband has left her because of her barrenness. One day, when Nathan has gone to attend the funeral of a relative, she avails herself the opportunity of meeting Dr. Kenny for the treatment of her daughter. Rukmani gives birth to her last child Kuti who proves to be a source of happiness to Ira.

Arjun, Thambi and Kali's sons are dismissed, as they go on strike against the employers' policies. Nathan favours his sons for fighting against injustice. Rukmani who is shocked at the decision of her sons' going to Ceylon for employment persuades them not to go but of no use. The drought destroys the crop and makes their sufferings deeper. Nathan and

Rukmani have to sell their household things to pay the landlord. Rukmani, who saved ten pounds of rice for difficult time, is blackmailed by Kunthi, who asks her to give her rice, otherwise she will let Nathan know her secret meetings with Kenny. Kunthi misrepresents the relationship of Rukmani and Kenny from a wrong angle—the angle of physical relationship. Poor innocent Rukmani is afraid and becomes Kunthi's victim. She is stunned when she comes to know that her own husband stole rice for Kunthi who had continued her relations with him even after marriage.

The store of rice is over. Now, they have to eat prickly pear, a sweet potato, a stick of sugarcane and, finally, eat grass. The youngest child Kuti asks for food in sleep. Death like a thief enters Rukmani's home and steals the life of Raja who is hit by the guard because of stealing a piece of skin. To save the life of Kuti, Ira sells her body but her self-sacrifice is considered as immoral. Rukmani has to accept Ira's ways. Her money keeps the family alive but her sacrifice fails to save the life of Kuti. Now, nature becomes favourable and blesses the fields with the rich crop. Nathan and Rukmani become hopeful and go to the temple where they worship the merciful God. Biswas lets Rukmani know that her benefactor Kenny has come. The comment that he knows about their relationship makes Rukmani angry. Now Rukmani goes to meet Kenny who has an ambition to improve the condition of poor Indian farmers. She informs about Ira's pregnancy. Selvam who does not like farming joins Kenny. It is Kenny who develops a kind of love-hate relationship with Rukmani and others. He does not like their surrender to injustice and suffering. Ira gives birth to an albino who is named Sacrabani. Old Granny dies of starvation. Kenny comes with food and medicine for Nathan who is suffering from rheumatism and fever. Because of his bad health, none goes to the city to attend the marriage of Murugan. A great shock comes to the family when Sivaji informs the family that the landlord has sold his land to the tannery. Two weeks are given to Nathan to vacate the land. Once again tannery becomes the source of trouble for the family.

Now Nathan and Rukmani decide to go to meet Murugan. Selvam takes responsibity to look after Ira and Sacrabani in their absence. After facing difficulties, with the help of Puli, they reach Murugan's dwelling place, where they meet Ammu, who informs them that their son has deserted her for gambling and other women. Now they bade goodbye to their daughter-in-law and children and take shelter in the temple. Nathan longs for his village where he wishes to die but he has no money for fare. Rukmani uses her learning and makes small money by writing letters for others. Rukmani gets inspiration from Puli, who in spite of being orphan and a patient of leprosy, is struggling. Following the advice of Puli, they work as stone-breakers and earn eight annas a day. Even in rain, they break stone but, on the seventh day, Nathan's condition becomes so worse that he becomes unconscious. People lift him and carry him to the temple. Nathan puts his head in Rukmani's lap and dies. Being alone and helpless, she returns with Puli to her village where she will get him treated in the hospital of Kenny. She introduces him to Selvam and Ira as her adopted son.

Divided in two parts with thirty chapters and one page of glossary of some Indian words, the novel *Nectar in a Sieve* begins with Rukmani's gentle nostalgia which presses the switch of her mind that displays the picture of the past:

> Sometimes at night I think that my husband is with me again, coming gently through the mists, and we are tranquil together. Then morning comes, the wavering grey turns to gold, there is a stirring within me as the sleepers awake, and he softly departs. (*Nectar in a Sieve* 7)

The very opening of the novel becomes the keynote which helps in peeping into the soul of Rukmani who feels a kind of tranquillity when she recalls that her husband is with her. Morning that brings hope to her stirs her from within when she sees him departing. Soon scenes come after one another and, finally, when she is in herself, she has no fear. "Yet I have no fears now: what is done is done, there can be no repining" (*Nectar in a Sieve* 7). She calls up memories of her wedding night and feels pain, as it was painful. 'First Person Narration' reveals her mental state regarding her first wedding night. "A woman, they say always remember her wedding night. Well, may be they do; but for me there are other nights I prefer to remember, sweeter, fuller, when I went to my husband matured in mind as well as in body, not as a pained and awkward child as I did on that first night" (*Nectar in a Sieve* 8-9). 'First Person Narration' mixes the third person statement in view when the novelist uses "they say" and "may be they do" and it provides juxtaposition to Rukmani who does not wish to recall her first night as they (people) do. She feels better when she is mature in mind as well as in body. As a child-bride, she feels awkward and pained.

Let me quote some narrative statements to highlight women characters in *Nectar in a Sieve.*

> It was my husband who woke me—my husband, whom I will call here Nathan, for that was his name, although in all the years of our marriage I never called him that, for it is not meet for a woman to address her husband except as "husband." (*Nectar in a Sieve* 9-10)

This narration reflects the image of the patriarchal attitude of the society particularly rural. Women are not allowed to call their husbands by their names. They are supposed to call them saying either husband (*patidev*) or their children's father (papa/apu etc.). Rukmani never calls Nathan Nathan but always husband as she knows that she is living in the traditional society.

Rukmani, who is accustomed to live in a big house, cries to see the mud hut where she has to live. But she never makes her husband worried about her assuring him: "No," I said, "I am not frightened. It suits me quite well to live here" (*Nectar in a Sieve* 10). She is overwhelmed when Kali informs that Nathan himself has built the hut without anybody's help. She tells Nathan: "Should I not be proud that you have built this house with your own hands" (*Nectar in a Sieve* 12)?

The following narration highlights Rukmani's inner nature that she values love more than the material things. She is a peace loving woman longing for a husband who sees beauty and provides her grain for hard times. Peace cannot live forever and is turned into disturbance at any slight change in circumstances. Sample the narration for revealing both—pleasure that gives her peace and pain that invades her life in the form of tannery:

> While the sun shines on you and the fields are green and beautiful to the eye, and your husband sees beauty in you which no one has seen before, and you have a good store of grain laid away for hard times, a roof over you and a sweet stirring in your body, what more can a woman ask for? My heart sang and my feet were light as I went about my work, getting up at sunrise and going to sleep content. Peace and quiet were ours. How well I recall it, how grateful I am that not all the clamour which invaded our lives late could subdue the memory or still the longing for it. (*Nectar in a Sieve* 12-13)

A change enters her life through tannery "in the twinkling of an eye" (*Nectar in a Sieve* 29). The tannery becomes the source of her undoing as it snatches her hut and the land. Rukmani narrates this loss in a pathetic manner. It is her heart that cries:

> This home my husband had built for me with his own hands in the time he was waiting for; brought me to it with a pride which I used to better living, had so very nearly crushed. In it, we had lain together and our children had been born. This hut with all its memories was to be taken from us for it stood on land that belonged to another. And the land itself by which we lived. It is a cruel thing, I thought. They do not know what they do to us. (*Nectar in a Sieve* 137)

Her emotional attachment with her home and the land reflects her concerns and sets her in an image of traditional wife whose roots are in the native soil. She struggles hard and helps her husband in increasing the income of the family. She proves herself that she is a "Karamyogi" or "Karyeshu Mantri".

She is quite aware of the male parameters in the male-oriented society where the first-born, if it is male one, is welcomed. When she gives birth to a female child, tears come out from her eyes though she does her best to gather herself. The narration reflects her mental state: "I turned away and, despite myself, the tears came, tears of weakness and disappointment; for what woman wants a girl for her first-born" (*Nectar in a Sieve* 19)? She names her daughter Irawaddy. In the beginning, her husband Nathan does not care for her as "he had wanted a son to continue his line and walk beside him on the land, not a puling infant who would take with her a dowry and leave nothing but memory behind" (*Nectar in a Sieve* 20).

Rukmani's narration reveals many prevalent wrong systems like dowry. The birth of a female child worries parents regarding dowry and also pain felt when girls leave at the time of marriage. Her saving money for Ira's marriage shows her foresight in meeting out the expenses for marriage. "Every month I put away a rupee or two against the time Ira would be married. So we still could not grumble" (*Nectar in a Sieve* 28). It is not the only concern of Rukmani but of every Indian woman. Besides dowry, physical beauty of the girl is also taken into consideration. Old Granny makes Rukmani believe that she will not have to spend a lot in Ira's marriage as "She is endowed with beauty," and "It will make up for a small dowry—in this case" (*Nectar in a Sieve* 40).

She meets Dr. Kenny and tells him that she has "no sons" and "Only one child, a girl" (*Nectar in a Sieve* 24). His treatment makes her able to give birth to sons. The birth of the first son makes Nathan and her father overjoyed: "My husband was overjoyed at the arrival of a son; no less so, my father. He came, an old man, all those miles by cart from our village, to hold his grandson" (*Nectar in a Sieve* 24). She is conscious of the value system of the society which never respects a barren woman and does not allow a woman to meet the man other than the husband or a close relative. To get treatment for Ira's barrenness, she meets Dr. Kenny in the absence of Nathan as she knows that her husband will not allow her to meet him. Her fear can be traced out in her statement to Dr. Kenny who asks her to come the next day: "I waited all day," I gasped. "I must see you. My husband will be back soon and then I cannot come" (*Nectar in a Sieve* 63). She is highly obliged to him because of treatment to her and her daughter's cure of barrenness. She has a kind of Platonic relationship for him and calls him her benefactor. She calls him 'lord' because she could get sons due to his treatment. That she has almost adorations for him is clear from the excerpt:

> "My lord, my benefactor," I cried. "Many a time I have longed to see you. Now at last you come," and I bent down to kiss his feet, shod as they were in leather shoes. He withdrew them quickly and told me to get up.
>
> "I am not a benefactor," he said, "nor a Lord. What ails you?"
>
> "You are my benefactor," I said stoutly, "Have I not five sons to prove it?" (*Nectar in a Sieve* 35-36)

Let me quote two excerpts from the text to assess Kali as a woman.

> Kali, big and plump, with ample hips and thrusting breasts, whose husband worked the next field to ours. (*Nectar in a Sieve* 11)
>
> ...
>
> You are Rukmani, are you not? Wife of the farmer Nathan. The whole village has been curious about you—heaven knows why, one woman is like another. The fuss your husband made! Why, for weeks he was as brittle as a bamboo before it bursts into flame! He built your hut with his own hands—yes, he would not even have my husband to help. (*Nectar in a Sieve* 12)

Rukmani's narration delineates Kali's physical personality in lively words: big and plump, with ample hips and thrusting breasts. She is homely with homely figure. When she meets Rukmani, she tells her about Nathan who built a hut with his own hands. Her statement "one woman is like another" reveals a kind of curiosity to see and meet Rukmani because of Nathan's affection for his would-be-wife. It also shows her inner patterns that reflect a kind of jealousy that she has when she sees Nathan's blooming of love in his heart for his would-be-wife. She feels that women are same and is surprised at "the fuss" Nathan has made by building the hut with his own hands without taking anybody's help. She is surprised at the changed behaviour of Nathan who was "as brittle as a bamboo before it bursts into flame." Hence, Kali is a simple village woman who is curious to know about the things around her and is very helpful in the time of need.

Kunthi is another female character who moves gracefully and looks "thin, slight girl". Rukmani finds her "quieter, more reserved" but she fails to understand why she is reserved against her. When she helps her at her delivery time, Kunthi asks her to go. In the end, she comes to know the reason of hostile treatment—the reason being Kunthi's relation with her husband Nathan. Both Rukmani and Kunthi differ on the issue of tannery. For Kunthi who does not wish to be called 'senseless peasant woman', tannery proves to be a boon as it has turned the village into a town. But, for Rukmani, it has spoiled the peace of the village life because of "noise and crowds everywhere and rude young hooligans idling in the street and dirty bazaars and uncouth behaviour, and no man thinks of another but schemes only for his money" (*Nectar in a Sieve* 50). How accurately and minutely, Rukmani paints Kunthi's physical features and the patterns of the behaviour that she notices in her! Sample the excerpt:

> I saw her head fall back, the thin sari she wore slipped from her shoulders. Then I saw that it was not tied at the waist but below the navel, like a strumpet's, and that she was naked below. Sandalwood paste smeared her swelling hips, under her breasts were dark painted shadows which gave them sensuous depth, the nipples were tipped with red. (*Nectar in a Sieve* 64)

Kamala Markandaya's 'First Person Narration' through her protagonist Rukmani presents Kunthi as a woman who considers herself superior to other village women because of her attractive figure that she uses as a commodity for earning money. Her dress and conduct show that she is a strumpet. As she has no scruple or qualm, she feels no hesitation in blackmailing Rukmani and Nathan. Rukmani's narration of Kunthi's breast, nipple, navel and hip create first-hand impression.

Kamala Markandaya peeps into inner psyche of her characters and reveals the waves that strike the mind. Ira, whose husband has left her because she could not give birth to a child, sees her mother's pregnancy with a feeling of jealousy which has a touch of hatred. Her mother's pregnancy reminds her own barrenness. Rukmani's words "As my pregnancy advanced she turned completely away from me. Sometimes I saw her looking at me with brooding, resentful eyes, and despite myself I could not help wondering if hatred lay behind her glance" (*Nectar in a Sieve* 65) narrate Ira's feeling of jealousy out of rivalry.

Rukmani has to adjust with the changes that occur in her life on account of tannery. Ira becomes a prostitute as she cannot see her brother dying of hunger. Rukmani has to accept the future and Ira's lot. While sleeping she finds herself "rebellious, protesting, rejecting, and no longer calm" (*Nectar in a Sieve* 66).

Rukmani is traditional in outlook regarding a woman's place which, for her, is with her husband. She does everything to console her husband and makes him relaxed. She becomes quite philosophic over the death of Old Granny who dies of hunger. She comments on her death and the way of the world that pays attention only when a person is dead. It is quite surprising as well as soothing to hear such meaningful words from the mouth of a village semi-literate woman Rukmani. Kamala Markandaya explores 'First Person Narration' and has the liberty to make her female protagonist her voice. Mark Rukmani's narration for philosophising over death:

> Once a human being is dead there are people enough to provide the last decencies; perhaps it is so because only then can there be no question of further or recurring assistance being sought. Death after all is final... . So it had been with my sons, so it was now with Old Granny,

> one day it might be the same for me, for all of us. A man might drift to his death before his time unnoticed, but when he was dead and beyond any care then at last he was sure of attention... . (*Nectar in a Sieve* 125)

The last page of the novel depicts the height of 'First Person Narrative Design.' Rukmani speaks through symbols and images which reveal her viewpoints of the journey of life. She believes in roots and no one can remain happy if one goes far away. When she returns to the village with Puli after the death of her husband, she feels the earth under her feet. Sample the narration:

> So good to be home at last, at last. The cart jolted to a standstill. I looked about me at the land and it was life to my starving spirit. I felt the earth beneath my feet and wept for happiness. The time of in-between, already a memory, coiled away like a snake within its hole. (*Nectar in a Sieve* 188)

The sight of the land gives food to her starving spirit. The jolting of the cart is the jolting of her experiences which she had in city and cart's standstill makes her life standstill finally leading her to peace. The time in between becomes a memory and like a snake, it coils away to take rest in its hole. The snake, its coiling and its hole are the symbols which represent the journey of her life. Rukmani's last sentence "It was a gentle passing," I said. "I will tell you later" (*Nectar in a Sieve* 189) is ironical. She tells Selvam that it was a gentle passing but she will let him and Ira know about life in the city later. She calls life gentle passing while the reality is that life in the city was quite disturbing and upsetting as it swallowed her husband and dreams. That's why she postpones saying that she will tell later while the fact is that she does not wish to recall those bitter experiences of the city.

Some Inner Fury

Kamala Markandaya also follows 'First Person Narrative Technique' in her second novel *Some Inner Fury* (1955). But here narration is refined—refined in the sense that now the narrator is an educated woman while in *Nectar in a Sieve*, Rukmani is a village woman who is semi-literate to the point of only reading and writing. Mirabai in *Some Inner Fury* narrates the story with effective touches as she, while narrating an incident, reflects over it. Narration becomes crystal clear through the reflective mind of Mira who narrates the story in a haphazard manner. The piece of cloth takes her into the past where she is found reflecting. Mark the first passage of the novel:

> I had not been home for a long time, and so I had forgotten the little silver box which lay in my cupboard which no one ever touched. A beautiful thing of filigree, with a raised design of lotus flowers which I knew was there, though I had to feel for it with my finger-tips, it was so worn away. I opened it, and inside was the scrap of material I saw torn from Richard's sleeve, from his upper arm where the flesh was like milk, and which I picked from the dusty when it was all over. The dust was still there—no reason why it should not be; not reddish hot and swirling madly as on that day, but faded in this sunless air and settled on the cloth in a fine greying powder. I trembled like a coward standing there, wondering if it would, and then the slow pain came seeping up, filling my throat with grief, flowing from throat to temple, I could feel it behind my eyes. I closed the box gently and put it away, waiting for the ebb; a little frightened that I could still be hurt so easily, that time should be so powerless to staunch that flow. (*Some Inner Fury* 7)

The passage illustrates some words that Mira has used for symbolising something precious about her life which she has locked in her memory. "The little silver box" is locked in the memory of her "cupboard" and in this bcx, there is "a beautiful thing of filigree with a raised design of lotus flowers". Mira uses the lotus that reflects the purity and also that drops of water cannot remain on its leave for ever though it may always remain in water—water of love. Through such narration, she makes the reader ready to go through the story of pure love and the last sentence proves her viewpoint. "Outside a wind was stirring; the reddish dust of car loosened by many feet, came swirling in, and at last turned to go" (*Some Inner Fury* 286). The wind comes and goes; the wind of love is stirred by the circumstances but finally it changes its direction. The drops fall down but water becomes the life of lotus that illustrates its indifference.

In the beginning of *Some Inner Fury*, Kamala Markandaya writes to make her stand clear: "In the struggle for independence in India non-violence was the rule. This book is based on the exception. No reference is, however, intended to any political party, past or present, even where specific names have been used." The statement clearly reflects that the novel is based on exception as it is set against the background of the 'Second World War' when the 'Quit India Movement' was at its height.

The fire of violence burns the love of Richard who belongs to the "ruler" class and Mirabai, the ruled one. Mirabai, though brought up in the Europeanised environment, believes in her Indian culture. She goes to the railway station to welcome her brother Kitsamy who has returned with his friend Richard. She welcomes Richard by presenting a garland and feels a kind of attraction towards him when she finds him imitating the Indian style by wearing a *dhoti* and *chappal*. She falls in love with him and goes to the club in his company. A gift from him makes her reflect and elated. The family plans for the marriage of anglicised Kitsamy with Premala who in spite of her roots in Indian tradition does her best to be ultramodern as her would-be -husband wishes to be. Kit who is posted in the state capital invites Mira to come asking her to avail herself of the opportunity of meeting Richard but the mother knowingly delays her journey so that she may not meet him.

Mira comes in contact with Roshan and is much impressed by her personality to the extent that she becomes ready to work for her paper. She is assigned to submit a report on a peasant resettlement in the neighbourhood. During this assignment, she unexpectedly comes in contact with Richard and the meeting ignites the old acquaintance turning into love affair. Premala adopts an orphan and makes herself busy in the progress of the school building. Govind who is accused of the burning the Gazette offices is rescued by Roshan through her swearing that he was with her. Though Mira is not married, she goes with Richard on a tour of the southern parts of the country enjoying life fully. Their romance is shattered when an acid bomb is thrown at Richard who was vexed at the posters meant for the English asking them to leave. Kit and Mira go to a party at the Government House but Kit does not feel good when he comes to know that Premala has gone to the village leaving a slip. Suddenly the power supply fails and a kind of scrimmage takes place with the natives who enter the hall forcibly.

Govind asks Kit about Premala and knowing that she has gone to the village, he advises them (Kit and Mira) to go to the village. But they are late as they come to know that Premala who was in the building was burnt to death by the terrorists who were supposed to be the associates of Govind. Kit turns to Govind accusing him of the death of Premala and rushes towards his car but is hit with a knife thrown at him among the crowd resulting in his death. Govind is charged with Kit's murder by Hickey, the missionary who says that he saw Govind throwing the dagger. But Mira swears that she had thrown her arms round Govind when Kit left the hut and, hence, the impossibility of his throwing the knife. As the natives start shouting the slogan, Govind is taken away. Mira associates herself with the crowd and leaves Richard behind.

First Person Narration offers a medium to the novelist who gives an outlet to his or her pent up feelings. Uma Parameswaran comments on the novel from this angle: "When I read it, I read it as a love story, and was duly carried away by the trials and tribulations of love, the possibilities and impossibilities of a happy ending. It is particularly moving because one assumes that some of its poignancy is due to an autobiographical element" (75). A curious thing can be noticed in this novel that the protagonist Mirabai leaves her lover Richard for the sake of the country while Kamala Markandaya leaves her country and marries an English man. Sometimes, Markandaya reflects her sorrow through Mirabai and the reader is inclined to connect an imaginary link with her life. It seems that she is correcting her mistake by making Mira leave the lover and settle with her countrymen.

Markandaya is the best cataloguer as her narration offers a telling depiction which evokes an image of the articles or things mentioned: "...the Club provided amenities such as no other place did, because there was a billiard room and a squash court and tennis courts which were infinitely better kept than the ones belonging to the Oriental Club, which a small group of Indians, tired of being black-balled from the English Club, has recently started" (*Some Inner Fury* 24). The novel is through the consciousness of Mira who goes to the clubs because of her training with the expectation of her marriage with a man of her class. "I went because I was taken; and to learn to mix with Europeans. This last was part of my training, for one day—soon – I would marry, a man of my own class who, like my brother, would have been educated abroad and who would expect his wife to move as freely in European circles as he himself did" (*Some Inner Fury* 24). The narration clearly reflects the future possibilities of her would-be-husband who would expect from her movement in European circle. Yet this type of training could not help her from feeling a traditional shy when she garlands Richard, the friend of her brother. "And yet the first time we meet I was so shy I hardly looked up until someone prodded me and I stumbled forward and garlanded him" (*Some Inner Fury* 8).

Mira wishes for freedom—freedom of thought and freedom of movement. In her exploration for identity, she has some doubts even when she goes with her lover Richard after crossing the threshold of tradition.

> Words which anyone might say to anyone, warned my wary suspicious self, instantly raising its guard against possible hurt, a formality, a courtesy, a manner of speaking, no more, but my other self, warm impetuous, unafraid, cried that these words for me meant more, much more—And I, the arbiter, placing the truth half-way between, found, even so, that the glow was not doused. (*Some Inner Fury* 91)

She believes that one can explore oneself only when one is free but fails to communicate it to the old generation that is deadly against the young ones with the feeling of possession. The forthcoming narration articulates her inability to convince the older generation though she votes for shared feelings and understanding—an understanding based not on reason but on instinct:

> It was more an instinctive understanding than a reasoned one: if anyone had asked me for an explanation. I should have been hard put to it supply a coherent one. But then none who belonged to my generation would have needed to do so, and to those who did not belong the sense and the spirit would alike have been incommunicable. It is this shared understanding, this common awareness, diffuse in the atmosphere, yet not absorbed by all, which makes the ground split, the crevasse to appear, between one generation and the next. (*Some Inner Fury* 189)

Philosophically she analyses her life and searches for choices that one makes in order to get peace.

> And it was our life, by our own choice, by being born when we were, even, if one were so minded by destiny. We created it, as much as it created us; belonged to it as much.... To keep our peace we would have to go back then to the world from which we come, to which we would always return because it was a part of us even as the earth was of these others who stayed, we could no more renounce it than a bird the air, or fish the sea, or any other creature its element.... (*Some Inner Fury* 192)

She is on the road that leads her to love and from there she takes a turn and chooses the thorny path that leads to the mature love as it is "a talisman that would somehow keep us together, protecting us against war, the world, everything" (*Some Inner Fury* 199). From mature love, she further traces out the way that leads to sacrifice—sacrifice for the sake of the country.

She explores her identity when she realises that in spite of love for Richard, she can not single out her people. She feels but fails to tell as "it was just beginning" and muses over the circumstances: "There is a time in one's life, they say, when one opens the door and lets the future in: I had the feeling I had done so, but had neither the power nor the courage to recognise the shape of things to come; and therefore I could not speak" (*Some Inner Fury* 218). She reaches the peak of love and feels that it is now time to go beyond this selfishness. She becomes one with the natives leaving her love behind. She states:

> ... it was simply the time for parting we had known love together, whatever happened the sweetness of that knowledge would always remain. We had drunk deeply of the chalice of happiness, which is not given to many even to hold. Now it was time to set it down, and go. (*Some Inner Fury* 285)

Before taking the decision, she thinks of her country that becomes more important for her than her love. The narration reflects the mental state of Mira who is passing through inner conflicts in her mind:

> Go? Leave the man I loved to go with these people? What did they mean to me, what could they mean, more than the man I loved? They were my people those others were his. ... and I know I would go, even as I know Richard must stay. For us, there was no other way, the forces that pulled us apart were too strong. (*Some Inner Fury* 285)

She believes in the thread that binds heart to heart and not merely body to body. She weeps inwardly and keeps mum before the world that is indifferent to such soft feelings. Sample 'First Person Narration' which reflects the controlled sentiments of the narrator who even talks to herself to convince her:

> It is all one ... . In a hundred years, it is all one; and still my heart wept tearless, desolate silently to itself. But what matter to universe, I said to myself, if now and then a world is born or a star should die, or what matter to the world, if here and there a man should fall or a head should break. (*Some Inner Fury* 286)

Kamala Markandaya has the unique knack to turn her "I" into "We" particularly when her characters are in love or when they are facing the ordeals of life. Let me quote first before making any comment:

> "We're alone," he said, holding me still. "Quite alone," and the skies were empty, the sands were bare, I listened and there was only the sound of the sea.
>
> "You see," he said softly, "there is nothing and no one. No one but us."
>
> Slowly my senses awoke and responded, the buds of feeling swelled and opened one by one. In the trembling silence, I heard the blood begin its clamour, felt its frantic irregular beat, then the world fell away, forgotten in this wild abandoned rhythm, lost in the sweep and surge of love. (*Some Inner Fury* 198-199)

This dialogue between Mira, the protagonist, and Richard state the spirit of "We" as he begins stating "We are alone", "quite alone" and attracts her making her ready to accept her for love rather physical one to explore the intensity which pierces her and she becomes ready to respond to the rhythm that she feels. The use of symbolical phrases like "skies were empty", "sands were bare", "sound of the sea", "buds of feelings" "trembling silence" and "surge of love" demonstrates the depth of intensity that fathoms such feelings that arise in the hearts when the lovers are alone. In depiction of such scene, Kamala Markandaya becomes quite poetic in mood. Such union binds the lovers more than ever. The spirit of "I" changes into "We" after such encounter and it seems that the novelist seems to make an attempt to reconcile the East with the West. Note the possibility of such reconciliation likely to occur in future:

> "I am so happy with you darling. You're wonderful to be with not just now, all the time."
>
> "I wish we could be together all the time."
>
> "We shall be, soon." (*Some Inner* Fury199)

Now come to the other character and let me see how far the following narration helps in forming an idea about Roshan:

> Born in one world, educated in another, she entered both and moved in both with ease and nonchalance. It was a dual citizenship, which few people had, which a few may have spurned, but many more envied, and which she herself simply took for granted. And curiously enough, both worlds were glad to welcome her in their midst. (*Some Inner Fury* 142-143)

In this narration, Kamala Markandaya has not used 'I' as it is narrated by Mira, the protagonist who sufficiently gives clues about Roshan that she must be comfortable in the two worlds—the East where she is born and the West where she has got education. 'Dual citizenship' is the right phrase that clearly reflects the personality of Roshan who is a liberated woman because of her nurture in the Western set-up. It is her love for freedom that she rebels and breaks marriage though she is on friendly terms with her husband. She feels a feeling of pride in going to jail and her remark to Mira shows her passion for political struggle against Britain. Mark the narration:

> Of course I'm not sorry! I'd rather go to the devil my own way than be led to heaven by anyone else. And I wouldn't give up being free like that for anything ...it hasn't always been that way— No, not even for me! (*Some Inner Fury*189)

She never follows the path that Govind has chosen for freedom. It is her faith that "There is no power in violence ...only destruction" (*Some Inner Fury* 126). She makes it clear to Govind stating: "Everybody is interested in freedom ... only, we do not all agree on the means to the end, as I think you know too" (*Some Inner* Fury 126). Mira appreciates Roshan's motivating force that persuaded her to follow her example. Very candidly she admits Roshan's influence on her:

> She gave me the chance to go and I took it; and though I left my home. I discovered at least the gateway to the freedoms of the mind and gazed entranced upon the vista of endless extensions of which the spirit is capable. (*Some Inner Fury* 71)

Now the next character in *Some Inner Fury* is Premala who with her "gentle and unassuming, and had tender pleasing ways" (*Some Inner Fury* 55) makes her place in everybody's heart except her husband who expects from her to be modern. Mira narrates her personality thus: "And Premala...? A lovely face, tenderly moulded, which never lost its tenderness because she could never learn to be tough" (*Some Inner Fury* 143). As she is a woman of compromising nature, she makes an adjustment in the world of her husband who wishes to see his wife in shorts, not in a sari. Keeping his liking in her mind, she goes to Mira to take shorts. Notice the passage for her modesty and shame that, like an Indian woman, she feels when someone (even though he may be her husband) looks at the naked parts. It also reflects that in the world of Kit there is no place for modesty.

> ... for she would have done anything for him- Premala came to borrow my shorts, put them in' blushing; blushed again, furiously, when Kit looked at her bare legs, for she had never worn anything but a sari. But this modesty, which is supposed to grace a woman, found little favour in Kit's eyes. (*Some Inner Fury* 53)

Mira notices in Premala a kind of innocence on her face while praying not once but several times. "Several times I saw her praying eyes closed, forgetful of the crowd, with that expression of desperate entreaty you sometimes see on the face of a small pleading child" (*Some Inner Fury* 72). She is religious to the core and whole-heartedly sympathetic to children. 'Goodness of heart' is a key through which she unlocks the gates of human beings. When she dies, she looks as beautiful as she always looks. Mira depicts her death: "But I could not believe she was dead. The feeling would not come, then I looked at her and she had always been beautiful and she was beautiful now" (*Some Inner Fury* 239).

These two novels *Nectar in a Sieve* and *Some Inner Fury* exhibit Kamala Markandaya's skill in exploiting 'First Person Narrative Technique'. This technique helps in delineating the first-hand impression well as everything is narrated only through the protagonist. It is the protagonist who presents other characters and only through her or him, the other characters are portrayed. This technique has its merits as well as demerits. The story narration is done well through this technique as one character narrates the story and, hence, the digression is least possible. The novelist gets a chance to make the protagonist say what he or she wishes. Its demerit lies in the fact that the reader misses others' points of view and has to confine his association with the protagonist. Rukmani in *Nectar in a Sieve* and Mira in *Some Inner Fury* have demoed Markandaya's viewpoints well. There are several occasions when they seem to be propagating the novelist.

Works Cited

Parameswaran, Uma. *Kamala Markandaya*. Jaipur: Rawat Publication, 2000. Print.

Markandaya, Kamala. *Nectar in Sieve*. New York: Signet Books, 1954. Print.

____ . *Some Inner Fury*. London: Putnam & Co., 1955. Print.

3

Third Person: Various Options and Liberty in Expression

Plurality of approaches is always welcome, as it offers fresh interpretations of the text and, hence, provides the reader various options for his understanding. Kamala Markandaya is aware of this, and so continues to experiment with her techniques. She employs 'Third Person Omniscient Narrative Technique' and 'Third Person Non-Omniscient Narrative Technique' after writing her first two novels: *Nectar in a Sieve* and *Some Inner Fury* in 'First Person Narrative Technique.' 'Third Person Narration' offers various options not only for the novelist who is at liberty in expression but also for the reader who gets various viewpoints that help him in forming his own attitude. Except *Possession* which employs 'Third Person Non-Omniscient Narration', She has used 'Third Person Omniscient Narration' in *A Silence of Desire*, *A Handful of Rice*, *The Coffer Dams*, *The Nowhere Man*, *Two Virgins*, *The Golden Honeycomb* and *Pleasure City*. Now let me discuss one by one to find out the usability of these techniques, and how far they are helpful in tracing out the trends regarding the fair sex and the contemporary landscape.

A Silence of Desire

The Epigraph "Three silences there are: the first of speech, the second of desire, the third of thought" (Longfellow) clearly reveals Kamala Markandaya's choice of the title for her third novel *A Silence of Desire* (1960) which displays the inner patterns of Saronji, a traditional housewife and her husband

Dandekar who, because of silence, suffer the torments and tortures of mind. The conflict of faith and reason creates a kind of space between them and speech is more desired than silence to fill the space. The blurb states:

> How men and women embroil themselves, and each other, by silence at times when their real need is to unburden their hearts! *A Silence of Desire* tells of Dandekar, a clerk in the 'new' India, who centres his whole peaceful life on his adored wife Sarojini, his love for her and their three children. They have never known luxury, but lead a comfortable life, happy in their mutual confidence. An evening comes when Sarojini is not at home; suspicions arise, confidence breaks—shocked and incredulous, Dandekar finds himself caught in the beginnings of a web of concealment, which he himself is soon helping to spin. Kamala Markandaya skillfully builds up a loving picture of a happy marriage in the India of today; and the tense situation that endangers it becomes a focus of ancient conflicts—science against 'superstition', religion against materialism, Eastern tradition against Western 'progress'. These are the forces that work on Dandekar and Sarojini, and the friends that surround them, as their unforeseen crisis develops.

The blurb clearly peeps into the novel and makes the reader ready for the story which runs thus: Dandekar, a clerk in a Government office is traditional in thinking on the sanctity of marriage in spite of his being Western outlook. He leads a happy married life with God-fearing Sarojini who begins her day with the worship of the *Tulasi* plant. One day when he does not find her at home; he is disturbed. Soon Sarojini comes and tells him that she went to meet her niece Rajam. Dandekar is satisfied but when he meets Rajam who tells him that Sarojini has not met her for the last four or five months, the suspicious scorpion bites his mind. While searching her box, he sees a photo that makes him more suspicious. She tells him that the photo is of the music teacher whom he has never met. He doubts her fidelity and spies on her movements. Following her, he reaches the place where he finds his wife sitting before the Swamy who was blessing her with his hand on her bent head.

Dandekar is stunned to know that Sarojini has a growth in her womb. He persuades her to go to hospital but she has a kind of fear-psychosis because of her mother's death in the hospital. She has more faith in the healing power of the Swamy than that of the doctors. Her continuing visits to the Swamy result in her neglect of household affairs and three children. Dandekar, who is upset because of Sarojini's attitude, fails to complete the office work. The officer Ghose threatens him with dismissal if he does not pay attention to work. The tranquility is disturbed.

He is afraid lest his eldest daughter should go astray. He is sad to see the condition of his son Chandrababa who is devoid of his mother's affection. In his frustration, he starts visiting prostitutes. He pleads the Swamy for not allowing Sarojini from visiting but he does not make any promise. He shares his feelings with his boss Chari who asks Ghose to make enquiry the Swamy's activities. Ghose concludes that the Swamy is an imposter but the people are divided in their opinions—some praise him while some belittle him.

The Swamy who has become a controversial figure advises Sarojini for the treatment in the hospital and then disappears. Mental peace is restored in the family but he feels guilty when the dwarf makes him realise that he is responsible for making the people 'derelict' without the Swamy. He feels small and kicks the dented silver vessels gently aside and goes out into the street remembering his children 'Ramabai and Lakshmi' who "would be leaving school about now". With this recollection that "He would go and meet them, with the good news about their mother" (*A Silence of Desire* 224), the novel ends.

Kamala Markandaya has employed 'Third Person Narrative Design' but its use is confined to the viewpoints of Dandekar. "Everything is seen only through Dandekar's eyes" (Parameswaran 91). Sarojini's viewpoint is drowned in the flood of Dandekar's doubts and suspicion. The narrator seems to be experiencing what he narrates. The omniscient narrator keeps the reader engrossed so much that he is curious to know about the turning points of the life of Dandekar and Sarojini. Let me analyse the first paragraph which runs thus:

> The six rooms that they rented were built round a courtyard, a square of about eight feet with an uneven cement floor in the middle of which stood the divine *tulasi* that his wife worshipped. It was a small evergreen plant, crammed into bright and decorative brass in which it languished, surviving without health, but with a sharp imperious smell that made you forget its looks—a smell that clung to your hands until you had washed and scrubbed, and even after, and could haunt you if you did not pray. Dandekar did not pray to it, he was always careful to say; it was a plant; one did not worship plants; but it was a symbol of God, whom one worshipped, and it was necessary that God should have symbols, since no man had the power or temerity to visualise Him. (*A Silence of Desire* 5)

The very first paragraph reveals the clash between thinking *tulasi* as divine plant—a plant for worshipping and the *tulasi* as merely plant—a plant not for worshipping. The narration makes the reader see the difference between viewpoints of Dandekar who is rational and Westernised in his thinking and Sarojini who is deeply religious to the core. The geography of the rooms exhibits the divine *Tulasi* plant which is worshipped by Dandekar's wife. Dandekar thinks that one does not worship the plant which is nothing but only symbol of God. The statement "It was necessary for God to have symbols" reflects Dandekar's sceptic nature. When the novel comes to a close, Dandekar is found kicking the "fallen, dented silver vessels" and thinks that "Ramabai and Lakshmi would be leaving school about now" (*A Silence of Desire* 224). He smiles as he got back Sarojini from the Swamy and now he "would go and meet them, with the good news about their mother" (*A Silence of Desire* 224).

These two paragraphs exhibit Kamala Markandaya's use of vocabulary and style. Her use of words is unique as they take the reader to the world where he also experiences the experience of the characters. The news of Sarojini's return that Dandekar will share with his daughters Ramabai and Lakshmi who would be leaving school make the reader go through his inner mind. N. Ramachandran Nair analyses factors responsible for the upheaval in their domestic life.

Kamala Markandaya seems to stress the point that there are times at which one has to keep silence and times at which one has to speak. Indiscretion in this regard may be detrimental to the preservation of joy and peace. Dandekar and Sarojini are victims of such an impasse. The root cause of their prolonged uneasiness is their inability to speak out. (238)

Mark the narration that unfolds the traditional facet of the character of Sarojini: "a good wife, good with children, an excellent cook, an efficient manager of his household, a woman who still gave him pleasure after fifteen years of marriage, less from the warmth of her response than from her unfailing acquiescence to his demands" (*A Silence of Desire* 7). Here, the image of the traditional Indian woman is depicted. Sarojini is a good wife for her husband, a good mother for her children, a good manager who manages the household, and above all, a woman who obeys her husband without protest. The walls of her house speak of her religiousness. The pictures of gods and goddesses are seen on these walls. "These were all of gods and goddesses singly and in groups, tableaus that showed them holding court in their heavens, or worrying, or being miraculously born of the earth or the sea" (*A Silence of Desire* 11).

But the same Sarojini, who believes in the *pati-paremeshwar* image of her husband, becomes rebellious when her husband calls her a 'soiled woman' doubting her character. She is deadly against Dandekar's spying on her. She states angrily: "You listened to the office gossip and you spied on me" (*A Silence of Desire* 72). She rebukes: "But you have eyes. If you wish to see you can. See for yourself—there is nothing to stop you" (*A Silence of Desire* 73). She is shocked to note Dandekar's changed behaviour towards her because of doubts that he had regarding her character.

Sarojini tells him that she goes to the Swamy for the cure of growth in her womb. Dandekar is shocked to hear this and asks her why she did not inform him about it. She tells him very frankly that if she had told him, he would have not allowed her to go to the Swamy for healing. Mark the narration for her honest confession for not letting him know about her going to the Swamy for the healing touch:

> Because you would have stopped me going to be healed... You would not have let me be – no! you would have reasoned with me until I lost my faith, because faith and reason did not go together and without faith. I shall not be healed. (*A Silence of Desire* 87)

There is one more reason for not sharing the fact of her disease with her husband. She knows that her husband has the Western notion that is against superstitions. His reason will struggle against her faith. He will force her to go to hospital for cure while she does not wish to go there. She has a kind of phobia because of her mother's death in the hospital. She is full confident that only healing touch of the Swamy will be effective in her case. Mark the narration for not revealing the fact because of her fear of the hospital:

> Yes, you can call it healing by faith, or healing by the grace of God, if you understand what that means. But I do not expect you to understand—you with your Western notions, your superior talk of ignorance and superstition when all it means is that you don't know what lies beyond reason and you prefer not to find out .... And none is a disease to be cured and so you would have sent me to hospital and I would have died there. (*A Silence of Desire* 87-88)

The Swamy's leaving the place is painful to her but she has become strong enough to assert:

> I formed an attachment, it is broken, that is all. One must accept it .... It would be sinful to batter oneself to pieces because one refuses to recognise that another's life is his own. If the Swamy chose to go, it was his decision. One must accept it in good heart. .... He prepared us for his going, I realise that now though I didn't at the time ... perhaps because I did not want to. He said there must be no repining; she said, "He was insistent on that." (*A Silence of Desire* 217)

It is she who has learnt acceptance from the Swamy. Her face is calm and so is her voice. When Dandekar consoles her that she will be cured even without the Swamy, she very calmly informs that she is not afraid of the hospital as she has got the strength from the Swamy. "I'm not afraid now of knives or doctors; or what they may do? All will be well. He said so. Her face was confident" (*A Silence of Desire* 218). Saying so, Sarojini makes Dandekar realise that he has not got victory in ousting the Swamy, rather, she has got a kind of etherising effect that has made her fearless of the knives and the doctors.

In the struggle of 'Faith' and 'Reason', faith has got upper hand as it is 'Faith' that has given strength to her to accept 'Reason'. Though the story is not from the points of view of Sarojini, she is able to impress the reader through her presence as a traditional woman and also through her protest when the integrity of character is doubted by her husband Dandekar. But it is surprising to note that even after so many years of marriage, she could not take her husband into confidence regarding the faith in the healing touch of the Swamy. If she had taken him into confidence, the picture might have been different.

Possession

Let me begin with the blurb that is on the first page of *Possession* (1967 published by Jaico).

> Anasuya first meets the beautiful and willful Lady Caroline Bell at a party—"rich, divorced, well-born, said fashionable Indian society, concentrating upon essentials". Lady Caroline is used to getting her own way: and Anasuya, an Indian writer, watches without astonishment as the humble peasant-boy Valmiki, who expresses himself in painting, is suddenly swept away from his village and his ragged little family, to London, Caroline's luxurious house, and smart society.
>
> Are Caroline's motives purely altruistic, simply her patronage of an artist and the development of his talent? Valmiki is a person as well as an artist, and his apprenticeship in Western ways takes some unorthodox forms. He also thinks to have possession: the love of women younger than Caroline, for instance, or even the adulation of the scarlet-jacketed Minou, that living symbol of possession.

> The roots of Val's, too, grow close to the wise and ascetic Swamy, who first recognised his gift. The Swamy will bide his time; but the clash of wills is inevitable, and will bring destruction with it.
>
> Kamala Markandaya writes with the penetrating observation and true craftsman's use of language to which her readers are accustomed; she has woven threads of poignant and somber hue into the fabric of this dramatic story of contemporary East and West.

The blurb quite attracts the attention of the reader who grabs the book to satisfy his quarries regarding the truth of colonial possession over the natives on the plea of Whiteman's burden. Let me go through the story before discussing such questions and the narrative techniques. The story of *Possession* runs thus:

Possession, narrated by Anasuya is a story of Caroline and her possessiveness over Valmiki, a goatherd. The novel opens with a party thrown by ex-Maharaja Jumbo and, here, Caroline comes in contact with one of her Indian friend Anasuya who takes her to a village for *arak,* a south Indian wine, which she (Caroline) longs for. By chance while wandering in her drunken state, she meets a Tamil boy Valmiki who is gifted with the talent of painting. Discerning the painting potential and future possibilities of further exploration in him, she buys him from his parents to whom she offers five thousand rupees as a part of compensation for his services as goatherd. Before going, he wishes to take farewell from the Swamy and the *devas* in the cave in hills. Then, she takes him to London where she makes him learn the way of her class. There he comes in contact with Ellie, a twenty-year Jewish girl who suffered a lot at the hand of Nazis in concentration camp. He finds a kind of thread that binds him with her as he feels that "she still bleeds within" (*Possession* 84).

He paints her portraits to reveal her inner pain and gets peace in her company. When Caroline finds Ellie pregnant with the child of Val, she removes her as she wishes to possess him wholly. She forces her Tamil cook to write letters to Val on behalf of the Swamy who has still an influence on his mind. She exploits him sexually and makes him introduce to the fashionable world as an artist of high order by displaying his paintings. She makes a tour of U.S.A. and returns with success. Now she thinks that she has possessed Val thoroughly but is stunned when she witnesses Val attracting towards Annabel, a girl of eighteen. This is intolerable for Caroline who with the intention of getting rid of her shows the clipping to her about Ellie who was pregnant with Val's child. She incites him in the name of racialism so that she may leave Val who will repeat it after enjoying her sexually. She believes in Caroline and breaks up her relation with him. Being frustrated and crushed, he meets Anasuya and comes back with her to India where he remains unknown. He goes to the Swamy when he receives a telegram. Caroline who never accepts defeat goes to meet the Swamy and claims for Val who declines the offer. She challenges the Swamy stating that today he belongs to him but she knows that one day he will be hers and she will return to claim him. To the question of the Swamy whether the day will come, she retorts: "Of course it will come."

The novel *Possession* breathes in different environment as it does not use 'Omniscient Narration' rather it uses 'Non-Omniscient Narration' which has its positive points as well as negative ones. In this novel, Markandaya has given the weakest link by making Anasuya, a minor character narrator. She has attempted to narrate the story through Indian viewpoint. It seems that she needed an Indian character who could be well-versed in both cultures: East and West. The story mainly focuses Caroline's possession over Val, the Indian artist boy. The story would have been narrated better if she had made Caroline narrator. Anasuya fails to link the situations and the novelist has made her non-omniscient in real sense. The presence of Caroline is felt right from the beginning to the end of the novel. Sample the narration:

The First Paragraph:

> I first met Caroline Bell at a party in Madras given by an old friend of mine, an ex-ruler of one of the smaller states of India who now cheerfully eked out his existence on parties and a pension of seventy-five thousand rupees a year.

> She was the first person I saw as I entered the room, partly because she was magnolia white and stood out in a company that was divided between brown and brick-red, partly because of the attention she was already attracting with her English good looks which, a rarity in India, passed there for a transcend loveliness. But perhaps she was beautiful in her own right as well. (*Possession* 1)

The Last Paragraph:

> "There is still one thing," she said at length, equably, "to be taken into account: Valmiki is yours now, but he has been mine. One day he will want to be mine again. I shall take care to make him want me again: and on that day I shall come back to claim him."
>
> The Swamy's eyes were troubled: "If that day comes," he said.
>
> Caroline came of a breed that never admitted defeat.
>
> "Of course it will come," she said with a faint contempt. (*Possession* 232-33)

Both the first and the last paragraphs obviously reveal the presence of Caroline who is expert in making her figure everywhere. In the party, she attracts the attention of all through her English looks and, in the end, she declares before the Swamy that the day comes when she will come to claim Val. Both the excerpts exhibit her dominating nature and her possessiveness which reveal the nature of the colonialism.

Anasuya presents Caroline's personality stating: "She was supremely confident, born and brought up to be so, with as little though of fallibility as a colonial in the first flush of empire, as a missionary in the full armour of his mission, dogged by none of the hesitancies that handicap lesser breeds" (*Possession* 15). This narration displays her bringing up that is meant only to rule whether by hook or crook. She knows how to maneuver. She searches for the possibilities in Val and manipulates in possessing him. The forthcoming narration shows her triumph in winning Val as she puts her arm round him as a part of her possession. "Caroline must have known at once she had won for she put her arm round the boy, as it were taking possession of him in full view of his family" (*Possession* 20).

She puts the Indian boy into the Western setup in order to uproot him culturally. She feels pride in doing her best in taking the Whiteman's burden while the hidden motive is only exploitation. She narrates with a feeling of pride and satisfaction that she is her mentor. "I discovered him in a cave. Oh yes, a real one. In India. Hideously bare and uncomfortable, except for those superb walls. And Val of course" (*Possession* 125). This narration shows her pride and possessiveness. Whenever she fails to control Val, she calls this relation a kind of an old 'classic ailment', 'that England and India never did understand one another" (*Possession* 77). Very candidly she confesses her relation with Val stating: "We go out of way to meet, and we squabble every time we do. It's a sort of love - hate relationship, don't you think? Like the kind British and India used to have" (*Possession* 70). She does not like the spiritualism of the Swamy who is her rival for Val. She states furiously: "It's a seduction, spiritual if you like. There's no place for it in England. He ought never to have been allowed in" (*Possession* 143). She belongs to those people who "do not easily give up what they think are their possessions" (*Possession* 198). Her exploiting nature is well narrated by Anasuya thus:

> Possession. I thought appalled: attenuated form of the powerful craving to have, to hold, which was so dominating and menacing a part of Caroline; which left grey and ugly trail of human misery such as, horribly swollen but not unrecognisable, one saw stumbling in the wake of power societies and empires. (*Possession* 217)

Anasuya's narration reveals the inner nature of Caroline who outwardly poses to be the benefactor while behind the fair skin, there is a black layer of selfishness and possessiveness. This possessive nature is quite immune to the pathetic appeal and misery of human beings. Possession becomes the 'dominating' and 'menacing' part of Caroline's nature.

The story of *Possession* is narrated by Anasuya who is a friend of Caroline. Though she narrates the story as an objective reporter, she remains enigmatic to the end. Regarding the role of Anasuya, Iyengar points out:

> Perhaps Anasuya (or Kamala Markandaya) is trying to make the story of Caroline and Valmiki something of a parable of colonialism, the passing of one empire, and the current insidious movement of new-colonialism. (444-45)

It is Anasuya who makes Caroline realise that Val has a family which may not wish to leave him. "You forget," I said, "he may have a family. He may not want him to leave them. They may not want him to leave" (*Possession* 10). She understands human values and the human beings who are not mere the things of possession. She clearly states it to Caroline and refuses to help her in this matter. Mark the narration for Anasuya's boldness and candidness:

> I meant I was not going to help you. This boy is a human being, even if he's a goatherd and a simpleton. He's not a toy to be picked up now and discarded when something else takes your fancy. (*Possession* 10)

Anasuya is a good reader who deciphers the words imprinted on the inner screen of Caroline's mind. She reads her mind that has a fear of losing Val at the hands of the Swamy. Caroline considers the Swamy her real adversary. She wishes to possess what she wants and does not like anyone crossing her path. Note Anasuya's narration that reflects the inner patterns of Caroline's viewpoints:

> I think she saw him as in the end the real adversary the one who could, more formidably than anyone else who had crossed her path, show up for shadows her authoritative declarations of an austere disinterestedness in and a legitimate entitlement to the boy; and resist her taking and keeping possession of what she wanted. (*Possession* 104)

Ellie is the twenty-year Jewish girl who comes in touch with Val who feels one with her and portraits her on the canvas. She bleeds within as she has been "a victim of European crime in European confine" (*Possession* 73). Mark the narration for her hopelessness and helplessness. "She had no parents, no state, no passport, no papers none of those hollow stacking blocks on which the acceptable social being is built. Her one asset was that she was trained and fully experienced domestic help" (*Possession* 72). She feels at ease with Val who loves her. She is unknown to the feeling of love as she was to lie with men in the concentration camp where she was raped. To lie with Val is somewhat different. She becomes pregnant with the seed of Val. Raping is not raping simply; it is colonial suppression. Her pregnancy with the child of Val is a kind of freedom that she feels. Her death-wish makes the narration pathetic.

> "First time with Valmiki," she said carefully, "but in the camp it was every night. They came for us every night. In the beginning I would ask them to kill me but they only laugh ... it made it worse" "... I was too dry. Also after a few months were not women any more ... the flow stopped, we looked like men no flesh, no hair." (*Possession* 116)

Annabel, a girl of eighteen, is "small, slim, ordinary-looking: bright brown eyes, brownish-gold hair cut in ragged urchin style, the short spiky ends appearing all over her head" (*Possession* 189). This is the pen portrait of Annabel who wishes to lead a free happy life with Val. But she sees the world through the eyes of Caroline who separates them as she wants to have complete possession over Val. It is Caroline who washes her brain stating: 'Emotional,' 'Unstable'. Foreigners are. Dear Annabel, you must realise they aren't like us ...you would never be able to rely on one of them" (*Possession* 206). Under Caroline's impression, she breaks her relationship with Val and goes away without knowing the trap.

Kamala Markandaya's 'Third Person Non-Omniscient Narration' does not create impression which is created through 'First Person Narration.' Anasuya narrates the story but fails to make a grip over the consciousness of the reader who bewilders at switching over from the Eastern atmosphere to the Western one. Caroline represents the colonial image of exploitation and suppression. Her narrations unfold the layers of her mind displaying the concealed motives in the name of Whiteman's burden.

A Handful of Rice

The blurb of the novel *A Handful of Rice* on the first page states:

> In this extremely fascinating novel Kamala Markandaya has succeeded introducing a work of art which is compulsively readable and gratifying in a most complete way. It depicts the hard struggle of life in a modern city and its demoralisation. Ravi, son of a peasant, joins in the general exodus to the city, and, floating through the indifferent streets, lands into the underworld of petty criminals. He falls in love with pretty Nalini, and marries her against all odds. She tries to change his way of life, but fate conspires against him... and the story moves to a memorable and a haunting climax.

The blurb gives the reader a clue about the type of novel he is going to read. Before making any comment on the factors that make this novel a gripping and gratifying reading, it is mandatory to go through its story which runs thus:

Ravi who is loitering on the road enters Apu's house forcibly to escape from the policeman. He threatens Apu and asks him to provide food and bed. When he wakes in the morning, he finds himself bound in chain. Jayamma, the wife of Apu beats him so much that the blood comes out from his head. He lets her know that he enters the house like a ruffian in order to eat something. She pities and gives breakfast to Ravi who goes to meet his criminal guru Damodar and tells everything. Next day he goes to Apu's house and, after his permission, he approaches Kannan, the blacksmith who sets the bars right. He thinks of spending five rupees which Jayamma gave for the bars but decides to return. He returns four rupees and fifty paisa to Jayamma as only fifty paisa was spent on cement and Kannan charged no paisa for the bars. He sees Nalini who attracts him like a magnet. He is lost in his dream of Nalini and wishes to meet her on an equal footing. He recalls his relatives who left the village for the city which does not provide jobs even to graduates. Ravi goes to meet Apu but Jayamma who keeps a watch on Nalini, is not happy to see Ravi. When he brings orange crush and kola for her and Nalini, she allows Nalini to go to the stall first and, then, to the cinema in her company. Ravi writes to his father Ram who meets Apu to finalise his son's engagement. Apu bears the expenses of marriage. Now, Ravi meets Nalini on the first night and feels ecstasy, as he feels different with her though he had enjoyed women in the past. He breaks the knot of virginity and blood is seen on the bed.

After blessing the couple, Ram, the father of Ravi, returns to the village and Ravi comes to his daily routine. Ravi wishes to provide all the comforts to his wife but she is satisfied with her present status and like a good wife, asks him not to worry. She never likes anyone to call her husband vagabond. The late night return of Ravi and idleness of Puttanna worry Apu. Ravi, who goes to Memsahib's house with Apu, sees the luxuries which make him lusty for wealth. Puttanna and Thangam sleep with babies between them. A quarrel arises between Puttanna and Jayamma and Ravi has to intervene. Nalini is not ready to hear any word against her sister Thangam from Ravi. Thangam is supposed to give birth to a child. Ravi, who thinks of going to the park first, goes to meet Damodar who thinks that only riches bring respect. Thangam gives birth to a female baby. Ravi reacts to Apu's decision that Thangam will share Nalini's room but Nalini obeys. He feels happy at the news of the birth of a male child to Nalini. Ravi wants to be rich but Nalini once again makes him understand that the rich have their own problems.

Apu's illness becomes the concern of the family. Thangam's pregnancy is unwelcome to Jayamma. Apu is shocked when he comes to know that all his savings are stolen by Puttanna. Ravi blames Thangam but faces protest from Nalini. Surprisingly, Thangam keeps contact with Puttanna and leaves Apu's house to join her husband. Apu takes the betrayal to his heart. Apu falls ill and dies. Now Ravi has to take the responsibility of the family. He goes to the house of Memsahib but she becomes angry for the delay and also for ill-fitting of a blouse. Ravi returns and is much disturbed enough to raise quarrel with his wife Nalini whom he beats for the first time. In the morning he feels sad and finds that his son Raju is against him as he loves his mother. Nalini falls ill and is hospitalised. It brings a lot of financial pressure on his mind. Nalini gives birth to female twins. Ravi goes to meet the memsahib and beats the Durban who does not permit to meet her.

The tailoring profession does not provide him sufficient earning, as his customers are taken over by the other tailors. Loneliness makes him its own. When Raju asks him if he loves him, he replies positively stating that he is the first-born child. Jayamma regrets that she wronged her husband. Ravi goes to Damodar who suggests him to return to the village as he is of no use to him. Ravi is frustrated every inch and when his wife asks him not to meet, he loses control over himself. Then, he goes out to be relaxed and returns drunk. He does not find Nalini at home and, so, asks Jayamma about Nalini. She rebukes and looks in a strange manner that results in igniting the passion in Ravi who suddenly rapes her. He feels sorry for the immoral act but Jayamma takes it indifferently. Raju falls ill and dies. His death is the shock that becomes unbearable to Ravi who loses not only faith in himself but also balance of his mind. He joins a crowd that is raiding a godown for rice. He takes a jagged brick but hesitates to throw it at the Nabobs' Row as he feels "the strength that had inflamed him, the strength of a suppressed, laminated anger, ebbed as quickly as it had risen."

In *A Handful of Rice*, Kamala Markandaya uses 'Third Person Narration.' The story progresses in a linear mode as the omniscient narrator narrates the story almost in a chronological order. The narration is not through a female character as is generally seen in her novels but through a male one—Ravi. Though the narration runs straight in a linear way, shots of flashback can be traced when the central character recalls the days of his village life. The novel begins with Ravi who is trying to escape from the policeman and ends with his indecision of not doing any violence because of his inner moral force.

It is Nalini who brings a change in Ravi's life. Ravi is attracted towards her as soon as he sees her and thinks that to have such a wife will make an end of all the troubles. He dreams of her and goes to Apu's house only to have her glimpse. He feels satisfaction even if he hears the "sound of her the swish of her sari as she whisked about the place at her mother's bidding or a glimpse of her sitting cross-legged like an inaccessible goddess in one of the inner rooms" (*A Handful of Rice* 34). After marriage, she makes him realise that peace is more valuable than wealth. She never runs after the city life which is full of pomp and show. She never demands for higher things which cost money. She is content with what she has.

> You are getting high and mighty; putting yourself on a level with high-class folk. How can we ever be like them? Why can't you be content with what we have? (*A Handful of Rice* 75)

Praising Nalini, Iyengar writes:

> What is, however, astonishing is the woman's power of patient endurance, her inexhaustible capacity for love, her simple tenderness. The sisters Nalini and Thangam are the salt of the earth and the character of Nalini is exquisitely drawn. She is the sort that can redeem even an errant husband like Ravi. Fallible he may be, but he does not cease to be a credible human being, always more sinned against than sinning. (446-47)

Nalini's attraction turns Ravi from a vagabond to be "a respectable house holder, a decent citizen with a decent job and a wife to support" (*A Handful of Rice* 25). A.V. Krishna Rao observes: "... Nalini symbolises the subtle fragrance of life, a clean, healthy and traditional life. She promises "sweet life but demands hard and honest labour" (Rao 14). It is the voice of realism and sanity that speaks through her: "Such ideas. Do you think we are grand people? Is not this good enough for us" (*A Handful of Rice*77)? She is a self-respecting woman who cannot tolerate anyone to call her husband 'a vagabond'. The statement "I just don't want to hear them calling you vagabond again, that's all" (*A Handful of Rice*77) clearly reflects her sense of respect for her husband.

The forthcoming narration reveals her nature of rebellion. It happens only when her tolerance exhausts. She shares with Kumaran: "I try and try. I swear to you. I try but it makes no difference. He is angry with me. All the time I don't know why. I can't bear it any more" (*A Handful of Rice* 224)? She presents ideal—the ideal of good sister when she opposes her husband who is abusing Thangam and her husband for the act of stealing Apu's hard earned money. She defends her sister stating: "You blame her, what about him, stealing, taking what wasn't his is there no such thing as right and wrong. What's the matter with you that you can't see it" (*A Handful of Rice* 177). She is a good mother who takes care of her child Raju, and when he dies, she is shocked. Being a good daughter, she looks after Apu in his illness. Hence, she is a traditional woman who succeeds in every relation of life—the relation of sister, daughter, mother and wife while her sister Thangam is selfish and mean.

Jayamma who is the mother of a virtuous daughter like Nalini and also a wicked one like Thangam, is referred as 'a bitch', 'a sow', 'an old cow', 'a many goat' by Ravi who finds her morally degrading particularly when he hears such statement. "What for last night? Do you think I care about that? Who cares what goes on between four walls" (*A Handful of Rice* 223)? He asks her to pardon him for raping her under the effect of liquor. But she shows that nothing has happened to her and believes that none cares what happens inside the house. Her statement reveals that she is morally depraved and, hence, remains hungry for sex. After the death of her husband, she feels guilty conscious in her wrong treatment to her husband. She shares this feeling with her daughter and, to some extent, shows her redeeming feature. Sample the narration:

> "Perhaps I wronged him," said Jayamma staring queerly at her daughter. "He was a good man your father, perhaps I did him wrong ... but he was an old man you know, he seemed old to me even when married.... No matter, it is over." (*A Handful of Rice* 202)

In *A Handful of Rice*, Kamala Markandaya bids farewell to 'First Person Narration.' She succeeds well in presenting the narration through the consciousness of a male character. She has broken her earlier image of depicting through the female protagonist. The novelist has suggested the life of Ravi in village and avoided from narrating it directly. She has used parallels and contrasting techniques in order to provide maximum exposure to the characters. The contrast between the life of the village and the city has been highlighted through juxtaposition. The novelist has created an environment for Nalini so that her traditional qualities may get exposure.

The Coffer Dams

Kamala Markandaya has poured the old wine of East-West clash in *The Coffer Dams* where it is bubbling to the brim but, finally, the bubbles burst and it comes to its former level. Nagendra Kumar Singh considers this novel inferior in quality stating: "Large parts of this novel are virtually unreadable and contribute nothing by way of development of the plot or growth of characters" (164). But, Uma Parmeswaran opines that *The Coffer Dams* is "a turning point in Markandaya's maturing as a novelist" and further she adds: "Gone is the correct simplicity of earlier novels and in its place is a power rich in overtones and undercurrents; gone is the distance of third person narrative in favour of stream of consciousness technique which plumbs the emotional working of characters in a language that cuts clean and sure as a surgeon's knife" (168).

Before going into the analysis of narrative technique, let me go through the story which runs thus: 'Clinton and Mackendrick Co.' has been given a project to construct a dam. Clinton and Mackendrick who work for the project under stress facing the blasts of nature and the non-cooperation of the Indian technician and workers on an issue related to the dead body of the workers. Clinton and Helen are the happy couple and have an understanding of not intruding each other's boundary. Clinton who sees himself as a builder, "a man whose conceptions of concrete and steel his highly polished and perfected technical skills could translate into reality. Though what; or where, the pursuit of this reality led him had become a matter of indifference" (*The Coffer Dams* 8). His wife Helen who has a curiosity to know the tribal people and mysteries of the forest comes in touch with Bashiam, a tribal technician, who is known as '*Jungly-wallah*'. To materialise the bird trapping, she goes to jungle with Bashiam and there is attracted towards him resulting in their physical relationship. She meets the tribal chief who is not happy because of his people's inclination towards materialism.

Clinton accelerates the work which he has to complete any how before the monsoon. The steel man turns the workers into machine to execute his mission without allowing them any rest. Human considerations are not above his work. But Helen treats the people as human beings. Two accidents—first the death of Bailey and Wilkins and second the blast that tolls forty two lives—become the cause of postponing the work. Bailey and Wilkins are given the Christian burial. When the second accident occurs, Clinton who has to complete the project seems to be unwilling to stop the work and his statement that "their bodies could be incorporated into the structure" infuriates the workers who stop working.

Finally Bashiam takes the responsibility to recover the two bodies lying under a boulder. Clinton is informed that the crane that Bashiam is to operate has a fault in the lugs. But, he does not stop him from operating it as somewhere in his mind he has jealousy against him on account of his intimacy with Helen. Bashiam lifts the boulder successfully with the crane and the bodies are recovered but the jib of the crane breaks resulting in the accident that makes him cripple. Helen accuses Clinton for the accident. Millie runs into the jungle and is found in the hysterical state. The monsoon approaches, and the water level in the river is rising high. The tribal are in danger. Helen and Mackendrick run to the tribal chief who dies with the last words on his lips "When the ridges rise clear". Helen returns to Clinton. Bashiam, a cripple will go in search of another project. Mackendrick sees that rains are over and the coffer dams are safe. The project is completed and the Clinton's prestige remains unspoiled.

The novel *The Coffer Dams* with its 34 chapters scattered over 222 pages begins with "It was a man's town" and ends with the following narration:

> 'The monsoon is over,' said Mackendrick to Helen, also soberly, but enclosing her hand in two jubilant palms.
>
> They picked their way out, into the watery landscape and through the aftermath of storm to the river to look, and saw that the banks held firm and the water levels were falling, which was of moment to them. While others who looked, their concerns being different, saw only the coffers, whose formidable ribs rose bleached and clean in the washed air above the turbulent river. (*The Coffer Dams* 221-22)

The beginning indicates that it was a man's town that shows the domination of man while the end reveals that the monsoon is over. Kamala Markandaya always equips her characters with double visions. Their own viewpoints seem to bc right in their own way. Undoubtedly, she has made Helen strong but equally she has depicted the steel man Clinton. Uma Parameswarn states: "Markandaya's final identification is with Helen, but she has made Clinton strong enough to accept that his view is perhaps as valid as hers" (168).

Helen is like Kenny of *Nectar in a Sieve* as she also associates herself with the tribal people considering them human beings. She develops a healthy relation with them while her husband hates them and human feelings have no meaning for him. She is mature in matters of developing human relations. Mark the lines:

> It's nothing to do with age. I just think of them as human being, that's all. You've got to get beyond their skies, darling. It's a bit of hurdle, but it is as essential one. (*The Coffer Dams* 12)

She scolds her husband for showing indifference to the non-whites. "Don't human beings matter anything to you? Do they have to be a special kind of flesh before they do" (*The Coffer Dams* 105). She treats human beings as human beings, not as white or black. She believes that there is no yardstick that differentiates people. She thinks: "These people aren't different clay, they're like me, like people like me. What is for me, is for them, there's no other kind of yard stick that's worth anything" (*The Coffer Dams* 49). She wishes to be intimated with the tribal people and, for this, she searches for a man who may be well acquainted with them and also with the new technology. She searches such possibilities in Bashiam. With the passage of time, she develops a soft corner in her heart for him. She makes him assure that he is like her. Mark the narration for making Bashiam comfortable in her company:

> Look at me, I've never been a memsahib. You're not some kind of freak to me. We're alike, we're freaks only to the caste we come from, not to each other. (*The Coffer Dams*136)

She has an inclination towards the Indian spiritualism. She has a kind of hatred towards the Western civilisation which she considers oppressive and exploitive in nature. She considers that the European are arrogant people and do what they like depriving of others' rights. Mark the frankness in narration:

> Our world. The one in which I live. Things are battened down in it. Under concrete and mortar, all sorts of things. The land. Our instincts. The people who work in our factories, they've forgotten what fresh air is like. Our animals—we could learn from them, but we're Christian you know, an arrogant people so we deprive them of their rights. (*The Coffer Dams* 138)

She experiences oneness with Bashiam through sex and feels satisfaction which she never got from her husband. A sense of belongingness is breathed by her. It seems that the East and the West have become one resulting into harmonious relationship that will bring peace and prosperity. Sample the narration for the touch of universal inclusiveness that brings peace to her mind through the union with Bashiam.

> I belong, I'm not alone. Everything is a part of me, and I'm a part of everything. And just a pop-up card-board

> figure. ... And felt the release as spoke, a peace that was to do with her mind as consummation had been for her body, the fusion making her whole in a way that she could not recall having achieved before. (*The Coffer Dams* 139)

Kamala Markandaya has adopted 'Third Person Narration' in *The Coffer Dams* in a different way. It is different in the sense that she goes into the inner psyche of her characters by using the questioning words: 'Which' or 'Who'. No doubt, there are some passages that do not add to the story but such passages give the taste of poetry. She has used selective words that create images on the mind of the reader who sometimes is lost in the labyrinthine of poetic words. "Her syntax lends itself to following the meanderings of thoughts and feelings within the characters" (Parameswaran 165). Notwithstanding, the novel *The Coffer Dams* is Kamala Markandaya's mature work that fuses the Indian and British attitudes into a genuine tale.

THE NOWHERE MAN

Kamala Markandaya's *The Nowhere Man* (1972) is story of Srinivas and Vasantha who feel a kind of dispossession which creates space in their heart on their coming to England in pre-Independence era. While discussing the theme of the novel, V. Rangan states:

> Though the predominant theme of the novel is displacement, alienation, and a search for identity in alien environs, it treats of larger human relations rendering the work and interesting psychological study of human relationship as well as of the essential human loneliness. (186)

Kamala Markandaya employs the flashback technique in narrating the story of displacement and alienation. Srinivas, the protagonist who belongs to a rich South Indian Brahmin family is the son of an unambitious lecturer Narayan. His father being Indian remains a lecturer while his junior teachers who were Englishmen supplanted him. He is betrothed to Vasantha whose brother Vasudev hides in a box to escape from the police because of his participation in the National

Movement against the British and there he dies. His father though actively is not associated with the National Movement, goes to the college in khadi. During the Governor's visit, he annoys the authorities by singing one of those hymns that ordinary people sang in place of anthem. The Governor who brings his hand down firmly on Narayan's shoulder to keep him away from the distressing sounds is surprised to hear "take your bloody hands off my father" from Srinivas. Narayan is sent to lunatic asylum while his son Srinivas is blacklisted and now for him "there is no future here." Mr. Patt who is kind to the family makes an arrangement for Srinivas' passage to England. Srinivas marries Vasantha hurriedly in order to go to England where he establishes his spice shop as soon as he reaches there. He is blessed with two sons—Laxman who is an Engineer in the British Army and Seshu who is working as a navigator in the Royal Air Force. This is reel of his life story that moves very fast displaying the picture on the screen of his mind.

Srinivas acquires a house: 5, Ashcroft Avenue, South London. The house is named Chandra Prasad after the name of original house in India. Vasantha demarcates areas for Laxman and Seshu. They are English in their attitude because of their bringing up in an alien environment. They consider such sentiments foolish. After leaving the job of the Royal Air Force, Seshu becomes a lorry driver but unfortunately is killed in an air raid. Laxman marries an English girl named Pat from Plymouth and becomes a partner in the business of his father-in-law. He has neither time nor any desire to look after his parents. Vasantha who is suffering from tuberculosis takes to her heart the behaviour of Laxman who did not care for inviting his parents on his wedding day. Her hope of reuniting the family comes to an end when Laxman does not invite at the birth of his child. Such behaviour from her son completely tells on Vasantha who feels heart-broken and, finally, leaves the world for ever leaving Srinivas alone to suffer loneliness and alienation to the period that was now "a dust bowl of being. Empty. Without meaning. Scooped out, picked clean, no climbing up the slippery sides. A skull from which all matter had gone" (*The Nowhere Man* 40). He does not join the business when his friend Zanzibari Abdul Bin Ahmed who is leading a life of prosperity with his French wife, persuades him.

Mrs. Prickering, a divorcee, comes in contact with Srinivas and a few meetings result in a kind of friendship that becomes an outlet for their pent-up feelings arising out of loneliness. Srinivas invites her to his house which she turns into cosy and comfortable one and, to a far extent, she succeeds in providing the company to him. She helps him in raising his income by her suggestion of converting the house into small flats for the poor. Laxman comes to meet his father and is shocked to see Mrs. Pickering but soon his doubts are over. The racial prejudice in air due to acute problem of unemployment and housing as a consequence of war swallows Srinivas who is harassed by his racist neighbour Fred Fletcher. Mrs. Fletcher and Mrs. Glass are not happy to see a black Indian to be their neighbour living happily though Mrs. Fletcher is a changed woman after the death of her husband.

Fred who returns as a failure from Australia holds African and Asian immigrants responsible for creating such problems. Hence, with his associates, he tortures Srinivas sometimes by putting human excreta and sometimes by placing a dead rat on the door steps. Srinivas is passive and tolerates the abuses of Fred. Frost bites his feet when he returns barefooted. It results in leprosy. He is conscious that the disease will be infectious and so asks the people residing in his house to vacate without letting them know any reason. It is unbearable to Fred. He throws hot tar coal on him but is not satisfied. With his associates, he plans to burn the whole building. To materalise his plan, he enters the basement and when he moves to fix the fuse, the cross belt of his coat is caught in the wire of an old disused boiler. The fuse gets a spark resulting in fire and the black man who is silently watching all the activities slips away from there without providing any help to Fred who burns in the fire as he fails to free himself from the coils. Mrs. Fletcher also becomes the victim of fire as she enters the basement to stop Fred from his plan. Laxman picks the body of Srinivas who opens his eyes only to speak the last word "Constable Kent" and then he is declared dead by Dr. Radcliffe.

Kamala Markandaya has shown her knack in depicting the life of an Indian expatriate in England. She has followed 'Third Person Narrative Technique' and the story is narrated from Srinivas' viewpoint. She has put vigour into narration to make it forceful. Due to its forceful narration, it has become a classic and is considered one of her best novels. It has 42 chapters scattered over 312 pages begins with "There was a screen behind which patients dressed and undressed" and ends with the conversation of Mrs. Glass with Mrs. Pickering.

> "You mustn't blame yourself," said Mrs. Glass, sweating.
>
> "Blame myself," said Mrs. Pickering. "Why should I? I cared for him."
>
> "And, indeed, that seemed to her to be core of it." (*The Nowhere Man* 312)

Mr. Srinivas who remains uncared in England feels alienated and displaced and, in the end, dies. There is one lady named Mrs. Pricking who cares for him and looks after him well. The novel keeps the reader captivated to the tragedy of Srinivas, who like a tragic hero, struggles, suffers and, finally, dies arousing the readers' sympathy for him.

The Nowhere Man is a forceful novel that narrates the story of Srinivas and Vasantha who are "fairly typical Indian immigrants, carrying Indian habits, dress and beliefs to an alien land and living peacefully but without in any way assimilating the culture of their adopted country" (Parameswarn 187). Kamala Markandaya depicts Vasantha thus: "a pretty girl who wouldn't be prettier still if she were not quite so thin, but then who wouldn't be after she'd been through, poor child" (*The Nowhere Man* 129). She is a traditional woman who remains in touch with the Indian ethos. She is fed up with the life like gypsies and, hence, asks her husband to possess a house. Mark the narration for her longing for a house:

> There is no nomadic strain in us, that forces us to wander. Although it may well manifest in our children if we

> continue this vagabond existence." "... We will buy a house. "We", she said, "my family, have for generations been accustomed to living in a house." (*The Nowhere Man* 17)

When her husband owns a house No. 5 Ashcroft Avenue, she feels overjoyed. She thinks that her husband has achieved something in alien surroundings. Her joy can be seen when she says:

> At last we have achieved something. A place of our own, where we can live according to our rights although in alien surroundings; and our children after us and after them theirs. (*The Nowhere Man* 21)

No doubt, she has owned up a house but she has not yet adopted the foreign way of life as Indian culture is flowing in her blood. She wishes to return to her native country India. She shares with her husband:

> When I am better, she said to her husband, we must return to our country. There is no reason, now that India is free, why we should not. Nor, she said painfully, is there anything, really to keep us here any more. (*The Nowhere Man* 38).

She is imbued with Indian spiritualism and in her declining years she follows the way of detachment that leads to the state of Nirvana. Later, she becomes calm and detached. Sample the narration that reveals her detachment in her later stage of life:

> She was very calm, very lucid, putting her affairs in order in so far as she could, though with a certain detachment, as if the concerns and liaisons of the world had fallen into peace, if not insignificance. Yet they were close; closer perhaps than many couples, since there had been no alternative vines and supports to which each might have attached. "It has been" said Vasantha hoarsely, the breath from her ruined lungs coming up rough, "a happy marriage." (*The Nowhere Man* 39)

Mrs. Fletcher who is the mother of Fred, sympathises with Mr. Srinivas and consoles him stating:

> You don't want to pay any attention to Fred. He doesn't know what he's talking about. You've got as much right to live here as he has. More. Even if you weren't born in this country, Mr. Srinivas, you belong here, and don't let anyone convince you different. (*The Nowhere Man* 174)

It shows that Mr. Fletcher is sympathetic to Mr. Srinivas and is free from the stigma of racism. She has consciousness that ever guides her to feel guilty for the crime that her son Fred has committed by insulting Srinivas.

Two Virgins

"I did not like it (*Two Virgins*), and that it seemed like a pot-boiler a novelist writes between real novels" (Parameswaran 199) are the words that were shared by Uma Parameswaran during a conversation with Kamala Markandaya who "smiled, and said she had spent quite some time thinking about it, and rather like it" (Parameswaran 199). Kamala Markandaya's eighth novel *Two Virgins* (1974) created a hullabaloo among the literati who branded it a book replete with exoticism and called it a "disappointing novel as an artistic achievement" (Nagendra Singh 173) while on the other hand it got the coveted Asian Prize.

The blurb—"The story, set in a village in India, is timeless and universal one, of growing up, and of love and conflict between parents and children, and of the lure of the big city. It is through the gentle yet shrewd eyes of Saroja, younger daughter of Appa and Amma, that we view that family, their neighbours and their fortunes and misfortunes. We experience the girl's growing awareness of the adult worlds and of the slow but irresistible encroachment of new and material values on the ancient beliefs and old established relationships within the family and the village" —makes the reader mentally equipped with what kind of story he is going to read. With the characters, like Appa, Amma, Lalitha, Saroja, Manikkam's wife, Aunt Alamelu, Chingleput, Mr. Gupta and minors like, Manikkam, the boys (sons), Rangu, Jaya, Miss Mendoza, Lachu, Jaya, idiot carpenter Kannan, Anand, Perumal, the moneylender, the Kallars, Mr. Jacobs, Nalini, Miss Krishnan, Bundi, Miss

Subramaniam, Devraj, Shelvankar and Curly, the novel *Two Virgins* peeps into the female world where the growing girls share the experience related to sex sometimes with traditional fears and sometimes with bold excitement resulting on the verge of covert lesbianism.

The story of basic human experiences particularly at the stage of adolescence is revealed through the consciousness of Lalitha's younger sister Saroja who passes through ignorance to self-awareness regarding sexual matters. The traditional values of Aunt Alamelu and Lalitha's tragedy which work somewhere in her mind help in resisting her steps from temptation that appears in the form of Devraj and Chingleput.

Chingleput, an orphan who is named after a railway station where he was found, runs "the only sweetshop in the village" (*Two Virgins* 3). He calls all the boys younger brother and the girls 'little sister' except Saroja whom he calls by her name because "her mother sold him buffalo milk for his extra-special fried milk sweet" (*Two Virgins* 5). Manikkam wishes to sell his barren cow to the butcher but his wife who is fond of it does not consent. Being poor, his wife gets the babies of rich breast-conscious women sucked in order to have money. Saroja's father Appa who had been freedom fighter instils in his children a sense of understanding and unity. Lalitha asks Saroja not to look at her mother's naked body while bathing. Aunt Alamelu, who being a widow has no status, never crosses her younger brother Appa. Lalitha, who has status even without having no husband, is fair in complexion, and so is liked and loved by all while her sister, being plain, remains under shadow, and often becomes the victim of partial behaviour from Appa, who gets Saroja admitted in a simple school, and Lalitha in 'Mission High School', better known as 'Three Kings School' where Miss Mendoza, a Christian develops the character of girls especially the moral side.

While going to school, Saroja sees Lachu who "sits by the roadside stretching out his hands to the girls on their way to school (*Two Virgins* 19) and is frightened. No one dares to go to file a complaint against him because of the avoidance of the evidences in the court. At night, she hears the quarrel of Appa and Amma who finally become silent in quarrelling leading to the other noise of charpoy that creaks away because of the sex act in which they are engaged. Though she is disturbed, she feels longing for such knowledge. Lalitha advises her to collect some pebbles like *lingams* to work herself and demonstrates how it works. She calls Saroja "a sissy, a baby, a mooncalf, an ice cube". She complains for not having modern amenities like a fridge. A quarrel arises between Appa and Aunt Alamelu on the issue of joint family. Manikkam's wife sends an emissary "pleading a silver bangle to God" for the safety of her child suffering from smallpox. Amma complains that Appa, being an unofficial moneylender, gives money to all but he has never bought her a sari. Perumal, the moneylender whose "breasts were like a woman's" (*Two Virgins* 42) charges high interest and employs the Kallars as night watchmen refraining himself from being robbed.

Saroja sees her mother making amorous glances with the Sikh hawker. Lalitha learns playing on the flute from Jacobs. Jaya spreads a rumour about the pregnancy of the widowed mother of Nalini who innocently believes. Aunt Alamelu is shocked to learn this and tells Saroja and Lalitha that "a woman's good name is her most precious possession" (*Two Virgins* 53). Saroja chooses the lady's bicycle named 'Raleigh' and learns riding from Chingleput. Lalitha learns it from Manikkam's son. Saroja admits that she is a peasant "with stiff wooden limb". She sees Lalitha's body and finds her limbs bold and free. Lalitha asks her to be quick and to seize the opportunity to get anywhere. She wishes to seize the opportunity of becoming a film star.

Aunt Alamelu is against Lalitha's decision of becoming an actress as she considers it improper. The film director Mr. Gupta with his assistant Devraj comes to the village with the intention of making a documentary film. Several shots of Lalitha are taken and when she is asked to tend the buffalo, she refuses to be a cow girl. When filming is done, Mr. Gupta comes to say good bye to the family of Lalitha who executes a colam pattern in saffron and white. The design looks like a dove on a trellis in a garden. Amma frowns when she sees the dove, which is Lalitha's her own creation. When Mr. Gupta shuffles from his feet, the dove gets blurred. Tears come out from Lalitha's eyes when she sees her lovely dove destroyed. Whenever Saroja gets confused, she moves towards "the path that led to Chingleput's sweetshop which was her escape route" (*Two Virgins* 124).

Miss Mendoza celebrates Deepavali with Mr. Gupta and Lalitha in the big city. Mr. Gupta's statement from Lalitha's lip "I am a natural" confuses Aunt Alamelu. Jaya displays her breasts to Saroja who finds them "advanced by comparison, rounded and thrusting, whereas hers were hardly more than swollen nipples" (*Two Virgins* 129). Aunt Alamelu forces Lalitha to eat saying that she looks like "a wraith, like one of those starving wretches that came over the border after the Partition" (*Two Virgins* 132). Lalitha leaves the village for her spiritual paradise, i.e., the city without informing anyone. Appa is furious and threatens Miss Mendoza for introducing her to Mr. Gupta. A packet which has gossamer tube falls from the folds of Manikkam's loincloth. When Saroja sees it, he cries: "it's nothing, nothing for girls. It's for men, it stops babies, takes away the danger. It takes away the fun as well." She imagines the same gossamer for her father's jigger and mother's aperture.

Lalitha, who is disillusioned, returns to the village. Due to her frustration over pregnancy, she tries to commit suicide but Saroja comes at the right time and saves her from taking such action. Appa and Amma with Saroja and Lalitha go to the city to meet Mr. Gupta who shows his indifference and advises for abortion. After abortion the family has to move to the village but Lalitha disappears leaving a note that she will remain in the city as the village life suffocates her. Parents make a futile search and finally they become penniless. Saroja asks them to return to the village where they belong. Devraj lures Saroja but Lalitha's experiences and Aunt Alamelu's traditional values help her in resisting the temptations. When Saroja returns with her parents, she goes to meet Chingleput who clasps her but now she is bold enough to draw away from him. She mounts her bike and skims down the "the path that led past the fields to the house" (*Two Virgins* 250).

The novel *Two Virgins* begins with "Chingleput ran the only sweetshop in the village" (*Two Virgins* 3) and ends with "She could hardly see for the tears that were cascading down her face, she couldn't have told for whom they were falling, for her, or Chingleput, or for what was ended. For a while she didn't try. She thought instead of when she was older, felt the wind in her face and the tears drying as she skimmed down the path that led past the fields to the house" (*Two Virgins* 250). Chingleput is the sweet seller with whom Saroja shares her feelings. In the end, when she returns to the village, she goes to him but is quite surprised, rather shocked to know his intention through his organ that was "nuzzling her body" (*Two Virgins* 250) and his statement that "I am a man"(*Two Virgins* 250). She is not afraid as she has learnt through the experience of her sister Lalitha. With tears in her eyes, she moves towards the path that leads her to the house. She is disillusioned from the snares of Chingleput.

The story is in 'Third Person Narration' or 'Omniscient Mode' and is narrated through the consciousness of Saroja. Saroja proves to be a weak narrator in telling the story and the reader is more interested in Lalitha than in her. As she is innocent and simple, her narration equally reflects her innocence about the experiences related to sex. She fails to justify her own experiences and is dominated by her sister Lalitha who is active and vivacious. Her narration is loose and not compact. She harps on the village life and its description. In *Possession*, it is not Anasuya, the narrator but Caroline who dominates the scene. Here, it is not Saroja but Lalitha who steals the show. The title *Two Virgins* is mocking and ironical as in the end only one sister Saroja remains virgin while her sister Lalitha loses virginity at the hands of Mr. Gupta. It seems that Kamala Markandaya calls the other sister virgin as Lalitha gets her child aborted. The story is dispersed over 250 pages that speak not only of the contrast of the village life and the city life but also of the various experiences and wonder at the first encounter with the matter related to the adolescence.

Lalitha who is of fair complexion has a status and becomes the favourite of Apu who sends her to Miss Mendoza's school where character formation is the first priority. She is a pleasure loving girl who wishes to enjoy comforts of city life. She thinks that fridge is not a luxury but a necessity. Mark her words: "It's barbaric, not having a fridge, it was not a luxury; it was a necessity in a tropical country" (*Two Virgins* 26). She calls Saroja "a sissy, a baby, a mooncalf, an ice cube" (*Two Virgins* 25). She is "brave, braver than Saroja" (*Two Virgins* 26) but is terrified not of the ghost but of spoiling of beauty. "She would rather have died than have her beauty spoiled" (*Two Virgins* 37). She dreams of becoming the actress and wishes to make the world her "oyster". She shows her body to Saroja who feels it lovely. She asks Saroja to "be quick" and states: "You have to seize your opportunity before it passes you by; you have to be quick with your answers if you want to get anywhere" (*Two Virgins* 77).

Mark the narration for her happiness which knows no bound as she acts in the documentary film of Mr. Gupta:

> I am happy, I feel like a dove on the wing, I could soar away, away like an eagle to the topmost peak of the sacred mountain. She trilled about the place. She flitted gracefully, creating new dance patterns. (*Two Virgins* 105-06)

In this narration words 'dove', 'an eagle', 'sacred mountain' and 'new dance patterns' are of importance as they reveal the future prospect of Lalitha. Lalitha who is a dove will be caught in talons of eagle Mr. Gupta who will take her to the peak of mountain that will provide comforts and luxuries and with him, she will create new dance patterns through sex. To welcome Mr. Gupta, Lalitha makes a *colam* pattern in saffron and white, and on this design, she creates a dove. When Mr. Gupta shuffles his feet, the dove gets blurred. The blurring of the dove is the sign that indicates her future which she will have from Mr. Gupta.

Sample the narration for Lalitha's love for the city:

> It is my spiritual country, she said, it is my spiritual home. What is? asked Saroja. The City, said Lalitha, and my acting, it is all jumbled up in one bright parcel. How

> bright? asked Saroja. Do you think you will become a star? Who knows? said Lalitha softly. I would like to think so, she said, hugging Saroja tightly; I would very much like to think so. (*Two Virgins* 128)

Lalitha calls city her spiritual country and spiritual home. City is the place which will give her what she longs for. She thinks that she will become a star. In her imagination she is so excited about her acting that she hugs her sister tightly. She thinks that "a city does add a certain luster" (*Two Virgins* 157). When she fails to get any call from Mr. Gupta, she leaves for the city. She returns from there and shares her experiences of the luxuries of the city life. She tells Saroja:

> There were electric fans in all the rooms, said Lalitha. With regulators, marked form 1 to 5, 5 was full on. I always had them on 5, I loved the blades whirring around at top speed though it created havoc with his papers. (*Two Virgins* 163)

The speed at 5 shows her own speed that she wishes to have. This is the speed—speed of sex that Mr. Gupta plays on her and makes her pregnant. She tries to commit suicide but is stopped by Saroja. When her parents ask Mr. Gupta about pregnancy, he denies any responsibility stating that "Lalitha had flung herself at him, he had never been so petered in his life" (*Two Virgins* 219).

Markandaya's 'Third Person Narration' makes imagination clear to the extent that abstract become concrete.

The following is the best instance to be intimated with Lalitha through Saroja's interpretations. Saroja recalls one sentence of Mr. Gupta and relates it with the life of Lalitha to get conclusion about her. Sample the narration:

> Saroja remembered he had told Lalitha she was a natural soon after they first met. She had interpreted it variously—a natural dancer, a natural actress, a natural woman. Or had he meant a 'natural' harlot? (*Two Virgins* 221-22)

Saroja connects the word 'natural' with many things which are true to some extent. After abortion, Lalitha goes away as she cannot live in village where she feels suffocation. She leaves with a note tucked in her bedding. Mark the note for the information that she writes about her whereabouts:

> This time she had taken nothing with her, not even a rupee was missing. Her bedroll was stacked against the wall. She had scrawled a note, left it tucked in her bedding. It said she couldn't face going back to the village: it stifled her, her talents, her ambition. She intended to stay in the city where she belonged. She could look after herself. They weren't to search for her, which in any case would be a waste of time because they would never find her. (*Two Virgins* 236)

This narration amply underscores Lalitha's way of life that she wishes to lead so that she may get what she longs for. The city is the place which will give an exposure to her talent. She is independent and knows what is good to her.

The following conversation between the two sisters is the key to understand the moral character of Saroja:

> I wish I were you, said Lalitha.
>
> Saroja stopped singing.
>
> I too could be happy, said Lalitha.
>
> Aren't you? asked Saroja.
>
> Of course, said Lalitha. (*Two Virgins* 209)

Lalitha is depressed and disillusioned. She wishes to be like Saroja who is quite innocent and simple. Artificiality is quite foreign to Saroja. She is not happy but wishes to be happy like her. The conversation reveals that Lalitha is not happy as she has lost her virginity in the brightness of the city life which blinded her. It also reveals the goodness and nobility of Saroja who is satisfied with the life of the village where she sees the colour that "changed with the seasons. The tender green of new crops, the tiny shades of harvest, the tints of freshly turned earth" (*Two Virgins* 243). She has her roots that makes her identity while the city swallows one's identity. It is in the village where one knows:

> each grove, each acre, each homestead on it, who owned then and the names of the owners. You knew every pathway. No one could ever be lost, not by trying. The wells, the fields, each had its name; the well by the banyan, the field next to the mill. You always knew where you were. You knew who you were. The city took it all away from you. You were one in a hundred, in a thousand.... You might have been an amoeba. You drifted, amoeba-like. (*Two Virgins* 243)

This narration from Saroja clearly indicates the contrast between the village and the city. Hence, *Two Virgins* has become the vignette of the village. It is the ability of Kamala Markandaya who has shown Saroja in the village that provides spiritualism. Mark the difference between the sisters. Heaven of one is hell for other and hell of one is heaven for other. The life of city is spiritual for Lalitha who is wrong in her conception as it is the materialism that attracts her. Spiritualism is lost in brightness of materialism.

Saroja knows that Appa likes Lalitha more than her. "She knew Lalitha was borne in Appa's mind more frequently than Saroja, from the number of times he brought home presents for her but forgot about Saroja" (*Two Virgins* 26). No doubt, she has no ill-will against her sister Lalitha but sometimes she feels when she sees the double way of treatment. Appa gets her admitted in a simple school while her sister in Miss Mendoza's school. Lalitha is beautiful and so wishes that Saroja should be like her. But Saroja is conscious of her weakness.

> Lalitha wishes her to become active, vivacious and smart like her. She is conscious of her weakness. Saroja knew she hadn't, she knew she was slow, she was often compared with Lalitha on the score and found wanting. (*Two Virgins* 77)

While making comparison with her sister she finds her lacking in the charm. She calls herself a peasant with wooden limbs.

She feels that her sister has the magnetic personality because of her personality-pruning done by Miss Mendoza's school.

> Saroja had to envy her, had to admit by comparison she was a peasant, with stiff wooden limbs. She wondered if it was going to Miss Mendoza's school that made the difference, or if it all came naturally to Lalitha, who was so gifted; she concluded it must be a bit of both. (*Two Virgins* 64)

Some people learn from experience after losing something while some learn from others' experience. To learn from others' experience is wise and Saroja is certainly wise as she learns from Lalitha's experience. She remains a virgin in the whorehouse. She remains so partly due to the traditional teaching of Aunt Alamelu and partly Lalitha's experience. Devraj seduces Saroja but she comes out of the temptations because of Lalitha's experience and Aunt Alamelu's advice. Mark the narration for Devraj's temptation and Saroja's reaction:

> He came close. He touched her. Please, he said, Saroja leapt up. Her flesh was molten. She knew what he was asking. She knew where it ended. She had dragged her bloated gravid sister out of the bog; she had seen the bloody pulp of the baby. Take your hands off me, she cried ... what do you take me for, she screamed, a virgin in your whorehouse. (*Two Virgins* 245)

In the end, it is she who rejects Chingleput when she comes to know about his evil design for sexual exploitation. Her faith in Chingleput is lost. Now she has become quite strong enough not to be afraid. "Saroja was not afraid, she knew too much, she had gone through too much to be afraid of anything. She knew she wasn't for him, she would never be. So, she drew away from him" (*Two Virgins* 250).

The Golden Honeycomb

The Golden Honeycomb (1977) with a Prologue in the beginning and an Epilogue, a Note and Acknowledgement in the end is divided into three parts each having Epigraph. The text records a story of three generations of Rajas of an erstwhile princely state of Devapur so accurately with the dates and events that it has become "a saga, told by a master story teller—a modern saga." (Appaswamy, 63)

Quoting from the appeal of Lord Raddolph Churchil to the Members of Parliament, the Prologue speaks of India as the "most truly bright and precious gem in the Crown of the Queen" and the concern "to watch with the most sedulous attention, to develop with most anxious care, to guard with the most united and undying resolution, that land and the people of Hindustan" (ix). The rulers followed this doctrine and attempted to get victory over the princely states scattering all over India.

This novel is a bit different from the earlier novels as the story is not narrated from the consciousness of one character that always tries to see from one subjective lens. "There is no narrative presence except for the omniscient author. Briefly she might enter one or other character, but most of the time she is there as narrator. Thus, all the sarcasm and satire she pumps in are her own comments" (Parameswaran 227).

A cursory glance over the story will be useful in proving my viewpoint regarding the novel. The story runs thus:

In Devapur state, the ruler Bawajiraj I is deposed and imprisoned for his so called seditious activities. The Agent, an Englishman and the Dewan, a shrewd Brahmin serving the State as Chief Minister find a commoner *Kshatria* bearing the same name and get him enthroned as Bawajiraj II who will be a puppet in the master hand of the Britishers. Bawajiraj II with his wife Manjula drinks life to the full and a son is born to them in 1870. This son (would be Bawajiraj III) is provided education according to the norms of the British Government for upbringing and education of the princes of native states. This European nurturing results in his acquaintance with the English manners that turn him into a brown Englishman who will be an intercessory between the ruler and the ruled. The Prince is installed on the throne as Bawajiraj III on the death of Bawajiraj II in an accident while hunting. He marries

Shanta, the dull and sedate princess of the neighbouring state. As Shanta has given birth to four daughters, Bawajiraj III turns towards Mohini whom he wants to make his junior Maharani because of his son Rabi by her but she is happy with her state of being merely a concubine and so declines the offer. She is satisfied because she is free to provide education to Rabi according to her wish.

She, with the Dowager Maharani, injects the national feeling into the veins of Rabi and makes him proud of India and her culture. He comes in contact with commoners and their lives and becomes friendly with Janaki and Das. He likes Dewan for his welfare outlook and feels irritated towards the Agent for not allowing his father to act freely. He goes to Delhi Durbar (1903) which makes him disillusioned when he sees his father Bawajiraj III bowing down before Viceroy and walking backward like a lackey. He goes to Simla with the Maharajah and his mother Mohini. From Simla, they move to Bombay where they are to receive the delivery of a fleet of Rolls-Royce cars. When they reach there, they feel upset to see the storm in the city blown by the strikes of mill-workers and dockers. The Maharaja is injured in an accident but anyhow manages to reach the Imperial hotel and is looked after by Mohini. Rabi joins labourers on Chowpatty beach and is wounded while facing the police. Jaya, the mill worker who was leading a life of seclusion because of her husband's imprisonment takes him to her hut where she nurses him and satisfies him sexually.

When Rabi returns to Devapur, he is a changed youth. The nationalist feelings start bubbling in him and the Independence movement gets force. Like a true vassal, the Maharaja participates in the First World War and is compelled by the Resident to impose the salt tax in order to raise the revenue for war. But, Rabi along with Usha, the daughter of Dewan sides with the common people who are raising their voice against the tax. Feeling the pulse of the changing time, the Maharaja lifts the taxes. Sophie, the daughter of Mr. Copeland, is disturbed with anti-British feelings and leaves Rabi. Rabi feels emotional attachment with Usha and with her is lost in making future plans. The reader is informed that Rabi, who is different from his father, will do constructive things to ameliorate the state of the common men. He is quite sympathetic and has a feel for them. The victory (India's independence) falls to the side of Mohini, Rabi and Usha who have their roots deep in the Indian soil.

The novel is undoubtedly one of the best novels of Kamala Markandaya who has shown her talent in presenting a historical theme with the woven tapestries of words and sentences. But Nagendra Singh has a different view in considering the tapestries of words and sentences as non-functional to the extent that they create hindrance in the narrative flow. He observes:

> *The Golden Honeycomb* would have become a major literary achievement had the author not dissipated much of her energy and time in weaving tapestries of words and sentences and describing in great and boring detail, the pomp and show of the royal place, the Resident's and the Dewan's establishments, the trivialities of manners and idiosyncrasies of many characters who are only of peripheral interest, and many other things which in no way contribute to the development of the theme of the novel. The directness of purpose, the easy flow of the narrative and the lucidity of style that one finds in Markandaya's two major novels (*The Nectar in a Sieve and A Handful of Rice*) are missing here. (179)

Sunaina Kumar comments on the narrative techniques:

> The events of *The Golden Honeycomb* span nine decades and three generations of an Indian Royal family. The events are viewed by several reflectors which include the members of the royal family, the royal mistress, the British Resident and his wife, the Indian Dewan and his family members and occasionally even the lowly servitors. This technique has been eminently successful in conjuring up both a horizontal and vertical perspective. (64)

Its story is narrated in an absorbing manner and the dialogues that encompass the layers of thoughts can be dissected for throwing light on characters. The male characters are what they are made by the female ones. Margaret P. Joseph appreciates Kamala Markandaya for 'Third Person Narrative Technique' and observes:

> Instead of identifying with one character however, she maintains an impersonal stance that gives the impression of complete detachment and objectivity (98).

Manjula, Mohini and Usha are three main female characters who make Rabi red hot iron to hit the colonialism. Manjula favours the common people but remains helpless in the system. In the beginning she is shown a giggling teenager but with the passage of time, she becomes "mature manifestation of Shakti". Though ordinary in appearance and without the accomplishments of courtesan, she attracts the attention of the maharajah who "discerns and worships the very essence of the valley left behind" in "her flesh, in the fragrance of her hair and the depths of her eyes and in the cadences of her speech and voice" (*The Golden Honeycomb* 11). It is she who instils the mind of Rabi with Indian history and its culture. She asks Mohini not to marry Bawajiraj III.

Mohini is the concubine whom Bawajiraj III loves wholeheartedly. Rabi is the fruit of their love. She is satisfied with her status of being concubine as it will give her right to bring up her son Rabi as she wishes. She inspires Bawajiraj not to be a slave of the British who are "the civilised wolves" (*The Golden Honeycomb* 401). To her, Sir Arthur is only a bania sahib. The British are interested in their self-interest, not in the welfare of the Indian people. When Bawajiraj III asks her to be his Queen, she refuses to accept the offer of being a Queen. Mark the dialogues between Bawajiraj III and Mohini:

> I beg you. Will you not marry me?'
>
> 'No'
>
> 'It would make me the happiest man alive.'
>
> 'I can make you happy without that. I have no wish to be your second wife either.'
>
> 'Can you not think of the child?'

> 'I often think of the child. It is precisely because I think of the child.'
>
> 'I cannot understand your objection.'
>
> 'I've explained it to you.'
>
> 'I must say I find it difficult. Even princesses do not baulk at becoming junior Maharanis.'
>
> 'I am not a princess.'
>
> 'You could be a queen.'
>
> 'I don't want to be your queen. I want to be free.' (*The Golden Honeycomb* 32)

This dialogue clearly exhibits Mohini's upperhand over Bawajiraj III. He pleads to marry but she does not accept the offer. If there had been any other concubine, she would have accepted the offer. She knows if she marries and becomes Queen, she will leave all the rights over Rabi. Then, Rabi will be brought up by the English who will instil the English culture into his veins. She does not wish so and, hence, kicks the offer of being the Queen by marrying. Uma Parameswaran writes: "Hindu smriti makes mothers responsible for children's moral education, and Mohini does what Manjula was not allowed to do from within the system" (238). She votes for freedom and neglects the alluring offer of being the Junior Maharani.

Independence is flowing in her veins. She persuades Bawajiraj III to think of the natives who are being exploited and oppressed by the British. She succeeds in her efforts to some extent. When she finds Bawajiraj III showing fatherly affection to the natives, she feels delighted. Mark the narration for her praise for Bawajiraj III:

> For once in your life you are behaving like a father to your people. You're actually letting them keep a fraction of what's theirs instead of grabbing the whole lot for yourself and your *bania* friends. You ought to be pleased for their sake. (*The Golden Honeycomb* 465)

This narration also shows that she is a woman who loves freedom and also likes others' freedom. She appreciates

Bawajiraj III when she sees him on the right tract. She is rebellious in spirit and makes her son Rabi a rebel against the British. Uma Parameswarn observes: "Mohini's practical good sense makes her question everything, and once one questions, one has to rebel if the answer requires it and she rebels" (238).

Usha, who is revolutionary to the core cooperates Rabi at every step and plans with him for future. She goes in procession and meetings with Rabi. She participates in Non-Coperation Movement. She tells her father about it.

> 'It was like a revelation. We didn't believe, you know never really believed how much force there could be, if you trust yourself. But there is I've never felt like that before. So powerful. All of us. All the fright gone. They couldn't have touched us whatever they did. I think they knew,' she said, 'but they arrested us.' (*The Golden Honeycomb* 383)

Sample the narration for her enthusiasm for revolution:

> This is a revolution. Who ever heard of a revolution for men only? No, it's everyone. Men and women. They do belong to the same species. (*The Golden Honeycomb* 432)

She utters these words before her mother who asks her not to talk of revolution which is meant only for men. She retorts and justifies her stand with logic. Men and women belong to the same species. There is no difference between them. What a man can do, can also be done by a woman. Hence, she always talks of revolution and cooperates Rabi in order to give it a practical shape. To Rabi, she proves to be *shakti* that works with him hand in hand. Uma Parameswaran is right when she talks of these three female characters in terms of *Shakti* power. These three *shakti* powers shower their *shakties* on Rabi who is "anointed with three different kinds of *Shakti* power—from Manjula, the value of the past with all its stories of individual and national identity; from Mohini, the importance of resisting authority and fighting for one's rights; and from Usha, the personal fulfilment of walking hand in hand with someone whose intellectual acumen and political idealism would help him be a good ruler and good man" (240).

Apart from these three women, there is one more character that needs attention. She is Tirumal Rao's wife Vatsala. Mark the excerpt for her portrayal:

> She is a woman of forward fashion, though not in Mohini's class. She will not beguile her husband as the concubine is reputed to do, nor does she claim those freedoms that would establish her identity apart from him. But if she is content to live in the shadow of her husband, it is more form than substance that is conceded.(*The Golden Honeycomb* 116)

She works while living within her female circle, the circle which she never thinks of crossing. She is not the titular head of her household but even then she has a decisive grip. She is respected as "the acme of Hindu womanhood without having actually to endure its rigours" (116)

The Golden Honeycomb is indeed a forceful narration as it highlights the events with such effect that they reveal the innate nature of characters. This is the miracle of the genius of Kamala Markandaya who has created a historical atmosphere. It seems that she has done a lot of homework before writing a novel of such stature. Regarding the technical aspects of the novel, A.N. Diwedi writes:

> The technique of Kamala Markandaya in *The Golden Honeycomb* is one of forceful narration and occasional description. Her style reveals the person behind the work. It tells us a lot about the author's educational and cultural background and about her love of the motherland. She changes her scenes frequently, and each change is indicated by three asterisks. It appears as though we are sitting in a cinema hall, witnessing frequent changes of scenes on the screen. Sometimes a scene is a little lengthy, but sometimes it is very brief, say of barely four or five lines. (218)

What strikes the reader in *The Golden Honeycomb* is the way of narration. No doubt, sometimes, she offers the details that are not needed. But, the phraseology she uses is spectacular. Mark the excerpt for the use of language:

> Mohani is eating peaches on the terrace. Her sharp white teeth bite into the soft fruit, the juice trickles down her rounded chin. Bawajiraj watches her tenderly. It gives him pleasure to witness her pleasure. At the same time he is critical; he considers her earthy to consume with such avid enjoyment. He compares, unfavourably, her uncouth way with the fruit to his own. At this moment he is engaged in peeling a peach for himself. (*The Golden Honeycomb* 53)

Markandaya does her best to indianise the novel by using the Indian words like 'feringhi' (6), 'tamasha' (23), 'kumkum' (26), 'thali' (26), 'nam-ke-waste' (36), 'gaddi' (44), 'ashram' (47), 'dhoti' (60), 'ghat' (77), 'Bania Raj' (76), 'Chaprasi' (191), 'punkah-wallah' (195), 'izzat' (204), 'stridhanna' (214), 'bandobust', (241), 'goondas' (246), 'shabash' (267), 'lota' (273).

Pleasure City

Kamala Markandaya's *Pleasure City* (1982) seems to be a "dream world in which there are no barriers of caste, colour and creed and in which human values are supreme" (Bhatnagar: 15). Before analysing the techniques of narration in *Pleasure City*, it is crucial to know its story which runs thus:

By the sea shore, there is a fishermen settlement where Mr. and Mrs. Benjamin Bridie runs a school meant for the fishermen's children. Rikki, a student of Mrs. Bride is orphaned but adopted by Apu and Amma who take care of him along with their children Muthu and Valli. A multinational company named 'The Atlas International Development Corporation' (AIDCORP) founded by Herbert Boyle is launched with the intention of building a luxury pleasure complex Shalimar. This corporation never allows "private feelings to interfere with business" and, hence, it "built anywhere, everywhere, almost anything, for anyone, with a virtuosity" (*Pleasure City* 21). Boyle, Cyrus Contractor and Tully, the grandson of Sir Copeland are on the Board of AIDCORP. Apu, the headman has no objection if there is no harm to their water and territory. The villagers show their curiosity in observing the activities. Rikki continues to go to the school of Mrs. Bridie who, being childless, loves him and teaches him her language. But, soon,

Mr. And Mrs. Bridie die and Rikki is left alone. He often goes to Shalimar and one day he warns Tully against the danger of rocks in the sea.

As soon as Tully meets Rikki who is behaving well and speaking English, he sees the potential in him. Rikki serves as a tea boy but leaves this job because of the 'mackerel season'. When the mackerel season is over, he builds a boat for Tully on his demand and is paid amply. While working he wins the heart of the officials of Shalimar. Zavera, the wife of Cyrus Contractor takes the rein of Shalimar and makes the opening ceremony successful. Corinna, the wife of Tully, Mrs. Pearl, Mrs. Lockwood, Carmen, Mrs. Lovat, Mrs. Chari etc., come to join Shalimar and enjoy. To celebrate the birthday party of Zavera, they go for a picnic to the caves where they find an infant. Mrs. Pearl decides to be the foster mother of the infant and names it Kali in order to invoke the goddess Kali who protects. Corinna who feels bored in India is attracted towards Ranji, the young lieutenant. When the work is finished in Shalimar, Zavera thinks of celebrating 'An Open Day', the brainchild of her mind. Competitions like 'surfing event' become the attraction for all.

When the 'Open Day' celebration comes to a close, a storm bursts out. Rikki who goes to save Corinna is caught in the cross current and is badly hurt. AIDCORP provides the basic facilities to the stormed affected people. Tully decides not to go till Rikki recovers. Rikki feels happy when Tully gifts the boat. He goes to the graves of the Bridies to pay homage and becomes emotional as he still realises their influence over him. He recalls Mrs. Bridie's words: "There was a time, and a season, for everything. A time to sow, and a time to reap" (*Pleasure City* 341)

The novel *Pleasure City* begins with "The boats went out before it was light, the nets were down before the sun came up" and ends with "Rikki's step quickened. He would hurry, and get to Prospect point in good time, and settle down to watch. The views from there were matchless—not to be had from anywhere else, as he and Tully had often agreed" (*Pleasure City* 341). The beginning with such words 'boats' 'nets' 'sun' and ending with 'step' 'Prospect point' refer to things associated more with the male characters than the female ones and make the reader ready to go through the story of Rikki and Tully. The female characters direct the life of Rikki and Tully but remain only the bricks of the foundation in the Rikki-Tully building.

In the name of the story, there is nothing except the bundle of the episodes, however they are interwoven in such manner as throw light on the friendship of Rikki and Tully representing the orient and the occident respectively. In her last novel *Pleasure City*, Kamala Markandaya fails to spellbound the readers as she did in her first novel *A Nectar in a Sieve* but she has displayed her knack in assimilating two cultures through cooperation and understanding with the reciprocal mindset. In it, she talks of mutual understanding and wiping out of the misery of the past in the manner of Shakespeare who in his *Tempest* echoes forgiveness and reconciliation.

In *Pleasure City*, Kamala Markandaya does not appear to be a grasping story teller as she is in *Nectar in a Sieve* but now she does not talk of poignant heart-rending tale of Indian village, rather, she talks of human relationships or in a wider sense, of universal bond between the East and the West. The novel is not compact and intact; sometimes it is digressive and dispersed but, finally, all the threads are woven into the single whole. All the different episodes are the integral parts of one theme—the theme of synthesis between the Orient and the Occident.

Let me take first Mrs. Bridie who influences the life of Rikki and whose presence is felt even after her death. She teaches Rikki whom she makes him realise that food is not everything in life. When she sees the galled palms, she says: "Your hands will have to heal before you do "any more writing" (*Pleasure City* 12). What she wishes from him, is to do a thing worth doing to the point of perfection. "If a thing is worth, it is worth doing well. You must always aim to be immaculate" (*Pleasure City* 16). Mark the narration between her and Rikki for the relationship between them:

> He would have been like you, you know Rikki:
>
> 'Who?' He could hardly guess whom she meant.
>
> "If I had had a son:" she replied looking him full in the face. (*Pleasure City*16)

The narration exhibits that she longs for a child and showers her love on Rikki. In Rikki, she sees the image of her child. Her last words "If I had had a son" with her looks "full in the face" reflect her poignancy for not having a son. That's why she pours her love and affection over Rikki who always remembers "That – yellow stick – of—a woman" (*Pleasure City* 341). Her words prove to be *brahma vakayas* that guide him from time to time. Her valuable sayings like "There was a time and a season, for everything. A time to sow and a time to reap" (*Pleasure City* 341) always haunt his mind. Her saying "A time to sow and a time to reap" emits out the Indian fragrance of spiritualism. 'Universal Mother' is the right phrase for her as she loves all the children like her own.

"Call me Amma, if you like, she said, busy with the bellows and charcoal so as not it embarrass the child. I am your mother now, and lucky to be" (*Pleasure City* 9) are the words that amply throw light on Amma who looks after Rikki after the death of his parents. Like a mother she takes care of him. Her motherly affection can be traced out in these words: "Eat and grow up big and strong, so that you can master the sea" (*Pleasure City* 18). Like a mother, she wishes that Rikki should also be strong enough to master the sea. She makes no difference between her son Muthu and foster one Rikki.

"I'm a hopeless case I know, but I've always wanted to be able" (*Pleasure City* 139) are the words from Mrs. Pearl who is a hopeless case in learning swimming but in developing human relationship she is hopeful. When Rikki returns the money to this lonely woman, she asks him to take it because he has spent his time. She values time and links it with money. "Why not Rikki? Time; she blunted, is money. She did not think it was. Time was mysterious stuff, not an issue from a human mint" (*Pleasure City* 141). But when Rikki refuses, she takes it to her heart and utters: "Is my money polluted, or something?" (*Pleasure City* 141) Note the narration for her loneliness:

> So am I sure; she said, and rose above the fumes to even higher reaches of honesty and self knowledge. I'm old. I'm rich. I'm alone in the world except for one niece by marriage. It pleases me to give. Why can't you take? (*Pleasure City* 142)

This narration gives a key to unlock the heart of Mrs. Pearl who despite her riches is alone. To help others through money gives her pleasure. In the cave, she finds an infant and takes the responsibility of looking after it. She feels that she is not alone. She names it 'Kali' with the feeling: "Where she is, she's looked after" (*Pleasure City* 214). She pours her affection on Kali and thinks of taking the child to England. "And who knows", said Mrs. Pearl now and then, to Kali, or anyone else within hearing. One of these days I might even carry you off to England with me." And rocked and tickled the child under the chin lovingly, only half playing with the lovely, crazy notion" (*Pleasure City* 215). With the passage of time, materialism on the pearl is removed by the water of Indian spiritualism. She values more to Avalon than to Shalimar. It is clear from this narration that reflects her praise for Avalon: "Neither love, nor hate went into its fabric. Meticulously built for selling itself, it fulfilled that purpose. Shalimar went whoring after money.... Shalimar did nothing of the sort. Its wiles were more courtly, those of a courtesan" (*Pleasure City* 332). In the end, her stay in India changes her viewpoints. Spiritualism touches her soul and materialism becomes secondary.

Valli is a transitional girl because she can be called neither purely modern nor purely traditional. She likes Shalimar and tells Muthu who asks her the cause of her happiness. Mark the narration: "The matter with you, said Valli, making her shoulders as sharp and scornful, as she could, is that you are simply incapable of appreciating beauty" (*Pleasure City* 115). Very frankly Valli shows Muthu his real image and tells him that he is not capable of appreciating beauty.

Her body language, that is, making of her shoulder shows her superiority in considering herself better than Muthu who is ignorant to the limit that he fails to appreciate beauty. She loves Shalimar and wishes to be lost "among the flowers and lights and the gentry, within the crimson ropes of the cordon" (*Pleasure City* 115). She knows that she has a passable appearance but is quite conscious of the fact that she looks divinely beautiful when she dances. She shares with Rikki that dancing gives her pleasure. Sample the narration for her sharing with her foster brother Rikki who is better than her real brother Muthu:

> Because when I dance it gives pleasure to – to whoever is watching, and the pleasure, reflects right back. I dance divinely then and I know I look divinely beautiful too, although, she heaved a sigh, "really I'm only passable – pretty. (*Pleasure City* 129)

She works as a sales assistant in the Shalimar Gift Shop and Emporium. She loves to work and is satisfied with the job that she is doing. Mark the narration for the joy that she feels in her job at Shalimar Gift Shop and Emporium:

> I am as blithe as a bird. It's a pleasure to be here, I just love it.... It makes such a nice change after slitting fish open the whole of one's life; she claimed. (*Pleasure City* 129)

Corinna, who is the wife of Tully, has an inclination to art. She teaches Rikki how to paint and asks him to carry the equipments not like a coolie but like a scholar. She states: "Not like a coolie, Rikki I've told you before, like scholar, neatly, under one arm" (*Pleasure City* 131). Though Tully respects her 'Self', he is not satisfied with his marriage which proved to be of body, not of soul. It is not their hearts that meet but their bodies. Mark 'Third Person Narration' that presents their broken relationship:

> She shared his feelings, in more than one way. She too began to be conscious of distance or division. A sense of

> wedge between herself and her husband, more pronounced than she could remember, for she could not honestly pretend it had not manifested before. But hardened, while running alongside the incendiary unions that sequelled, as usual, their separation. The marriage is unsuccessful one. (*Pleasure City* 263)

This narration depicts the truth of their married life. Tully was conscious of a kind of distance from her. She also experiences it and very honestly she feels a kind of wedge between her and her husband. Mutual understanding is missing in their relation. She is obstinate as she goes for swimming in spite of Rikki's warning. Rikki saves her life throwing his life in danger. Later, she realises her mistake and feels sorry for Rikki. "I am sorry, Toby. About Rikki, I mean. It was unforgivable. I must have been mad" (*Pleasure City* 317). She is a weak link as she fails to make any relationship with any Indian. "She would never know Rikki, or perhaps the country he was bound up with, were equally outside her reach" (*Pleasure City* 318). Tully, when he goes to see her off, kisses her but the feeling of love is absent. Tully holds the country responsible for developing this coldness in relation. Sample the narration for isolation and alienation:

> When they kissed at the barren their lips were affectionate, but cool. So cool and unimpassioned that Tully momentarily rebelled, furiously charging the country with extracting its last pound of flesh; but as this was not true, as indeed he knew, the fury died even as it was kindled. (*Pleasure City* 319)

In kissing, they feel coldness. This coldness is the outcome of their misunderstanding but Tully holds the country responsible for this. 'Barren', 'cool' and 'impassioned' are the appropriate words employed by the novelist to depict their relationship.

Mrs. Contractor is the "brain wave" as she handles all the activities of Shalimar. It is she who has turned Shalimar into a world of its own and, with her cordial nature, she influences customers who are provided all the facilities for entertainment. Her managerial skill and strict control over her staff can be traced out in her statement which she utters before the staff-members: "If no one comes to Shalimar, let me tell you, you will all be out of a job" (*Pleasure City* 150). Her sociable nature is reflected in her treatment with guests who come to thank her. "Would you not do the same for me if I were a stranger in your country? No, no it is nothing it is simply do unto others" (*Pleasure City* 151).

Mrs. Lovat, a writer, who is writing a book about India, comes to Shalimar. She is much fascinated towards India as is clear from her narration to Rikki: "It is just that your country fascinates me. I'd like to find out as much as I can, that's all" (*Pleasure City* 154). It is Rikki who helps her in making her understand India. Her indebtedness to Rikki can be seen when she leaves India. "I want to finish my book. And don't be surprised; she said archly. If you find yourself in it" (*Pleasure City* 333). She feels much obliged and so promises that she will write about his help in the book.

The discussion demonstrates that 'Third Person Narration' gets upper hand over 'First Person Narration' but remains dry and uninteresting regarding the story telling which can be done best in 'First Person Narration.' 'Third Person Narration' does not provide an outlet to the novelist to project his or her personality. Women are seen from their own angles and not from anyone's angle. Here lies the greatness of Kamala Markandaya who has displayed her women in their colours so that they may be the role model to women.

Works Cited

Appaswami, S. P. "The Golden Honeycomb: A Saga of Princely Life in India by Kamala Markandaya." *The Journal of Indian Writing in English.* Vol. 6 No. 2. July 1978: 63. Print.

Arora. Sudhir Kumar. *A Study of Kamala Markandaya's Women.* New Delhi: Atlantic, 2006. Print.

Bhatnagar M. K., ed. *Kamala Markandaya: A Critical Spectrum.* New Delhi: Atlantic Publishers, 1995. Print.

Dwivedi, A. N. "The Golden Honeycomb: A Critical Appraisal." *Perspectives on Kamala Markandaya.* Ed. Madhusudan Prasad. Ghaziabad: Vimal Prakashan, 1984:208-220. Print.

Iyengar, Srinivasa K. R. *Indian Writings in English*, New Delhi: Sterling Publishers Pvt. Ltd. Print.

Joseph, Margaret P. *Kamala Markandaya*. New Delhi: Arnold Heinemann, 1980. Print.

Kumar, Sunaina. "Technique and Theme in the Novels of Kamala Markandaya." *Indian Women Novelists* Set II, Vol. II. Ed. R. K. Dhawan. New Delhi: Prestige, 1993: 53-69. Print.

Markandaya, Kamala. *A Silence of Desire*. London: Putnam & Co., 1960. Print.

____. *Possession*. London: Putnam & Co., 1963. Print.

____ . *A Handful of Rice*. New Delhi: Orient Paper backs, 1966. Print.

____ . *The Coffer Dams*. Delhi: Hind Pocket Books, 1969. Print

____ . *The Nowhere Man*. 1972. Bombay: Orient Longman (Sangam Books), 1975. Print.

____ . *Two Virgins*. 1973. Vikas Publishing House, 1975. Print.

____ . *The Golden Honeycomb*. New Delhi: B. I. Publication, 1977. Print.

____ . *Pleasure City*. London: Chatto and Windus, 1982. Print.

Nair, Ramchandran N. "Anatomy of Silence in A Silence of Desire." *Indian Women Novelists* Set II, Vol. II. Ed. R. K. Dhawan, New Delhi: Prestige, 1993: 238. Print.

Parameswaran, Uma. *Kamala Markandaya*. Jaipur: Rawat Publication, 2000. Print.

Rangan V. "The Nowhere Man: A Critical Analysis." *Perspectives on Kamala Markandaya*. Ed. Madhusudan Prasad. Ghaziabad: Vimal Prakashan, 1984: 186-197. Print.

Rao, Krishna A. V. "Continuity and Change in the Novels of Kamala Markandaya." *Perspectives on Kamala Markandaya*. Ed. Madhusudan Prasad. Ghaziabad: Vimal Prakashan, 1984:1-27. Print.

Singh, Nagendra Kumar. *Society and Self in the Novels of Ruth Prawer Jhabvala and Kamala Markandaya*. New Delhi: Sarup and Sons, 2005. Print.

4

Male Narration: Women's Passion

Narration is an art which needs labour to acquire. Kamala Markandaya is gifted with the art of narration. She has attempted all the narrative paradigms successfully. To explore the technical aspects is itself a technique that requires plurality of approaches. One vision will be partial. Looking through one vision may be right from one point of view. But none can shut his eyes from other approaches which may be equally valid for exposition and exploration. One may be right from one's own angle but the others' angle cannot be ignored. It is a fashion to search out the various facets of woman in the novels of a novelist, particularly when the novelist is a woman.

Studying woman from woman's angle is common. But, studying women from male narration is a new approach which is equally valid. If male narrations are taken into consideration, they may also be helpful in throwing light on female characters. If male narrations are properly deconstructed, they will themselves reveal what they think of women. In this chapter, some male narrations are deconstructed in order to trace out the forms of the image of women.

Nectar in a Sieve

Let me start with Kamala Markandaya's popular novel *Nectar in a Sieve* which is a story of Rukmani's struggle against the odds of life. "It is a thing that might happen to anybody," he said. "Do not fret. Come, dry your eyes and sit up here beside me" (*Nectar in a Sieve* 9). This statement of Nathan shows his innate goodness and his cooperative attitude towards his wife

Rukmani. He consoles her that every girl has to leave her house. He asks her not to worry and soothes her inviting her to sit beside him. The narration shows that Nathan has a kind of respect for woman and is mentally prepared to treat his wife as a companion. When Nathan is in a joyful mood, he takes Rukmani in his arms and raises her up. He shows her love before the onlookers and his happiness can be seen in his statement which also reveals the importance of Rukmani in his life. "I am happy because life is good and the children are good, and you are the best of all" (*Nectar in a Sieve* 61). Life seems to be good because of wife and children. He calls her the best of all. He states that it is due to Rukmani that life has become good.

When Rukmani tells Nathan about the young men who are eyeing Ira, Nathan becomes angry and says: "My daughter is no wanton...Not only men but women look at her, for she is beautiful" (*Nectar in a Sieve* 34). He is proud of his daughter who is beautiful but when he sees the same daughter parading at night, he asks her not to go. Ira replies that she will not let anyone die from hunger and for this she will parade. At this he loses his control and calls her "A common strumpet" (*Nectar in a Sieve* 103). Actually in society one who sells her body for any cause is treated to be a strumpet. When he calls her so, he wishes to show the mirror of the society where such woman is not respected.

Now let me quote four narrations to point out what a man thinks of a barren woman:

> "Mother-in-law," he said, "I intend no discourtesy, but this is no ordinary visit. You gave me your daughter in marriage. I have brought her back to you. She is a barren woman." (*Nectar in a Sieve* 54)
>
> ...
>
> "I have waited five years," he replied. "She has not borne in her first blooming, who can say she will conceive later? I need sons." (*Nectar in a Sieve* 54)
>
> ...
>
> "I do not blame him," Nathan said. "He is justified for a man needs children. He has been patient." (*Nectar in a Sieve* 54)

> ...
>
> "I would," he replied, with a hint of sorrow in his eyes, "for she was a good wife to me, and a comely one, but I have waited long and now I have taken another woman." (*Nectar in a Sieve* 65)

These four narrations clearly indicate one thing that only a fertile woman has a status while a barren one is treated like a barren land. Ira's husband comes to return Ira because she is a barren woman. He frankly tells Rukmani that he has waited for five years and cannot wait now. There is no guarantee that she may conceive. He needs sons. His statement "I need sons" shows his concern for growing his tree of his family and only son can continue it. He does not say "I need daughters". It shows the patriarchal nature of the society where a son is preferred to daughter. Nathan also considers his case right and does not blame him. His statement— "He is justified for a man needs children. He has been patient"— seals the way of the patriarchal society which allows a man to re-marry for producing sons. Ira's husband does not wait for long and takes another woman. A barren woman, however, may be good wife and comely one, is neglected and returned to the family.

Some Inner Fury

Some Inner Fury is mainly a narration of the love story of Mira and Richard but along with it, other plots are inserted. On the one hand there is love of Mira and Richard while on the other hand there is a pair of Kit and Premela whose chemistry does not tally. Mira and Richard, while loving, respect each other's identities. There is no possession in their case but in the case of Kit and Premela there is more of possession than of person. Mark the narration for a wide gap that he has made because of his incommunicativeness:

> Kit was equally incommunicative: there is a tradition, perhaps not only in India, that the best way to ensure this is to keep them as far as possible in ignorance and so now Kit insisted, blandly, that there was nothing to tell. (*Some Inner Fury* 117)

This narration takes the reader to the male viewpoint that it is better not to share with the women. Kit follows it and does not let anything know to Premela. He follows this tradition which does not allow even sharing with the wife. He believes that there are certain domains in which women should not interfere or encroach. He tells his wife nothing as he does not wish any encroachment on her part. In a very dominating tone, the forthcoming narration seals her points of view:

> Certain domains belong to men alone, and Indian women learn early not to encroach. Kit knew he would not have to remind Premela a second time. (*Some Inner Fury* 117)

It is Govind, the freedom fighter who puts a mirror before Kit in order to show his true image. He blames him for the death of Premela. Premela loved her husband Kit who never loved her. It is Kit who does not know the meaning of love. Mark Govind's narration that presents the insensitivity of Kit towards his wife Premela:

> "She loved you," he said. "You never loved her—you do not even know the meaning of love. You gave nothing—not even a home. You drove her to the village—you drove her to her death." (*Some Inner Fury* 240)

Kit is dominating and over-possessive to the point that he never offers to his wife what she deserves. His narrations depict his notion of the inferiority of women to men.

A Silence of Desire

A Silence of Desire is the story of Dandekar and Sarojini who desire to silence their queries but are themselves silenced because of misunderstanding which is responsible for digging a trench in their relation. When silence becomes communicative, misunderstanding is removed and harmony is restored in their relations. In the beginning, Dandekar is satisfied with his domestic life as his wife provides him all the essential things that are expected by him. Though he poses to be modern, he is traditional regarding the Indian women. He differentiates between Indian women and Western women when he says: "Our women are not like that. They do not flaunt themselves in front of men either before marriage or after. They are brought up differently" (*A Silence of Desire* 24).

Seeing a photograph, Dandekar becomes suspicious of Sarojini. He imagines: "A married woman did not have men friends who were not known to the husband, the family one of the girl's idols perhaps a teacher, a film actor" (*A Silence of Desire* 34)? He goes to the office and is much disturbed to hear the remark of Joseph that "Women are sly cats, you never know what they're going to be up to next" (*A Silence of Desire* 37). When he comes to know that Sarojini did not visit Rajam, he becomes more suspicious. The remark of Joseph about women tortures his mind and inwardly he experiences a kind of depression that makes him feel "dispirited, vulnerable, and somewhere around the perimeter of his mind, seeking entry, snuffled the thought: all women are the same" (*A Silence of Desire* 37). Under such impression, he calls his wife "a soiled woman" and spies on her. He expresses his anger before her: "Yes. And if I had watched you sooner, it would have been better for us, all of us, because a soiled woman is no good to anyone, not even to her children, do you understand that" (*A Silence of Desire* 71). Such narration is nothing except his depression which he feels out of insecurity.

Mark Dandekar's narration for his attempt to show his male supremacy:

> What were you doing? You say you, a married woman, were with this man in his house but you do not say why or what for. Am I not your husband, entitled to know? Or am I some kind of hireling gigolo to be told only as much as is good for him? (*A Silence of Desire* 85)

Dandekar who is suspicious of Sarojini's behaviour interrogates her. He makes her realise that she is a married woman who is not expected with any other man except her husband. He asks her what she was doing with the man. He makes her remember that he is her husband and being a husband he is entitled to know about her whereabouts. If she does not let him know, what is he to her? Is he only a hireling gigolo or libertine? The excerpt clearly reflects the dominating nature of Dandekar, who while living in male-dominated society, talks only of rights over woman. His jealousy is quite clear here as he cannot tolerate his wife with any man. It also reflects that Sarojini has not shared the secret with her husband. If she had shared, it would have been better.

When the same Dandekar comes to know the truth about the growth in his wife's womb, he feels stunned and wishes: "If only you had told me ... why could you not tell me" (*A Silence of Desire* 87)? He persuades her to get it operated but Sarojini has faith in the healing touch of the Swamy. He shares with Chari and tells him about his incompleteness without her. He asks her to relieve his wife from the talon of the Swamy. Mark the narration for his love for Sarojini: "My wife is part of me now—I did not realise it in all the years it has been happening, but I know now that without her I'm not whole" (*A Silence of Desire* 140). This narration shows that he loves her and without her he is incomplete.

Dandekar sees the world with the specks that he wears. He never tries to see his wife with her specs. If he had seen her through her specks, he would have not found her a soiled woman. The narration mode is better in this novel as it takes the reader into the mind of Dandekar. With Dandekar, he goes through the same experiences. The image that Dandekar offers about woman is partially true as he never sees the things from Sarojini's points of view.

Possession

Possession is the possession not only of talent of a young boy Val but also of his body over which Caroline claims and exploits it for her physical satisfaction. Mark the narration for exploitative nature of Caroline:

> He said, bitterly, speaking in Tamil so that the rush of thought should not be dammed by dearth of words: "She does not care for me. She cares only for what I can do, and if I do it well it is like one more diamond she can put on the necklace round her throat for her friends to admire:

> but when I do nothing I am nothing to her, no more than a small insect in a small crack in the ground. It was not a slip of the tongue, a manner of speaking: it is what she thinks of me when I am as I am now." (*Possession* 55)

This narration traces out some hidden factors of the hypocrite nature of Caroline who presents her as the well-wisher and guardian of Val's talent but, in reality, she is not so. She does not care for him. What she cares is his art which she exploits for her personal gain. It is pity that he is no more than a small insect in a small crack for her if he does not produce anything unique. His use of words like 'insect', 'crack' and 'ground' clearly reveal his pain over the exploitation. Through the narration of Val, Caroline seems to be possessive and hypocrite.

But the same Val is obliged to Ellie as she is the inspiration for his art. He takes her to the triumphal tours as he considers her right to go with him because she has been his model. His success is her success. Sample the narration for the honour he gives to Ellie:

> Between conscience and care, Valmiki made Ellie accompany him on his triumphal tours. He insisted that she should. It was her right, she had been his inspiration, his model, his success was at least partly hers. (*Possession* 123)

A Handful of Rice

A Handful of Rice is a story of the vagabond Ravi who is transformed into a householder on account of the love of Nalini. When he sees Nalini, he utters: "Take a girl like that, and half a man's troubles would be over" (*A Handful of Rice* 25). He imagines that his troubles will automatically come to an end if he gets such a girl for his wife. While eating, he dreams of a family and a house for him and his wife. Mark the narration for his dream of a wife and a house for her: "If I had a wife, he thought as he ate, she would cook for me, it would like this every day—but what had he to offer to get himself a wife?—I'll buy her a little house, small but nice" (*A Handful of Rice* 11). This is the image of a girl that he thinks about. He wishes to give him for someone and that someone will be his wife. For her, he dreams of buying a small but nice house. He thinks of a time-honoured image of woman who will cook for him and create an atmosphere of love that will release him from troubles.

Now take one more Ravi's narration to point out image of women:

> Ravi had sisters and so he knew the strict watch that was kept on young unmarried girls in their community, in all communities except shameless ones like the Europeans.
> (*A Handful of Rice* 40)

This narration exhibits clearly that strict watch is kept over the girls in Indian society which is male-oriented in nature. It also offers a difference between European women and Indian women. The European women are said to be shameless on account of their shamelessness. Ravi has the first-hand experience because of his sisters who are kept under strict watch. The narration offers a customary picture of Indian young unmarried girls who are strictly watched lest they should go astray.

The Coffer Dams

The Coffer Dams is the story of the builder Clinton who has a passion for "His work. The Dam" (*The Coffer Dams* 26) and neglects his wife "Unpredictable Helen" (*The Coffer Dams* 25). As a builder he succeeds but, as a husband, he fails. He is jealous and possessive by nature. He is jealous of Bashiam because Helen goes to meet him in order to have first-hand knowledge of the native people. Note the narration for his over-possessive nature:

> She is mine, he said, stubbornly; why should I let her go? What I have I hold. But knew this to be an illusion, having touched the emptiness where she had fled him, so that the bolsters began to sag under the weight of knowledge. (*The Coffer Dams* 126)

The narration shows his mastering nature. He thinks that his wife is his wife and he has the right over her body and soul. Notwithstanding educated, he does not consider her a person. He succeeds in making the dams but fails to make the building of relations. Being husband, he does not take her into confidence and in his drunken state, rapes her.

On the other hand, there is Bashiam who is cooperative and feels the pulse of Helen. Mark the narration for his affection that he feels for Helen when she is shivering with cold:

> They rose. She was shivering. Bashiam said, 'Are you cold?' and without waiting for an answer put a shawl around her, draping it over her head and shoulders. (*The Coffer Dams* 83)

Seeing Helen shivering with cold, Bashiam puts a shawl around her. Offering the shawl is not important. What is important is his feeling for Helen. This mutual feeling is missing in Helen-Clinton relation. If there had been Clinton in place of Bashiam, he would have not noticed Helen. For Bashiam, Helen is a person—living person who has her identity.

The Nowhere Man

The Nowhere Man is Srinivas who loves his wife Vasantha so much that in his later years he misses her and the gap is not filled even by the presence of Mrs. Pickering. Even in her company he feels spiritually isolated. When he throws her ashes into the river, he recalls the memorable moments that he passed with her. To him, she was a thoroughly Indian as is clear from the narration:

> ... he could not help feeling with Vasantha, who in her breath and bones had remained wholly Indian. She would have liked her remains committed to the currents of an Indian river, though she had scrupulously refrained from such onerous impositions; and now, watching her ashes drift away downstream. (*The Nowhere Man* 40).

The policeman tells Srinivas that the river is not meant for throwing the rubbish. Srinivas reacts to the statement of the policeman and very emotionally replies: "It was not rubbish," said Srinivas, and found to his dismay that his throat was working painfully. "It was my wife" (*The Nowhere Man* 41). The last sentence "It was my wife" shows his love for his wife. The death of Vasantha leaves a gap that becomes wider in spite of the company of Mrs. Pickering. In the end, he feels that he is a nowhere man looking for a nowhere city. He praises Mrs. Pickering who shares with him. For him, she is a friend who shares his house and keeps it well. Laxman asks him about her identity. Srinivas introduces her thus: "A friend", and adds "She shares the house with me. Have you not noticed how well kept it is? A pigsty," he said slyly, "no more" (*The Nowhere Man* 64).

Two Virgins

The scenery of *Two Virgins* reveals lesbianism, sex, dance, abortion and amorous glances, etc. Women dominate this novel as the title clearly reveals that it is the story of two virgins. However, male characters like Appa, Devraj, Mr. Gupta, Chingleput, Manikkam, etc. have registered their presence but mostly they are introduced through the consciousness of the sisters. Mr. Gupta is the film director who comes to the village for a documentary film. Lalitha acts and impresses Mr. Gupta who invites her to the city for being actress. She reaches the city where she is exploited sexually by Mr. Gupta. Mark the narration for his taking an advantage of innocent girl:

> "Lalitha is a woman with the natural desires of a woman," he said. His voice was very hoarse.
>
> "Of which you took advantage," Appa accused.
>
> "I am not made of stone," said Mr. Gupta, huskily.
>
> (*Two Virgins* 220)

This narration throws light on his nature of exploiting the girls. He calls Lalitha a woman with the natural desires of a woman. It may be true that Lalitha comes to the front to press the sex-button and Mr. Gupta takes an advantage of her innocence. When Appa charges him with the exploitation of his daughter, he very frankly tells him that he is not made of stone. Hence, Mr. Gupta treats girls only as a possession or a means for entertainment. He is greedy for sex and does not feel any scruple for exploiting the girls for sex in the name of roles in the film. Today, in the society there are thousands of Mr. Guptas who make many Lalithas victim of their lust, tempting them with the roles in the films.

The devil always appears in pleasing shape. This is true in case of Chingleput who is the well-wisher of Saroja. Appa calls him "a shrewd man" (*Two Virgins* 103) but Saroja sees in him a companion with whom she shares her troubles and take guidance from him. But the same man shows his real motives when he clasps her. Mark the words that he utters before Saroja:

> "Your whole life is in front of you." He clasped her. His organ was hard, was nuzzling her body. "Don't be afraid, I'm a man, I can't help it," said Chingleput. (*Two Virgins* 250)

This narration reflects the inner working of his mind that somewhere there is a hidden pattern that jumps through his organ against her body while clasping. If he had been her real well-wisher, the feeling of lust would have never come out. Why does he tempt her saying that the whole life is before her. Mr. Gupta took the advantage of Lalitha who could not gather herself and drowned in the river of his temptations. But Saroja is not a girl to be tempted easily because of Lalitha's case. She understands Chingleput's real motives when she feels her organ nuzzling her body. He shows that he is a man and asks her not to be afraid. But Saroja becomes fearless and is not trapped. The narration peeps into the mind of Chingleput who shows that he is Saroja's adviser and friend while he is a man waiting for an opportunity to exploit her sexually.

The Golden Honeycomb

The Golden Honeycomb has the three main inspiring (female) native bees—Manjula, Mohini and Usha who provide honey of Indian culture to Rabi who motivates other bees—the masses for a revolution against the foreign bees who were stealing the Indian golden honey to take it to their soil. Mark the narration for embracing the native (female) bee Usha in place of the foreign one, Sophie:

> A woman of a pared and lucid grace with whom he could talk, or be still, who could move him, and move with them, effortlessly picking up where he left off their common strand. A woman who was at one with him, their lives interlocking at more than one level, with whom it pleased him to feel, he could wait, or not, to come together. In their own country, in their own time. (*The Golden Honeycomb* 455)

This narration reveals that Rabi feels good in the company of Usha who makes him relaxed by providing an outlet for his viewpoints. He moves with her and discusses with her. He plans for future with her. She is a woman who will prove not only to be a good wife for him but also a companion with whom he can share his feelings. This narration shows that a woman proves to be a companion for man sharing with him in joys and sorrows.

The Dewan shows his broadmindedness in allowing Usha to talk and move with Rabi. When Vatsala informs him about the relationship of Usha with Rabi, he says: "It's natural ....Their attitudes are not dissimilar. It's bound to bring them together" (*The Golden Honeycomb* 385). When two persons of similar attitude meet, none can stop them to meet them. Hence, he thinks that there is no harm in meeting Usha with Rabi.

Bawajiraj feels that "women have simply no conception" (143) but he proves to be wrong in his thinking. He has to bow down before Mohini who defeats him with her logic and makes him dependent to the extent that without her, he feels like "a ghost of himself" (90). She calls him "tormentor". She reproaches him that he has provided everything to his wife Shanta Devi except himself. As she is not selfish, she thinks of other women and their miserable plight. She silences him with her remarks. When he says that he is free, she mocks at him realising him that he is a slave to the British. She says:

"The truth is you're not master in your own house. You're only a *naam-ke-vaste* king" (36). He calls her silly and remarks: "You're a woman, women don't understand these things" (36). She retorts: "I do. I understand very well. I'm not like your other women" (36). This response from her makes him annoyed though he remains controlled.

Rabi thinks of the strike which gave him a chance to come in contact with Jaya, a mill-hand who helped him. She told him about the causes of the strike which came from "the empty-belly race" (462). The girl did not belong to any caste or craft or sex; she simply belongs to "empty-belly race", "a race that would always be defeated" (462). It is Usha who makes him believe that this crowd is different saying: "That crowd didn't know its own strength. This one does" (462). The male narration becomes inferior to the female narration particularly in *The Golden Honeycomb*.

Pleasure City

Pleasure City is mainly a story of friendship between Tully and Rikki in a changed atmosphere. Rikki is much influenced by the female characters and also influences them. Let me begin with Mrs. Bridie who influences Rikki. Rikki portrays Mrs. Bridie thus:

> ...tall, bony woman with her yellowing skin and her tired eyes, who looked so different from everyone around.... He thought about her bosom. So flat, he could feel through the stuff of her dress, not at all like the full globes of his mother. He thought it must be so from never having brimmed with milk for children. (*Pleasure City* 6)

From this narration, the picture of Mrs. Bridie's physical features comes before the readers. Mrs. Bridie is different from other women because of her physique which is of tall stature. She is bony with yellowing skin and tired eyes. Her tired eyes indicate that she feels a kind of isolation in life. She has not freshness in her personality partly because of her physical frame and partly because of her discontented life. Rikki observes her bosom which is flat and not like his mother's. He surmises that her breasts are not global because of her being childless, they were never brimmed with milk. She is the woman who is responsible in shaping his personality. She has potential for moulding the character. She possesses "the key to locked, mysterious boxes that he barely knew existed except for the barest outlines that were showing up hazily in the distance" (*Pleasure City* 6).

Note the narration for the image of Mrs. Pearl:

> Grey curls with blue lights in them, a dumpy figure not improved by the flowered costume—a glance and he had placed her firmly in the brigade of aged and authoritative ladies that overflowed the camp. (*Pleasure City* 137)

This narration is from Rikki about Mrs. Pearl who is a new arrival at Shalimar. From this narration, she appears to be not only short and plump but also aged and authoritative lady. She is wearing the flowered costume but it does not make her impressive.

Corinna, the wife of Tully comes to Shalimar to meet her husband. To Rikki, she seems to be a horseman. He presents her as a horseman with a woman's long flowing hair. The outfits—the turban, the shirt and the trousers—she was wearing gave the impression of a horseman. "It was long and silky, a woman's flowing hair; the turban, and the shirt and trousers she was wearing, had led him to suppose a horseman" (*Pleasure City* 106). Tully appreciates her for her confidence and balance. Her riding is worth seeing as she keeps balance. For Tully, she has:

> poise, confidence, command, comes up superbly from initial crouch to upright and hold the position. Balancing finely, she rides the skimming plank with her body, guides it in subtle diagonals, her first work is dazzling. (*Pleasure City* 131-132)

After analysing male narrations about women, it can be said that somewhere in their mind in spite of asserting their favour for women, is the seed of male dominance and they wish to grow it as far as possible. But when they counteract women, they have to retreat and finally make an adjustment with them.

Nathan in *Nectar in a Sieve* has illicit relations with Kunthi even after marriage and does not feel guilty. Rukmani who has not the physical relations with Kenny has a kind of fear in her mind and does not let her husband know of it though this platonic kind of relation is an outcome of his treatment. Nathan favours Ira's husband when he comes to return his daughter as she is barren. Somewhere they have developed the feeling that they are men. Yet, Nathan loves his wife, praises her for her skill in running the family and recognises her importance in family. He respects woman in Rukmani and that is the reason that Rukmani lives with her happily facing all the odds in life.

Kitsamy in *Some Inner Fury* is possessive by nature while Richard is cooperative. He does not love Premela and expects from her to be modern. He does not allow her to interfere in his matter and asks her to be busy with her own affairs. It is Richard who loves Mira and treats her in a friendly way even after her leaving him for the sake of the countrymen.

Dandekar in *A Silence of Desire* expects Sarojini to be submissive. In the beginning she is modest and submissive. He is jealous by nature and does not wish to be disturbed in his daily routine. He fails to fathom Sarojini's faith and fidelity and doubts her for having relation with the Swamy. But, when he comes to know the reality, he shows his care for his wife and asks her to go to hospital for cure. He works on doubts and does not listen to what his heart says. Sarojini makes him realise that she is still faithful to the family. He has to accept her significance in the family and without her, he thinks that home is not home.

In *Possession*, Val is a Tamil Brahmin boy who does not exploit but is exploited by Caroline physically and mentally. He is shown with the three women—Caroline, Ellie and Annabel. He makes physical relations with all these three women though Caroline forces him to be in such a relation. He respects Ellie as he feels that she is bleeding inside and has many things in her nature that are similar to him. Where is his code of conduct when he makes relations with other than Caroline? No doubt, Caroline forced him to be indulged in illicit relation but what about his relations with Ellie and Annabel?

Ravi in *A Handful of Rice* falls in love with Nalini at first sight and wishes to make her his wife. He feels that she will bring changes in his life and make an end of his trouble. No doubt, she changes his life and proves to be a sheet anchor. He rapes his mother-in-law in his drunken state though he feels sorry after it. In his frustrated condition, he beats his wife but is ashamed of his behaviour.

In *The Coffer Dams*, Clinton is thoroughly possessive and greedy for sex and work. He wants to have dominance over Helen but she makes him disillusion and goes to Bashiam for exploring her space.

Mr. Srinivas in *The Nowhere Man* is indeed a cool and calculative man who loves his wife for her devotion and friendly nature.

In *Two Virgins*, Mr. Gupta, Devraj and Chingleput belong to the world where men have hunger for sex. They think women only as commodities and will not miss any opportunity to exploit whenever they find it favourable.

Rabi in *The Golden Honeycomb* is a young man who respects woman in his mother and woman in his beloved Usha. When he has sex-encounter with Jaya, he regrets.

In *Pleasure City*, Rikki again respects woman in Mrs. Bridie and is helpful to every woman who comes in his contact. Male narration displays many designs of the image of women. To men like Nathan, Richard, Ravi, Mr. Srinivas and Rabi, women are 'Persons' who have the potential to run the family and support men whenever the situation demands while there is the other category of men like Dandekar, Clinton and Mr. Gupta who think of woman as 'Possession'.

The discussion clearly exhibits women through 'Male Narration' which is an innovative technique that Markandaya has used. She makes her male characters speak so that their comments may reveal the facts which they have in their mind concerning women. No doubt, her male characters show their dominance over women but her women characters pierce the needle into the balloon of their ego and air comes out. Her male characters realise their incapability in running home smoothly.

First they are proud but later on they become meek and submissive to the women who make them understand that they are not commodities that can be purchased, used and thrown.

Works Cited

Markandaya, Kamala. *Nectar in a Sieve*. New York: Signet Books, 1954. Print.

____ . Some *Inner Fury*. London: Putnam & Co., 1955. Print.

____ . *A Silence of Desire*. London: Putnam & Co., 1960. Print.

____ . *Possession*. London: Putnam & Co., 1963. Print.

____ . *A Handful of Rice*. New Delhi: Orient Paper backs, 1966. Print.

____ . *The Coffer Dams*. Delhi: Hind Pocket Books, 1969. Print.

____ . *The Nowhere Man*. 1972. Bombay: Orient Longman (Sangam Books), 1975. Print.

____ . *Two Virgins*. 1973. Vikas Publishing House, 1975. Print.

____ . *The Golden Honeycomb*. New Delhi: B. I. Publication, 1977. Print.

____ . *Pleasure City*. London: Chatto and Windus, 1982. Print.

5

Bed Narration: Sex for Sale

Kamala Markandaya narrates social landscapes that emit out Indianness. But her erotic landscapes do not smell Indian perfume. Though she has touched the string of feminine sensibility, she has presented a naked and obscure picture of woman vis-à-vis sex. It seems that she cares for the Western readers for whom she writes. While presenting sex, she forgets that she belongs to India where it is taboo. Her sex-landscapes are erotic, animated and sizzling. They are displayed in the Western gallery where the Britishers enjoy to their fill. Her bed-narrations are picturesque. It is her genius that she paints the picture through words. Uma Paramewaran finds her writing "very visual, as though the reader is seeing a movie" (188). Her bed narrations seem to be bad to some critics while some search for the aesthetic sense.

In India, sex is a forbidden landscape that can't be viewed during day but can be frensied during night. It is not open as it is in the Western countries. Love, the root that makes the family tree strong is nurtured and watered by sex while in Western countries sex that forms the root nurtured by love often shakes the family. 'Love for sex' is not the Indian way of life. 'Sex for love' is the culmination of the emotional bond and integrity. Kamala Markandaya is well aware of the fact of sex which is not a forbidden fruit but surely a forbidden subject in India. She also knows that sex is responsible for the fertility motive and the concept of families and home would have been impossible without it. Purity of sex in Indian life gives rise to the concept of sweet home and families. Without purity and integrity in response, the world would have had animal like sex.

'Body' is the mechanism and 'Sex' is the soul that drives and inspires man. Sex becomes the primary drive next to hunger. Hence, it cannot be low and vulgar as it is certainly the divine gift of God to human beings. Praising the need of sex, Mrs. Mary Wood writes:

> Instead, then, of looking at sex circumscribed, and perhaps as something low and vulgar, to be thought of and spoken of only with whispers or questionable mirth, we should see that sex is God's divinest gift to humanity, the power through which we come into the nearest likeness to Himself - the function by which we become creators and transmitters of our powers of body, mind and soul. (110)

Now, let me decode the landscapes that Kamala Markandaya has portrayed with the forbidden subject on the canvas of her fictional world. How far has she painted them? How far is she professional or commercial in selling the Indian erotic landscape? What she has painted is within Indian moral code or she has crossed the limit in order to be saleable in the Western market. Uma Parameswaran writes: "It is interesting to note that in Markandaya's novels, women often take the first step towards sexual consummation" (176).

The very first novel *Nectar in a Sieve* that made her popular is the story of a village woman Rukmani who with her courage and rocky patience struggles against life and becomes larger than life. She is married to a farmer Nathan who is poor in everything except in love. She does not like to remember the scene of her first night but prefers to remember the other nights when she became quite mature in mind and body. Mark the narration:

> I prefer to remember, sweeter, fuller, when I went to my husband matured in mind as well as in body, not as a pained and awkward child as I did on that first night.
>
> (*Nectar in a Sieve* 8-9)

This narration shows that at the time of marriage she was a pained child. On the first night, she was awkward, as she did not know what to do and pained because of the sexual act about which she did not know. No Indian woman enjoys sex on the first night, so is the case with Rukmani who feels pain on account of the cyclic rhythm of sex about which she has no experience. But with the passage of time, the same painful night turns into the fruitful night when the 'woman' in her offers to the 'man' with whom she is united. She gives her whole to the man. Rukmani recalls some of the unforgettable moments that offered fruits of love. She recalls the scene of Deepawali night when she offered herself wholly—physically as well as mentally to her husband. Mark the narration for frankness in the depiction of sex:

> I stretched myself out beside him, close to him in the darkness, and as we touched he turned abruptly towards me. Words died away, the listening air was very still, the black night waited. In the straining darkness I felt his body moving with desire, his hands on me were trembling, and I felt my senses opening like flower to his urgency. I closed my eyes and waited, waited in the darkness while my being filled with a wild ecstatic fluttering waited for him to come to me. (*Nectar in a Sieve* 61)

How artistically Kamala Markandaya has painted the erotic landscape of Rukmani who is waiting for her husband for sex! Rukmani stretches herself beside Nathan in darkness. Kamala Markandaya has now used the word 'darkness' as she knows it is darkness that is quite suitable from Indian point of view. "As we touched" clearly reflects the sensation that both of them feel resulting in turning of Nathan to her. "Words died away, the listening air was very still, the black night waited" (*Nectar in a Sieve* 61). When both have an irresistible desire for sex, they do not speak, words die and their desires are ready for translation. The black night waits. She has used the word 'black' before night, as sex is more erotic in the darkest night when everything remains invisible except sex. In the straining darkness Rukmani feels Nathan's body that creates a passionate desire. His hands start working like the fingers of the player on the string of musical instrument. The sexual music opens her like a flower to his demands for sex. The artistic beauty in "I felt my senses opening like a flower to his urgency" is incomparable. She has shown this new desirable longing for sex against that first night when she felt pained. Now closing her eyes, she is waiting for her husband. Sex becomes the black desire crying for its realisation in the darkness. As she is filled with wild ecstatic pleasure, she waits for her husband to come to her for sexual act. 'Black Desire Fruitful' on this day of Deepawali and 'Black Desire Painful' on the first night are the two landscapes in the world of *Nectar in a Sieve*. The landscape 'Black Desire Fruitful' is symbolic as it is the night of Deepawali, the blackest night but *diyas* are lighted and the victory of Ram over Ravan is celebrated. Here Nathan returns to her as victor after defeating Ravan of lust and Rukmani offers her body to be lighted with love to spread the ecstatic pleasure.

The second novel *Some Inner Fury* that has the inner fury of Mirabai's love for Richard who, though a Britisher proves to be a true lover. But the love that she feels for him is sacrificed for the sake of the country. By the time of Govind's trial, Mira sacrifices her love. But before Govind's trial, both Mira and Richard enjoy life sucking the last drop of love. For her Richard becomes "a creature of gold" (*Some Inner Fury* 196). She finds his flawless sculptured body and feels it can "make you melt, or set you on fire and burn with an incandescent heat itself" (*Some Inner Fury* 197). Both of them enjoy and behave as married couple though not married. Richard starts bubbling with sex and talks of 'fever' and 'ache' and persuades her for intercourse on the uninhibited coast. Their bodies feel fiery and ultimately Richard has to say:

> "We're alone," he said, holding me still, "quite alone," and the skies were empty, the sands were bare, I listened and there was only the sound of the sea.
>
> "You see," he said softly, "there is nothing and no one. No one but us."
>
> Slowly my senses awoke and responded, the buds of feeling swelled and opened one by one. In the trembling silence, I heard the blood begin its clamour, felt its frantic irregular beat, then the world fell away, forgotten in this wild abandoned rhythm, lost in the sweep and surge of love. (*Some Inner Fury* 198-199)

This narration of the erotic landscape unfolds its meaning itself. 'Empty sky', 'bare sands' and 'sounding sea' are the words that indicate lovers' mentality. There is nothing in the mind except the desire to soar in the sky of love and sex that gives the strength to their wings helping them in soaring high. Sand is bare which indicates the sculptured body of Richard seen by Mira. It creates a desire in her to be nude like sand so that the water of the sea that is alluring her by its sound may quench the body. The line "You see, there is nothing and no one but us" is a dose powerful enough to resist the desire of Mira to eat the forbidden fruit of sex through love. Now Mira responds Richard positively as the buds of feeling swell and open one by one. It is the genius of Kamala Markandaya that she has sketched the landscape with such colouring words that speak and create frantic irregular beats in the hearts of the readers like the beats in the hearts of the two lovers. The two lovers are lost in the sweep and surge of love and the world ceases to be for them. "then the world fell away, forgotten in this wild abandoned rhythm, lost in the sweep and surge of love" (*Some Inner Fury* 198-199).

The third novel *A Silence of Desire* is silent in bed-narration and Kamala Markandaya is more interested in presenting the silence of relation on account of misunderstanding than in sketching the erotic landscape, which does not require silence but the uproar of blood that is missing in this novel.

The fourth novel *Possession* presents the erotic landscape but now it is a British lady Caroline who is hungry for sex. She wishes to show her colonial nature of exploitation in the name of welfare. She squeezes the young Indian boy Valmiki, the painter in the name of cultural relation through painting but she shows her true nature of possession, an attribute of colonial culture to exploit. She does not allow Val to have sex even with Ellie and Annabel. The erotic landscape that attracts the attention is the landscape where Anasuya presents the scene of sex between Annabel and Valmiki. Sample the bed-narration for its visual picture:

> Spread-eagled on a rug in front of the electric fire lay Annabel. Valmiki covered her. They were closely locked from mouth to loins until the firm white legs flared away from under him. Both were naked, and their bodies moved as if they were a unity, with a beautifully articulated urgent rhythm "... I was shivering, partly from cold, partly no doubt from what I had seen: yet why? I had seen enough fucking in the over crowded desperate hovels of India, and had not developed any emphatic attitudes either way ..." (*Possession* 194)

The narration of sex of Valmiki with Annabel is highly erotic and electrifying. Anasuya who is presenting the scene of intercourse of Val and Annabel seems to be affected and it is surprising that a serious novelist like Kamala Markandaya has used the word 'fucking' which is considered to be the most offensive in the English language. 'Spread-eagled on a rug in front of the electric fire' is the erotic imagery that the mind itself visualises the intercourse. The phrase "Closely locked from mouth to loins" makes the image more well-defined. The sex cycling is on the smooth bodily road giving the jerk to the two lovers but "they were a unity, with a beautifully articulated urgent rhythm ..."

The fifth novel *A Handful of Rice* though a novel of hunger and relationship is dotted with the red colours of sex and sensuality. *A Handful of Rice* that is food is needed to satisfy the hunger of the body that, in return, satisfies the hunger of hunger—sexual hunger through copulation. Kamala Markandaya is expert in depiction of the landscape of the first night. How realistically and immaculately she has sketched the erotic landscape of the newly wedded couple—Ravi and Nalini!

> The sudden darkness was blinding. He groped his way back, and felt his outstretched hand touch warm smooth skin, her soft-bare nape beneath the upswept voluptuous coils of hair. Instantly his senses leapt into life, he could hardly contain himself. He pressed her back on the bed and began caressing her, thrusting aside the filmy hampering folds of the muslin sari into which she had changed until he could feel her body and it was everything

> he wanted, warm, soft, long, fine, supple legs, a belly that arched under his hand, and a skin like satin - he heard himself cry out as he covered her, spreading her thighs to receive him. He did not know if he was hurting her - he could not have stopped if he was. He heard her sharp indrawn breath, but otherwise she lay passively under him.
>
> In the morning—he looked for it—there was blood on the bed. (*A Handful of Rice* 64)

The first night scene of Ravi and Nalini clearly reveals Kamala Markandaya's genius and her art of narration. It seems that she has made a live telecast of the first night. Artistically it may be convincing and pleasure-giving but to present the nudity as such is not expected from a sober novelist like Kamala Markandaya who is on the path of transforming her women from 'possession' to 'person'.

Decoding the text of the first night of Ravi and Nalini is itself a sensation. Somewhere it seems that she is on the verge of pornography. The text: "The sudden darkness was blinding" illustrates the desire to be lost in sex through love via purified lust. The word 'sudden' before darkness is noteworthy as the senses unfold their folds awakening a desire to have sex and charging the body with currents of lust. In this sudden darkness, Ravi's hands start working touching her smooth nape. "his outstretched hand touch warm smooth skin, her self-bare nape beneath the upswept voluptuous coils of hair" (*A Handful of Rice* 64). As he touched her, he could not control himself and flowed in the sexual currents that sucked his energy. He could hardly "contain himself" and heard himself cry out "as he covered her, spreading her thighs to receive him." When the night is over, Ravi sees the blood on the bed. "In the morning — he looked for it —there was blood on the bed." The blood is the blood of virginity that indicates that she did not enjoy sex earlier. Kamala Markandaya displays the bed sheet with drops of blood to the Western readers.

It is the phobia of the first night that keeps a woman passive and she does not reciprocate as she does afterwards.

The same Nalini who was so shy and passive on the first nigh becomes so active in the art of lovemaking.

> Now she was beginning to respond to him, making love as he, encouraged by her willingness, thought her to learning to abandon herself, to give her body without shame to him to do, with as he willed, so that now instead of a passive submission they came together joyously. (*A Handful of Rice* 66)

'Sex without shame and fear' is the mantra that the male characters chant and expect talks of love from women. It is Indian way that they do not talk openly but they cooperate in the game. Kamala Markandaya's first night landscapes are matchless but the landscapes of foreplay are equally haunting and worth noticing. This is the landscape from *A Handful of Rice* where Ravi is seen caressing his wife waiting for her till her longing for the game.

> His wife, he thought with a surge of possession, his to have, his to hold ... his excitement grew, externals fell away, there was nothing at all in the world beyond this feeling between him and this woman. (*A Handful of Rice* 77)

The texts "his to have, his to hold" and "externals fell away" prove to be charging words that make us visualise the sex act.

In India characters like Puttanna impregnate their wives in spite of not getting any privacy. Puttanna makes his wife Thangam pregnant under cover of shawls and coverlets in spite of the fact of sleeping with Apu and Jayamma.

> While Puttanna who could scarcely support the child he already had, who seldom had any privacy in the quarters he shared away and asleep with Apu and Jayamma, had somehow succeeded under cover of shawls and coverlets in impregnating his wife who had not imagined she would conceive with a baby still at the breast. (*A Handful of Rice* 91)

This erotic landscape that can be titled as "Under cover of shawls and coverlets" makes us imagined of the unseen scene.

Very surprising and equally shocking is the erotic rape landscape that Kamala Markandaya portrays with bold and unwomanly shades. Jayamma who is the mother-in-law of Ravi has a veiled lust somewhere in her mind and imagines to be satisfied by a masculine man like Ravi. As he is her son-in-law, she conceals the desire. Her own husband could not satisfy her whole being. Whenever Ravi beats her daughter, she praises his masculinity inwardly and feels the blows on her and wishes to be in place of her daughter. The tide of lust always strikes her body and rebels to be satisfied.

> She shivered a little thinking of Ravi's masculinity: and there was even the seed of a thought in her mind, though she would not let it grow, that in her daughter's place she would have welcomed her wounds. (*A Handful of Rice* 188)

Ravi knows that Jayamma is a starving woman longing for sex. When he is drunk and is not in himself, he sees Jayamma and the earlier ignited passions get flamed. He frankly declares:

> Why should I? You've wanted it for months, for years. All the time you lay with your husband. Every time you looked at me. (*A Handful of Rice* 221)

He takes her in his masculine grip while she tries to come out calling him a 'Ruffian Thug' (*A Handful of Rice* 221) but in vain.

> She was struggling. He held her and his excitement grew with her movements; her arms and breasts were soft and pulpy under his hands. (*A Handful of Rice* 221)

He feels her arms and breast that are soft and pulpy and becomes intoxicated to such point that he forgets she is his mother-in-law who, now, seems to be only an object of lust. Again and again he recalls her former activities of looking at him with sexual craving.

> "You like it," he said, his mouth rough on her nipples, bringing them up hard and erect. "Do you think your body doesn't give you away? Do you think I don't know how you have been starved?" (*A Handful of Rice* 221)

This is the dark erotic landscape as no Indian is expected to rape his mother-in-law. The sensuous implication and imagery can be noticed in "his mouth rough on her nipples, bringing them up hard and erect." Sucking makes her nipples up and erect.

The landscape 'Raping the Mother-in-Law' is the raping of Indian sensibility. The landscape is shocking as well as horrible but the more horrible and hurting is that she does not make Jayamma repent. It is surprising that being a man Ravi asks for forgiveness as he repents while Jayamma does not care about it.

> "What for - last night?" she said, and stared at him. "Do you think I care about that? Who cares what goes on between four walls?" (*A Handful of Rice* 223)

The plea that Kamala Markandaya paints sex painting through words for the aesthetic pleasure is not true as there is no aesthetic pleasure in raping a woman.

Her sixth novel *The Coffer Dams* presents the sexual affair of Helen with Bashiam for the realisation of self against the background of her mechanic and boring life with Clinton. The novel narrates two bed-scenes—one when Clinton almost rapes his wife to possess her body to satisfy his lust and the other when Bashiam enjoys sex with Helen. Sample the bed-narration when Clinton forcibly rapes her:

> She rose to go and he seized her wrist. "Stay away," he said, passionately, and the feel of her flesh twisting inflamed him and he bore down on her until he prevailed. Then he carried the listless body to his bed. (*The Coffer Dams* 126)

It is Helen who pushes the switch that runs the sexy fan of Bashiam electrifying both. Mark the narration for recording the sex-act but it is not as open as it is in *Two Virgins*.

> She glanced at Bashiam and his eyes were brilliant, lust lay like a heavy bloom on his lips which were parted over sharp white teeth like an animal close on quarry and she knew then that she was like that too, that that was how she looked; and it was not a judging but a recording.
>
> Then it was over. It had not been so long after all. The bird catcher stood up and stretched, working his fingers and blowing out his cheeks to relieve the cramp. (*The Coffer Dams* 86)

For Kamala Markandaya, sex is almost a religion that becomes a key to open the door of true love that leads to the home of Eternal bliss. She paints Vasantha on the canvas of *The Nowhere Man* as "a pretty girl who wouldn't be prettier still if she were not quite so thin, but then who wouldn't be after she'd been through, poor child" (*The Nowhere Man* 129). Like the first night landscape of Ravi and Nalini, the landscape of Srinivas and Vasantha equally vibrates the sensations and creates a commotion in the body. Srinivas sees rose-looking Vasantha whom he takes her in his arms and is lost in the sensual pleasure with her.

Sample the narration for the photographic narration of bed-scene of the first night:

> When he touched his bride he was so suffused with love for her - for flesh and spirit that were so beautifully conjoined - that he could not hold back. Forgive me, forgive me, some part of his brain cried, but soon he was lost, flooded with sensation which obliterated mind. Through it all, she complied. Her body opened for him, accepted his. That was the sum of it. The exultance that he demanded, the heartbeat and tumult, were all absent. It will come, he panted, striving as he had striven in his dreams, sinking himself deep into her flesh until he touched the pulp of her womb. But, it did not, then or ever.
>
> In the morning, there was blood on the sheets. It seemed like a symbol to him. He showed it to her, full of tenderness, which replaced the night's urgencies.

> "Your virginity", he said gently, "surrendered to me. Immaculate, unsullied by anyone or anything before." She gazed at him, compromised, uncompromising, the look he learned to know very well later, in England.
>
> "That is the physical fact of the matter," she said.
>
> (*The Nowhere Man* 157)

This landscape shows more maturity on the part of Kamala Markandaya in portrayal. For the first time she has used her brush in proper manner in placing 'flesh' with 'spirit' " for flesh and spirit that were so beautifully conjoined" (*The Nowhere Man* 157). Her sketching is more disciplined, more controlled and more artistic. The sentence "Her body opened for him, accepted his" is not hurting and reveals the desired effect. By using the phrase "pulp of her womb", she enters the depth of portrayal.

"The blood on the bed" of the landscape of *A Handful of Rice* is also here "on the sheets" of *The Nowhere Man*. But the difference is that Ravi shows blood to Nalini with a feeling of pride but here Srinivas tenderly shows her the blood calling it "your virginity surrendered to me." He further recognises her purity with the words "Immaculate, unsullied by anyone or anything before." But the right thing that Kamala Markandaya has done is that she makes an Indian woman say that it is not the whole, it is simply a physical affair. "That is the physical fact of the matter" (*The Nowhere Man* 157).

The novel *Two Virgins*, as the title connotes, is the story of two adolescent sisters Lalitha and Saroja who like the girls of their ages have the secret dreams and longing for sex. Kamala Markandaya is not only expert in the portrayal of first night scene but also in the portrayal of a growing young girl's secret yearning for sex. Sample the narration for experiencing the feelings as are narrated in a very imaginative manner:

> His hands were terrible; they were puffy and fat and they looked like a bunch of bananas, Jaya said. What terrible things those fingers, could do if they reached up under your skirts. Saroja closed up her thighs and asked exactly, but Jaya only said it was not to be described. Jaya's eyes

> shone when she told; she was older than Saroja, but in the same class. Saroja could not interpret that sheer disturbed her, made her feel she was missing out. (*Two Virgins* 19-20)

Jaya's narration of "What terrible things those fingers, could do if they reached up under your skirts" makes Saroja "closed up her thighs". Here Kamala Markandaya leaves Saroja to dream over as "it was not to be described."

Saroja is more sensible than her sister Lalitha who becomes a victim of the victimiser. She boldly rejects the temptation of Devraj as she sees the evil intention. When he comes near her and touches her, she leaps up because:

> She knew what he was asking. She knew where it ended. She had dragged her bloated gravid sister out of the bog; she had seen the bloody pulp of the baby. "Take your hands off me," she cried ... "what do you take me for," she screamed, "a virgin in your whorehouse?" (*Two Virgins* 245)

Kamala Markandaya's *Two Virgins* is generally charged with obscenity, lesbianism and open sex. It is considered to be merely documentary about rural life. But it is neither purely documentary except a few touches nor purely obscene. It is purely an aesthetic novel which has discussed the adolescence experiences of two sisters who are discriminated by their father. Kamala Markandaya has peeped into those experiences which are depicted in the decent words. It is her genius that she has used the decent words and the reader finds no difficulty in making out the meaning out of the narration. Saroja's innocent way to look to the sex of Appa and Amma is arresting and she feels happy that their quarrels end in love making. Mark the narration for the photographic presentation and the use of 'inner lips' for 'vagina' is purely aesthetic.

> In the night Appa and Amma quarreled, each saying false and terrible things about the other's scrounger. Saroja was dreadfully frightened, she always was when Amma and Appa hissed at each other like this, but Lalitha said not

> to be a baby, they were only working themselves up and it would all end in the same old way. When Saroja heard the charpoy creaking away she knew Lalitha was right, her parents were making love. They made love quietly to start with, but then it got frensied, the cot strings twanged although they were only made of rope and the wooden frame groaned. One of the charpoy legs was loose, it groaned most fearfully. Sometimes Amma would hiss that she could bear it no longer and they would bounce off onto the floor. Saroja knew she ought to be pleased her parents, quarrels ended in love-making and in a way she was. In another way, though, it disturbed her, made her thighs flutter and her inner lips moist; she longed to know what it was like for Amma, who was constructed like her, same openings only larger, Manikkam's wife told her, because of the babies pushing out, not to mention what was pushed in. (*Two Virgins* 24-25)

The novel *The Golden Honeycomb* has a few erotic landscapes that emit out the sensuous fragrance and also abusive dots like 'fucking thing' (213) and 'banchot' (266). Bawajiraj wishes to enjoy sex with Manjula but cannot do so because of the pregnancy. He controls himself and feels elated by rubbing his face between the breasts and feels a kind of anointing. Mark the excerpt for presenting the condition of a husband who wishes to have sex but cannot do so because of the life of the child which will be at stake:

> At night she lies beside him, in the four-poster bed of ornate mahogany, in a night-robe of finest mull. When he parts the mull, which is split downwards from the embroidered corsage, and places his hand between pubes and navel, he can feel the lunge and thrust of the child she is carrying. The engulf him in a medley of emotions: of love for his wife and the pulsing life he can feel, and awe for the dynasty which he believes between them they are creating, and lust that seizes his loins as his fingers encounter the springy pubic curls. It makes him ache; he longs for the consummation that is forbidden. Her body is sacrosanct; it has been so for one lunar month and will be until she is delivered and cleansed after birth. He will not breach the interdict. It is not only the life of the child

> which is at stake but, it has been impressed on him, the continuity of the royal line. The size of it overpowers, sharply exacts obedience. He groans and buries his face in her breasts, nuzzles the warm plump flesh. A thin colostrum issues, beads against his cheek. It seems to him like an anointing. (*The Golden Honeycomb* 12)

She gives birth to the son but being a maharajakumar, the child is taken away from her. She becomes restless because of the breasts which are full of milk. She becomes dishevelled and weeps out of frustration. She puts her hands upon "her breasts and squeezes them brutally. The milk spurts out rich and abundant; the bed-clothes are drenched" (14).

The second chapter demonstrates the scene of conception. It seems to be preplanned and later it happens exactly. The copulation between Bawajiraj and Mohini results in the conception of Rabi. In the beginning, the name of Mohini is not mentioned. It is mentioned only when she becomes pregnant. It is a technique that makes the reader quite curious to know about the woman who is being copulated by Bawajiraj. Mark the excerpt for raising the curiosity in the mind of the reader and the preparations made for conceiving the child, would-be protagonist:

> The child who is the protagonist of this story or history was born in January 1895, the natural son of the Bawajiraj who acceded to the throne as the third of his line.
>
> At this moment, a fine day in the spring of 1894, he has yet to be conceived. He lives, divided, between his future: between his mother and his father to whom the present is all-powerful. They lie, entwined, in the tall grass on the verge of woodlands that form part of the Palace estates. The woman is pale and lithe. Her shyness has gone with her virginity, which Bawajiraj has taken a full month since. It allows her to use her limbs in a manner which brings them both to the pitch of ecstasy. When she raises her legs and crosses them both over his torso both are lost. Neither can control the dazzling issue of their climax, which in the prelude has actually been their intention.
>
> Afterwards—a little afterwards—they lie quiescent in the grass, which their energies have tamped down into a bed...

> He rolls over onto her and bites her lip. She rouses and answers his vehemence. Quite soon a fresh orgasm is achieved.
>
> Afterwards—long afterwards—they pinpoint this as the moment of conception of their child. The child does not know—except perhaps in that incandescent instant of fusion when his two halves are joined; but the triumphant, dolorous paean, if there is one, is buried and lost in the womb. (*The Golden Honeycomb* 29-30)

This is the living visual picture of conceiving the child. It seems that characters know beforehand what is to happen. Everything is in their hand. But, the reality is that Markandaya is displaying even the minute details for the sake of the Western reader who is more interested in seeing the Indian women being copulated. When Mohini is conceived, she tells the Maharajah that "there is no flow" (30).

Quite contrary to Mohini is Shanta Devi who surrenders herself to her husband even without communication. Their copulation is more mechanical than sentimental.

> When they copulate it sinks, on his part, to moans and grunts. For her part she has long given up those cries of ecstasy feigned for his pleasure during early married days. Now she merely surrenders herself without ceremony and dissociates her mind, a technique she has perfected to meet the situation. (*The Golden Honeycomb* 144)

Kamala Markandaya knows that the reader takes pleasure in observing the ribs of a young girl. She also makes a display of a girl's ribs being observed by a young boy and of boy's by the girl. Rabi forces Janaki to show her ribs. She does not wish to show because she has become older now. But, Rabi does not give her any alternative as he thrusts her on the ground forcing her to show her ribs. Mark the excerpt:

> "I only want to look at your ribs."
>
> She yields. Actually she has no alternative, for he has thrust her onto the ground and pins her there with a knee. He is so urgent that the buttons fly; it is a mercy that a girl's only bodice has not been ripped to pieces. Janaki

> squints up at Rabi and notes he is indeed doing only what he said he would. He is inspecting her rib-cage, which still heaves from her exertions, if not her emotions. The swell of her breasts, which has engaged her lately, seems to interest him not at all. She sits up abruptly.
>
> "Seen all you want?" (*The Golden Honeycomb* 111)

Kamala Markandaya who is not satisfied with the episode of rib-cages shows the copulation of Rabi with a mature woman Jaya. Jaya gives him pleasures of sex to Rabi who is a 'bachcha' for her. She is making him expert in the art of sex. It seems that she is teaching *Kamasutra* practically. Again, the forbidden landscape is open to all and particularly to the Western reader.

> Hands on her thighs, he forces himself between and enters.
>
> His uppermost thought on completion, before he falls asleep, is that bodies are beautifully carpentered for their purpose. ..
>
> When he wakes Jaya is lying, awake, beside him. Their bodies touch at points: shoulders, hips, her bronze, his creamy, the delicate sleeping triangle, the colour of pitch, that he has compelled to meet his ardour. Leaning up on an elbow he hovers over her, proprietorially.
>
> 'Was it good for you?'
>
> 'Very good. Rabi, bachcha...'
>
> 'Mm?'
>
> 'Was it the first time for you?'
>
> 'Do you mean with a woman?'
>
> 'Have there been boys?'
>
> 'No. There are other ways.'
>
> 'I mean with a woman ...was it the first time?'
>
> 'Can't you tell?'
>
> 'Not always. Some men never learn. Some men are always bunglers.'

> 'I've never taken a woman before.'
>
> 'You weren't disappointed?'
>
> 'It was better than anything.'
>
> 'Rabi?'
>
> 'Uh?'
>
> 'Will you believe me?'
>
> 'Anything you say.'
>
> 'It can be better. Much better. Like this. Will you let me?'
>
> Her face is close to his. Her eyes are brilliant, bearing down on him.
>
> Like this. Erectile frills in the wake of her lips and stroking fingers. Like this. Moving in tender circles, apex like plush pushing up against him, her flesh like silk, like drawing slippery silk over polished cones. He is beginning to judder, but she holds and brings him into her rhythm. Coordinating superbly, they climax together. (*The Golden Honeycomb* 281-82)

The Golden Honeycomb, no doubt, is a historical novel. But, it seems to be more a novel of sex and pleasure than a lesson from a history. The way Kamala Markandaya has displayed sex as commodity in the Western mall is praiseworthy as it is sold like hot cakes. The Indian nudity from the pen of a woman novelist is a first-hand experience enjoyed by the reader who is himself sensuous.

In her last novel *Pleasure City*, Kamala Markandaya has painted a western erotic landscape that reveals body and the emptiness of the soul. Corinna who comes to India to meet her husband Tully meets him and remains isolated. Tully when he comes to know about her coming, he thinks of her lovely, plangent flesh and the dream of enjoying it. The landscape of the relation of Tully and Corinna unfolds the reality and the emptiness of their relations.

> Corinna had gone to bed, earning early retirement after the most charming genuflections that had everyone,

> virtually yearning to construct a litter. She would probably be asleep; but would always wake, and make available, to him her lovely, plangent flesh. (*Pleasure City* 114)

When words like 'asleep', 'wake', 'make available', 'plangent flesh' are decoded, they reveal materialistic and utilitarian theory of relation. It is not the healthy relation but the relation that becomes a burden to be carried. Corinna would be 'asleep' in spirit but 'wake' in body making 'available' her 'plangent flesh' for Tully. Here Kamala Markandaya has shown the difference between what an Indian feels and what a Westerner feels regarding sex. The body is a commodity that is enjoyed and forgotten. The heart is missing in bodily relation. It is only lust that dominates and as soon as it is satisfied its connection with the body snaps. Rikki is surprised to see Tully and Corinna who, in spite of being husband and wife, are standing face to face but the ego makes them dumb. Their bodies speak, as they require food, the food of sex.

> ... lovely arms inviting. "Come to bed, darling." Luckily he never needed a second invitation; and the molten experience made it easier for both of them, postponing franker exchanges. (*Pleasure City*124)

It seems that she has come only for bodily pleasures. She finds him marvelous and positively blooming. She asks no question and is lost with him.

> 'Don't know - about you - never have - but between kisses, lips full on his, stopping him up. He getting clear, pining her flat so he can look at her.
>
> 'But what?'
>
> 'But I don't care. Does for me, darling. Totally. Beautifully. - Toby?'
>
> Inviting him again. He accepting, as he wants to. Every sign, as she says; and the encounter has never been less than delightful. However, it has to stop. Limits for a man, though not, she makes it clear, for Corinna.
>
> (*Pleasure City* 253-254)

'Inviting him again', 'He accepting, as he wants to', 'the encounter' and 'Limits for a man' are the words that clearly interpret the Western outlook towards sex. It happens that in physical relations, one of them invites, the other is ever ready to accept, the result of acceptance is certainly the delightful encounter of flesh and finally there is the limit for man. In Tully-Corinna landscape, Rukmani's assimilation is missing, Mira's fire is extinguished, Nalini's heart is lost and Vasantha's devotion is absent.

The bed-narration decodes the forbidden landscapes which reveal that Kamala Markandaya has offered the Eastern food mixed with the Western spicy nudity. The Western readers have relished these spicy dishes with pleasure and contentment. It is said that she is aesthetic and artistic in her presentation. B.K. Das defends Kamala Markandaya saying: "She is never shy of describing sex and sensuality in her fiction. But it can be said with authority that she does not favour the vulgar display of sex. She only gives an artistic presentation of love and sex" (28). But a close scrutiny does not verify this truth. The bed-scenes that she has narrated are electrifyingly sensational. Sex mixed with love is a sacred urge while it becomes impious when it is mixed with lust. Above all, bed-narrations make Kamala Markandaya saleable in the Western gallery.

Works Cited

Allen, Mrs. Mary Wood. *What A Young Woman Ought To Know*. London: The Vir Publishing Company. Print.

Das, B. K. "Sex and sensuality in *A Handful of Rice*." *A Handful of Rice a Critical Study*. Bareilly: PBD, 1994: 28. Print.

Naik, M.K. "Post-Independence Indo- English Fiction." *Commonwealth Fiction*. New Delhi: Classical Publishing Company, 1988: 63. Print.

Parameswaran, Uma. *Kamala Markandaya*. Jaipur: Rawat Publication, 2000. Print.

Markandaya, Kamala. *Nectar in a Sieve*. New York: Signet Books, 1954. Print.

____ . Some *Inner Fury*. London: Putnam & Co., 1955. Print.

____ . *A Silence of Desire*. London: Putnam & Co., 1960. Print.

____ . *Possession*. London: Putnam & Co., 1963. Print.
____ . *A Handful of Rice*. New Delhi: Orient Paperbacks, 1966. Print.
____ . *The Coffer Dams*. Delhi: Hind Pocket Books, 1969. Print.
____ . *The Nowhere Man*. 1972. Bombay: Orient Longman (Sangam Books), 1975. Print.
____ . *Two Virgins*. 1973. Vikas Publishing House, 1975. Print.
____ . *The Golden Honeycomb*. New Delhi: B. I. Publication, 1977. Print.
____ . *Pleasure City*. London: Chatto and Windus, 1982. Print.

6

Some More Narrative Designs

Kamala Markandaya who made a niche in Indian English Fiction through her substance and techniques is now no more but her novels have become a perpetual source of inspiration to the countless women who have learnt how to explore themselves in the male-oriented society. Her novel *Nectar in a Sieve* and *The Nowhere Man* are the classics because of the depiction of the struggle of a village woman and the experiences of a man in an alien land, respectively. Before coming to any conclusion of her techniques, there are some other aspects of her narrative techniques which may be helpful in making an assessment. Some facets which are not yet explored in the earlier chapters are: 'Presentation of Dreams', 'Recollection of Remembrances', 'Stream of Consciousness', 'Dialogues', 'Monologues', 'Camera scene', 'Movie scene', etc. These are some of the facets that make Markandaya's novels a satisfactory reading from every angle. She has something for everyone. One who is fond of reading sex may trace out in her novels. One who is fond of social realism may also find it in them. Her novels make the reader social conscious and offer some issues that can be discussed further.

Let me quote two dreams one of male and the other of female to know how far they help in forming an image of women. The first excerpt is from *Nectar in a Sieve* where Nathan dreams. Sample the excerpt:

> Once Nathan cried out loudly and sprang up in his sleep. I went to him, and he woke then and clung to me.
>
> "Only a dream," I said. "Sleep, my dear one."

> "A nightmare," he said sweating. "I saw the paddy turned to straw, the grain lost....Oh God, all was lost."
>
> His voice was stark, bereft of the power of dissembling which full consciousness brings.
>
> "Never fear," I said with a false courage lest panic should swoop down on us. "All will be well."
>
> He composed himself for sleep again.
>
> "You are a good wife," he murmured. "I would not have any other." (*Nectar in a Sieve* 84)

This dream of Nathan highlights Rukmani's devotion to her husband who loves her considering her a good wife. The narration through 'Dream' is indeed a new innovation to demonstrate the character's personality. Kamala Markandaya has made her female protagonist Rukmani strong enough to instill courage in her husband's heart. She convinces Nathan with a false courage because of her own fear but she never lets him know otherwise he will be much worried. The nightmare seen by Nathan makes her worried as she already cares for the family and wishes her best to remove hurdles that come on the way of happiness of her family. To a great extent, she succeeds in doing so but there are some powers like nature over which she has no control. She asks her husband to sleep and not be disturbed by the dream convincing him that all will be well. Nathan murmurs while sleeping and his murmuring shows that he recognises Rukmani's value in family. He calls her a good wife as he gets support—moral as well as active from her. The two sentences "Never fear" and "All will be well" console Nathan while the fact is that Rukmani herself is much worried over Nathan's dream of the loss of the grain. Nathan's dream divulges Rukmani's courage and her stamina for tolerance.

Now the excerpt from *Two Virgins* is to be taken into consideration for dream-analysis. Here Saroja dreams about Devraj who tries to engage in sexual act with her. Note the excerpt:

> It was more the turmoil of her mind that slid into a dream, but it was sweeter, went further, went too far and turned

> into a nightmare. She was home, lying in the shade of the tamarind tree, watching the bright blue sky through criss-crossed fingers. Devraj appeared. She was not in the least surprised to see him, he and the country went well together. I followed you, he said. I knew you would, she replied. He lay down beside her and started to caress her. She allowed him to, she discovered she had no sense of shame in revealing, in yielding to him. Each caress was like a passing flame. The sensations were exquisite, were mounting, she could not bear them but she wanted more, she begged him to pierce her entirely and give her peace. "I will," he cried, and lunged. Lalitha appeared. She was naked, her belly was enormous but she didn't seem to mind. Her eyes were shining, rainwet, diamonds hung on the lashes. "It's so lovely," she said, "there's nothing like it when they spill their seed." Saroja burst into tears. She twisted herself away from Devraj, his sucking, clinging, spilling body. "You're killing me," he cried. "You're killing my baby," Saroja shouted at him. She woke. She was alone in the room. There was almond-milk moisture between her legs, her flesh was swollen and quivering. She wiped herself dry and got up, convinced she must still be dreaming, but in fact Amma and Lalitha were gone. Their sleeping mats were rolled up and disposed neatly against the wall. (*Two Virgins* 227-28)

This excerpt shoots the picture of Saroja's dream. The narration is on the verge of pornography which makes the reader dream. Saroja sees Devraj and is attracted towards him but does not reveal any feeling to him because she has experienced the case of her sister Lalitha who was made pregnant by Mr. Gupta. Saroja represses the feelings but they work on the mind and through subconscious they take the form of dream which displays what she wishes. In her dream, she sees Devraj and is not surprised to see him. He lies down with her and starts caressing her body. His caressing creates sensation in her body. A kind of flame is felt in her body. She bears the sensations but when she does not bear them, she begs him to pierce her so that she may get peace through sex. He becomes ready to follow what is desired by her. Then, Lalitha comes there naked and says that it is lovely when men spill their seed into the womb. Saroja is shocked and starts weeping. She moves away from Devraj who asks her to enjoy sex. She cannot leave him till climax. But she cries out stating that he is killing her baby. The two aspects—her attraction towards Devraj and Lalitha's unwanted pregnancy—which are working on her mind result in this dream.

Markandaya's narration is movie scene as even after the dream she presents "almond-milk moisture between Saroja's legs" and her flesh "swelling and quivering". To create an impression of reality, she shoots Saroja while wiping herself and getting up. Such scenes are not expected in a work of art but Markandaya feels pleasure in depicting them to the extent that they become visual to the reader who, being a man of sensation, feels pleasure inwardly though outwardly he may criticise such a pornographic scene. Uma Parameswaran writes: "I have said often enough that Markandaya's writing is very visual, as though the reader is seeing a movie" (188). But the dream of Saroja when deconstructed displays some inner qualities of her character.

It reveals that Saroja has a moral sense and knows well that it is not proper for her to repeat the mistake of her sister. She knows what happens when an unmarried girl becomes pregnant with a child. She represses her sexual feelings that break the dam and start flowing through the river of her dream. Experience is the best teacher but its fees are very high. A man who learns from others' experiences is a wise man. Certainly Saroja is wise as she learns from the example of her sister Lalitha who got knowledge of the way of the world after losing her virginity.

Kamala Markandaya has employed the technique of 'Recollection of Remembrances' which shows her path that leads her characters to the past remembrances—pleasant and unpleasant. Through this, she peeps into the past and lets the reader know what is going on in the mind of her characters. The past incidents prepare path for future action. When he recalls the remembrances to his mind, he feels wounded if they are unpleasant and elated when they are pleasant. One excerpt from *Some Inner Fury* is taken to prove the usability of the technique of 'Recollecting Remembrances':

> "A whole year lies between us, which had hardly begun when we met and is now a thing of the past, a whole struggle whose beginnings we did not see, which used us and wrenched us apart and is now best forgotten. When this is all over," I said to him—though I could scarcely move my lips, they were so stiff—"When all this is over we can still be friends." "Do you think so, darling," he said gently, and put his arms about me and held me, without passion, compassionately; and he did not have to tell me, nor I to say, that my words were foolish mouthings, fashioned out of despair, empty, and between us meaningless. And yet the first time we met I was so shy I hardly looked up until someone prodded me and I stumbled forward and garlanded him. (*Some Inner Fury* 7-8)

The narration displays the picture of Mira's love with Richard. The utterance "A whole year lies between us" shows her deep-felt pain that she inwardly feels. No doubt, it is a thing of past. Even then, her lips become stiff on uttering "when this is all over". Richard completes the incomplete utterance with "we can still be friends". Richard utters this and places her hand on her arms but there is no passion. She knows that she has sacrificed her love for the sake of her countrymen. Now, she is frank with her lover who asks her to continue friendship. She is lost in the layers of the past and picks up the moment when she met him for the first time. At that time she was so shy that she had no courage even to look his face. She was there with garland to welcome. She recalls that someone prodded her and as a result of prodding, she stumbled forward and, hence, could garland him. The narration through the technique of 'Recollecting Remembrances' opens the layers that display that in the beginning, Mira was shy and also reveals the inward pain that she felt when she left him for her country. Her country gets the upper hand over her love.

Kamala Markandaya has employed 'Stream of Consciousness' in her novels but not so as is practised by Virginia Woolf. She makes her characters lost in thought and when they do so, they dip in the river of thought flowing somewhere in their consciousness. Mark the excerpt for the flow of stream of consciousness:

> Underneath was a child's exercise book with stiff covers. He opened it, flicking the leaves and wondering which of his daughters' brilliant outpourings their mother wished to preserve, and as he did so a photograph fell out. He picked it up, staring at the face that gazed benignly back at him, his heart thumping loudly as his mind raced in mounting agitation. He did not know the man, he was sure of that. He was equally sure it was not one of his wife's relatives—after fifteen years of marriage he knew the lot. A friend then? He dismissed the thought. A married woman did not have men friends who were not known to the husband, the family. One of the girl's idols perhaps—a teacher, a film actor? Well, it might be, he said to himself, while his uncompromising mind withdrew into some forbidding fastness of its own, from where it emerged later, and again and again without cease, until at last he frantically repudiated the lie with which he had hoped to buy his peace. (*A Silence of Desire* 33-34)

This excerpt is from *A Silence of Desire* which tells the story of the domestic life of Dandekar and Sarojini. Their life is running smoothly but when he finds her absent and sees a photo that falls from the exercise book, he feels that his domestic building is slipping. Picking up the photo, he is drowned in the river of his thought. His mind feels agitation as he does not know whose photo it is. After fifteen years of domestic life, he knows a lot about her relatives. First he thinks that the photo may be of her friend but rejects the thought thinking that a married woman does not have any friend who is not in the knowledge of her husband. He is drowned in the river of consciousness deeply and there he thinks that the photo may be of her idol—perhaps teacher or film actor. He persuades himself so but his mind remains uncompromising and, hence, his mind runs to different conclusions. For the time being, he falsely rejects such thoughts in order to lie down and so may get peace. The excerpt takes the reader into the mind of Dandekar and shows him patterns that are taking place there. His suspicious nature along with the approach of the society that it adopts for women is revealed in this excerpt.

Kamala Markandaya's dialogues open the window to the mind of the characters who display their behavioural patterns.

Sample the dialogue which reveals the innate nature of Rukmani and Nathan:

> "Do you not think a man must choose his work?"
>
> "Such a man as you, yes," I replied.
>
> "What then if his wife can not accompany him?"
>
> "Cannot?" I said. "She must. A woman's place is with her husband."
>
> He sighed impatiently. "You simplify everything, being without understanding. Your views are so limited it is impossible to explain to you."
>
> "Limited, yes," I agree. "Yet not wholly without understanding. Our ways are not your ways."
>
> "You have sound instincts," he said.
>
> For the first time since I had known him I saw a spark of admiration in his eyes. (*Nectar in a Sieve* 111)

The narration in dialogic form is noted for clarity of expression as it has provided ample scope for the exposure of substance. Nathan asks Rukmani whether a man has the choice of work. She replies that a man like him has the choice. She also lets him know that a woman's place is with her husband. Saying so she reflects the traditional attitude of woman. In a male-orientated society, it is supposed that a woman's place is by the side of her husband. She cannot come out of this tradition. If she comes, she does not get the respect. He appreciates her for her way of simplifying things without understanding. He charges that her views are limited and it will not be possible for him to make her understand. She reacts to it stating that certainly her views are limited but they are not without understanding. Her ways are not his ways. He cannot understand them. Her statement shows that a man cannot understand the way of woman. Are the ways of woman so intricate that they are beyond the understanding of man? Here she tries to show her superiority stating that a man does not know a woman inwardly. But, Nathan appreciates her for wit and the way she replies saying that she has sound instincts.

Nathan's appraisal makes her see a spark of admiration in his eyes.

Kamala Markandaya has also used monologues and asides which make the reader know what is in their mind. They also show characters' mindset, and the reader is mentally prepared for their reaction to a particular situation. There is nothing hidden. If there are some secret things, they come out either through monologue or aside. Mark the excerpt for the use of the inner working of the mind of Dandekar in *A Silence of Desire*:

> There was a time—why, less than a week ago, he said to himself queerly—when his life had stretched before him even and serene, and he could say with assurance that at this time in the morning he could be in the office, that at such a time he would wake with Sarojini by his side. It was an assurance that comforted him—a certainty of living which he craved and which he had never coveted until now that he had touched the extreme fringe of its ephemerality.
>
> (*A Silence of Desire* 49-50)

Dandekar talks to himself or to his own personality in the inner room of his head. He thinks of the difference that has occurred in his life due to the absence of his wife. A week ago, it was quite easy for him to tell anything with surety. Today he cannot do so. His dream world that was based on the foundation of Sarojini is shattered by her absence. He was assured then to tell about the time when he would be in office and when he would wake with Sarojini by her side. He could tell anything but now such world proved to be ephemeral. The patterns of his mind reflect his disturbance and shock that he has felt on account of Sarojini's absence. No man wishes to come out from cosy nest woven by a wife. She is expected to weave it for her husband and for her children. She cannot come out of this nest if she wishes so. The male-oriented society particularly Indian society does not allow crossing the threshold.

Aside is equally effective to know the character. The following is the excerpt that shows Markandaya's use of aside.

> The women, she told Saroja, used her because they did not want to spoil the shape of their breasts, which suckling did. They wanted to keep them firm and round for their husbands. *Saroja wondered, if she had a husband, if she would put him or her baby first. She was certain she would never give away her milk to another woman's baby.*
>
> (*Two Virgins* 6)

The aside in italics (*emphatic mine*) takes the reader to the mind of Saroja who applies what she listens and tries to conclude how she will react to the situation if it comes to her. Manikkam's wife sells her milk for money and the women buy her milk because of the roundness of their breasts which they do not want to lose. Women are breast-conscious and want to keep them tight for their husbands. Now, she peeps into her own mind and wonders what she will do if she faces the same situation. She thinks through aside and comes to conclusion that she will give priority to her baby first and not to her husband. She will not sell her milk to any woman's baby. This excerpt shows that a poor woman like Manikkam's wife has to sell her milk for money. The rich women are conscious to beauty and do not like to feed their children for the fear of losing shape of their breasts. Saroja's goodness comes before the reader. Such experiences make her ready for the situation in future. She will not sell her milk under any circumstance. Her priority to her baby is worth noticing.

Speaking highly of the photographic quality of her novel, Uma Paremeswaran writes: "I have repeated several times that Markandaya's descriptions are photographically visual. The camera picks up exactly the right angle, zooms in to focus in sharpest detail the centre of action" (227). Kamala Markandaya has a rare ability to click with the camera of words that release the original photo. It seems that the picture that she shoots turns out to be a real picture with all its hues.

The excerpt displays the different shots taken from all angles:

> They pulled up their sleeves to show the nurse at the health center the marks on their arms, but Lalitha had

> to lift her skirts because the marks were high on her thigh. She had been done there to avoid disfiguring her arms which were shapely and beautiful. Lalitha blushed when she showed her marks, not from having to lift her skirts but because of the compliments she was paid. A lovely girl, the nurse said, such wise parents to have had her vaccinated, her lovely skin would never be pitied and scarred. (*Two Virgins* 37)

Here, Kamala Markandaya as a photographer shoots picture of Lalitha with the effect of originality. Here is the scene of health centre where everyone has to show whether he or she is vaccinated. Appa has already got his daughter vaccinated. At the centre all pull up sleeves to show marks on their arms to the nurse. But the case of Lalitha is different as she does not pull up her sleeve because she is not vaccinated on her arms but on her thigh.

Now the camera is on and Markandaya, the photographer clicks and takes shots first. She shoots Lalitha lifting her skirts. She shoots the mark on her thigh. The beauty of thigh is revealed to everyone. She is shown blushing and her blush is original. She is shown blushing at the compliments regarding her beauty. In the photo the nurse is shown praising her for her beauty. The novelist succeeds in shooting her with her camera of words and her photo gives an aesthetic pleasure. The excerpt also brings another aspect into limelight. Quite different to Saroja, Lalitha cares for beauty. Lalitha is afraid of nothing except disfiguring of her beauty. She wishes to keep the beauty of arms that are shapely and beautiful. She gets her vaccinated on her thigh and her parents are also careful of her beauty. The nurse calls Lalitha a lovely girl and her parents wise. Just as the rich women are careful of their breast, Lalitha is equally careful of her beauty and is aware of her attractions. What makes her blushing is not her lifting the skirt but the words of appreciation make her so.

Now, to take some more excerpts of male and female narrations to give the final touch will be useful in assessing the techniques used in the novels of Kamala Markandaya. First of all, I quote a male narration from *A Silence of Desire*:

> What were you doing? You say you, a married woman, were with this man in his house but you do not say why or what for. Am I not your husband, entitled to know? Or am I some kind of hireling gigolo to be told only as much as is good for him? (*A Silence of Desire* 85)

Dandekar who is suspicious of Sarojini's behaviour interrogates her. He makes her realise that she is a married woman and is not expected with any other man except her husband. He asks her what she was doing with the man. He makes her remember that he is her husband and, being a husband, he is entitled to know about her whereabouts. If she does not let him know, what is he to her? Is he only a hireling gigolo or libertine? The excerpt clearly reflects the dominating nature of Dandekar, who while living in male dominated society, talks only of rights over woman. His jealousy is quite clear here as he cannot tolerate his wife with any man. It also reflects that Sarojini has not shared the secret with her husband. If she had shared, it would have been better.

Note the excerpt from *The Golden Honeycomb*:

> You do not have to worry about that either....I'm not a nun, no one expects me to live like one either, not around here. I find for myself, I have to. Do you understand? (*The Golden Honeycomb* 283)

This is narrated by Jaya to Rabi. Rabi enjoys sex with her at her provoking. When he comes to himself, he realises that he has committed sin by copulating with Jaya. When the excerpt is deconstructed, it reveals Jaya in her true nature. She asks him not to feel guilty over the sex-act and makes him see in practical way that she is not a nun. None expects that she will live a life of a nun in absence of her husband. She has her own way of thinking and so thinks as she wishes. Hence, he must not be conscious of the sin of sex-act. The excerpt shows that Jaya is hungry for sex as she has been living alone for the last five years. Rabi is not strong enough to resist the sexual charm when provoked.

> *Your* people. They *were*. *Now* you can count your people on the fingers of one hand and all of them are toadies. They're Rabi's people. (*The Golden Honeycomb* 401)

This excerpt is spoken by Mohini to Bawajiraj III. She is a woman of strong determination. She is determined not to marry and so does not marry. She is satisfied with her present position of being a concubine. She instills courage and patriotism in her son Rabi who fights against the British for the sake of his countrymen. She feels happy to see her son and asks Bawajiraj III that the countrymen are not his people as they have become her son's people. So far as the people who are in his favour can be counted on fingers. These men are only toadies or bootlickers. She is proud of her son who succeeds in winning the hearts of his countrymen with his devotion and work.

> A love-nest for her and her son in which you will be welcome. That's what you want. That's what you're asking me for. Why do you ask? I do not want to know. Take what you want. You will anyway. You always do. (*The Golden Honeycomb* 43)

This excerpt is spoken by Shanta Devi to Bawajiraj III. Shanta Devi is the wife of Bawajiraj III and Mohini is the concubine. She registers her protest before her husband when he asks for the Summer Palace for Mohini. She says angrily that he needs the palace for Mohini and her son. He wishes to change her palace into a love-nest. She knows his intention and does not wish to know from him. After registering her protest, she asks him to take what he wants. She also makes him realise that he always does what he likes. The excerpt reveals that Shanta Devi, in spite of being the wife, cannot stop him from going to his concubine. It also displays the possessiveness of Bawajiraj III who acts according to his whims in personal matters.

The discussion of her techniques demonstrates that Kamala Markandaya is genius in narrative techniques. On account of these techniques, she succeeds in creating a desired effect on her readers who feel spell bound by contents and narrative designs. She has touched 'First Person Narrative Technique',

Third Person Narrative Technique' 'Male Narration', 'Bed Narration', 'Photographic Presentation' 'Recollecting Recollection', 'Stream of Consciousness' and 'Interior Monologue' with equal mastery. Sunaina Kumar writers in this connection: "In her narrative methods she tends to approach Henry James in her use of reflector- characters and to Faulkner in her psychological analysis of character motivation. Her success lies in her choice of the person, the perspective and the mode of narration, and her occasional failure results from inappropriate selection and arrangement of events coupled with obscurity and allusiveness" (68).

Other minor narrative techniques like monologues, asides, stream of consciousness, recollecting recollections, dreams, camera scene and movie scene are applied by Markandaya in her novels that reveal the various dimensions of her female protagonists. Monologues and aside prove to be the windows that open to the mind which displays the conflict arising out of a particular situation which exposes the mental stamina and their approach to life. Stream of Consciousness is better used in *The Coffer Dams* that takes the reader into the deep stream of thought where, he with the character, swims though the stream does not provide him much depth to be lost completely as is the case with Virginia Woolf.

Recollecting recollections becomes a habit with Markandaya who makes her characters lost in nostalgia that makes them recall the incidents that happened in the past. Rukmani, Mira and Vasantha recall the past experiences and feel either elated or depressing according to the incidents. Markandaya has also exploited the technique of dreams in *Nectar in a Sieve* and *Two Virgins* that reflect the character's internal patterns that are the result of suppression of desires or unfulfilled wishes that work at night on consciousness. Movie Scene and Camera shots are clicked through poetic words. She makes the scene visible before the reader who feels spellbound by the quality of her shoots as they display features sharply and clearly. Hence, these minor techniques are the devices that unfold the behavioural patterns of characters.

Her core techniques: 'First Person Narrative Technique' and 'Third Person Narrative Technique' are functional in nature as they reveal the concealed motives and provide the characters particularly female ones an outlet that make them quite straightforward in releasing out utterances. Her women characters utter what they have to utter frankly and forcibly. 'First Person Narration' makes the reader associate with the character more intimately than 'Third Person Narration'. But, in 'First Person Narration', the novelist has a kind of inclination to the protagonist through whom he or she pours out his or her viewpoints.

It seems that the protagonist becomes the mouthpiece of the novelist. Rukmani and Mirabai are the protagonists who, no doubt, appeal the reader for their freshness and poignancy of feelings but sometimes it seems that it is not they but is Kamala Markandaya who is voicing her viewpoints through them. Nevertheless, 'First Person Narration' tells story in a more gripping manner than either 'Third Person Narration' or 'Stream of Consciousness.' 'Third Person Narration' is reader friendly as he finds the narration not through only one protagonist but through every character who has his or her own way of expression and, thus, stating his or her individuality. Varieties of viewpoints are provided to the reader who walks through the viewpoints of every character and not like through one viewpoint of protagonist who presents every character. Though the story telling is more effective in 'First Person Narration' because of knitting the different threads in one string, 'Third Person Narration' provides liberty to the reader. The protagonist introduces the reader with the character and leaves him. Now it is character who speaks in his or her voice with complete freedom of expression.

'First Person Narrative Design', 'Third Person Narrative Design' and 'Third Person Non-Omniscient Design' illustrate the innate goodness of Kamala Markandaya's female characters. These Narrative Techniques divulge Markandaya's female characters who are on the journey to realise and explore themselves in male-oriented society where they search for their space which is reserved for them. Rukmani (*Nectar in a Sieve*), a firm lady who adjusts and face in adverse circumstances, Caroline (*Possession*), a self-centred lady who exploits Val for her benefits, Sarojini (*A Silence of Desire*), a homely lady who is traditional but has the stamina to silence her husband when the situation demands, Mira (*Some Inner Fury*), a girl who crosses the threshold in love but retreats for her country, Helen (*The Coffer Dams*), an English woman who explores her 'self' with the tribal, Nalini (*A Handful of Rice*), a lovely woman who brings back her husband on the right track, Saroja (*Two Virgins*), a girl who resists all temptations and remains a virgin, Vasantha (*The Nowhere Man*), an Indian who lives in an alien land embracing Indianness, Mohini and Usha (*The Golden Honeycomb*), two Indian women who have potential to energise Rabi for fighting against the British rule, and Valli, Mrs. Bridie, Mrs. Tully and Mrs. Pearl (*Pleasure City*), who assert their individuality in their own way, are her women whose traits are demonstrated through the narrative designs mentioned above.

These women make the reader aware of Indian ethos and sensibility. Markandaya's women who are certainly Indian in temperament and behaviour become a spring of inspiration. She has her own limits when she presents Indian scenario. Sometimes she becomes partial in depiction of her women as Indian women. The limit is her limit of the place and the motive. For whom is she writing whether for an Indian who never likes her bed-narration or for a Westerner who is interested to know the secret of Indian women? It seems that she has written her novels with a view to keeping the Western reader in her mind. She has narrated the bed-scenes so openly that they have come to the point of pornography. She has presented "the Indian food in the western plate" and when she does so, she crosses "the limit and forgets the ethos of Indian culture in order to please the Western reader for whom she was writing" (Arora 138). In presentation of sex, she is not liked, if not hated by an Indian (who himself enjoys such shots in his mind but has no courage to talk it openly) while she becomes favourite for the Western reader who searches for aesthetic and sexual pleasure. But she cannot be overlooked only on account of her depiction of sex. One's paradise is other's hell and other's hell is one's paradise. Hence, her other merits cannot be ignored.

Works Cited

Arora, Sudhir K. *A Study of Kamala Markandaya's Women*. New Delhi: Atlantic, 2006. Print.

Kumar Sunaina. "Technique and Theme in the Novels of Kamala Markandaya." *Indian Women Novelists*. Set II, Vol. II. Ed. R. K. Dhawan. New Delhi: Prestige Books, 1993: 53-69. Print.

Parameswaran, Uma. *Kamala Markandaya*. Jaipur: Rawat Publication, 2000. Print.

Markandaya, Kamala. *Nectar in a Sieve*. New York: Signet Books, 1954. Print.

____ . Some *Inner Fury*. London: Putnam & Co., 1955. Print.

____ . *A Silence of Desire*. London: Putnam & Co., 1960. Print.

____ . *Possession*. London: Putnam & Co., 1963. Print.

____ . *A Handful of Rice*. New Delhi: Orient Paperbacks, 1966. Print.

____ . *The Coffer Dams*. Delhi: Hind Pocket Books, 1969. Print.

____ . *The Nowhere Man*. 1972. Bombay: Orient Longman (Sangam Books), 1975. Print.

____ . *Two Virgins*. 1973. Vikas Publishing House, 1975. Print.

____ . *The Golden Honeycomb*. New Delhi: B. I. Publication, 1977. Print.

____ . *Pleasure City*. London: Chatto and Windus, 1982. Print.

7

The Orient and the Occident in *The Pleasure City*

Rudyard Kipling's viewpoint vis-à-vis the incompatibility of the Orient and the Occident is now not in vogue as the magic of globalisation has reduced the space and provided an environment quite proper to the flowering of the proximity which has made them understand each other and, consequently, reciprocate the best that they have. In the present time, for a purposeful and peaceful life the materialism of the Occident is to be assimilated with the spiritualism of the Orient. It is soul, that is, spiritualism that can work better in a sound body, that is materialism and, hence, a balance is always required. It is the West that knows that it cannot be happy without the Indian spiritualism and India also needs to make her body burly with the help of Western materialism without losing the touch of her spiritual identity.

Kamala Markandaya is the leading woman novelist who has experienced both cultures—the East and the West—and, hence, as a diasporic novelist is qualified for the depiction of the state of those who survive on a foreign land while feeling alien in an alien country and bearing affliction on account of recalling the memories of the native country. To make the life worthwhile the approach of compromise is always sought and Kamala Markandaya is the best instance as she dreams of India and in her texts she offers the solution—the concept of giving and taking the best. She has become a synthesis-seeker who unites both the cultures on the basis of zero loss of identity. Calling her insider outsider, M.K. Bhatnagar writes: "She is an impressive explorer of human consciousness and of the convolutions of intimate interpersonal relationships, caught in the whirlpool of disparate and divergent cultures" (2).

As a diasporic writer she has endeavoured her best to bring East and West together in her novels and more particularly in *Pleasure City*. Her *Pleasure City* becomes the pleasure city on account of the environment that it provides to the natives and the foreigners who come together and reciprocate the best. The friendship of Rikki and Tully is the ideal one in the changed independent atmosphere. Tully, the English officer is the representative of the transcontinental consortium with the touch of modern technology. He comes to a fishing village in South India with the intention of transforming its face by building a holiday complex 'Shalimar'. The imperialists cross the threshold in the disguise of technocrats in the name of modernity and progress. Kamala Markandaya has presented them with the promise of fresh areas of understanding and co-operation and it is the only approach that can bring the East and the West together resulting in the development and prosperity of each other. It is Tully, the representative of the West who acknowledges Rikki's perception of beauty and his honesty and the sense of spiritualism that characterises Indian culture. Knowing that there is an ocean between the East and the West, Kamala Markandaya suggests the mantra that will be helpful in crossing the cultural barriers.

In *Pleasure City*, Kamala Markandaya is not as fresh as she was in *Nectar in a Sieve*. She does not talk of story but of relationships particularly relationship of the East and the West. All the different episodes in the novel are the integral parts of one theme—the theme of synthesis between the Orient and Occident. A multinational company 'The Atlas International Development Corporation' founded by Herbert Boyle is launched in independent India to build a luxury pleasure complex "which at blue print stage, with rare unity, and not entirely cynically, got to be called Shalimar by everyone concerned" (*The Pleasure City* 20). It was the corporation that never allowed "private feelings to interfere with business" and, hence, it "built anywhere, everywhere, almost anything, for anyone, with a virtuosity" (*The Pleasure City* 21). This transcontinental consortium consisted "with an admirably distilled purity, of purely technological mercenaries" (*The Pleasure City* 21). Boyle, Cyrus Contractor and Tully are the on the Board of AIDCORP. Apu, the headman has no objection if there is no harm to their water and territory. "This is our territory. The waters are ours, to a five fathom depth" (*The Pleasure City* 26).

In the name of the story, there is nothing except the bundle of the episodes. However, they throw light on the friendship of Rikki and Tully representing the Orient and the Occident respectively. No doubt, the East and the West dichotomy has been the theme of her earlier novels like *Possession*, *The Coffer Dams* and *The Golden Honeycomb* as, in the words of Lakshmi Kumari, "the area of divergence between the East and the West therefore is readily identifiable" Further, she writes:

> The East signifies a sort of orientation that cares eventually more for the inner and the unseen, the categorical and the absolute. The values are associated with, or may be interpreted as passivity, stagnation, rootedness and a kind of conservatism that seems antithetical to progress and material attainments. The West likewise signifies a skeptical; hardheaded, if not cynical, attitude towards the problems of the world (116).

Though the East is somewhat orthodox and has the touch of traditionalism, it can now pace with the pragmatic West if it approaches wiping out the prejudiced feelings. The West also can learn spiritualism from the East. In the novel *Pleasure City* she has shown the possibility of fusion of the East and the West if both reciprocate genuinely and remain unprejudiced in taking the best. The friendship of Rikki-Tully is the foundation on which she makes the castle of 'Assimilation' in a new surrounding where there is the fresh breeze of independence and identity. A.K. Bhatnagar writes:

> The friendship of Tully and Rikki is actually a friendship of moderns and traditionals in the changed environment.

> Through this friendship Markandaya points to fresh areas of understanding and co-operation between the West and the East in the post-colonial period. She suggests that this is how the two parts of the world can contribute their might of the development and prosperity of each other. (49)

D. Maya offers a fresh interpretation of the friendship of Tully with Rikki as she feels that Tully is the "decolonised Prospero returning to expiate the crimes of the past, searching for a spiritual home and place. The spiritual journey undertaken by Tully in the company of Rikki, is a regressive journey from civilisation, but a journey of progression towards complete decolonisation" (111). Now Tully has entered the Indian subcontinent to make amends to the wrong done previously and when Boyle reminds him that "the sun never set on the British Empire" he offers some flip transatlantic gibe replying, "God so ordained it because he didn't trust the British in the dark" (*The Pleasure City* 170). Actually, his grandfather's remark "My dear boy, India was never an occupied country. Mistake to imagine. They never felt that" (*The Pleasure City* 30) echo and re-echo in his mind. He has not come to dominate the country but to reciprocate what is best. He learns what he can about the sea and the fishing colony from Rikki in whom he searches all the possibilities and confides in his instinctive knowledge. He asks to make a boat that will symbolise the friendship and, in this way, he is healing the past wounds. The following dialogue reflects the unflinching faith of Tully in Rikki who equally responds.

> 'I'm looking for a boat. An old love,' said Tully; and it was. 'Will you build me one?' he said.
>
> 'Will you trust me to?' asked Rikki
>
> 'There'll be reasons not to,' said Tully, 'when you supply them.' (*The Pleasure City* 61)

Rikki is not selfish in his relations, as he believes in the bond of humanity. He presents a flower to Tully as a token of love. He tells his sister Valli that Tully is as "human as you or me" (*The Pleasure City* 73). Tully returns the boat to Rikki as he realises that it belongs to him. Rikki deserves the boat as he is the true owner and here Tully sees the whole scenario with the lens of equality. "The boat belonged to him" and he "would bequeath it to its proper owner, a proper resolution of at least one equation" (*The Pleasure City* 328). He feels sad when Tully decides to go and very emotionally he asks: "Will you come back, Mr. Tully?" Hearing this, Tully also becomes emotional and expresses his desire saying: "'I wish I could" (*The Pleasure City* 340). Now their friendship is on equal footing and it is too firm to be broken and he realises that "they shared a language that went beyond English, and was outside the scope of mere words. As, of course, did Tully" (*The Pleasure City* 340).

The crucial role in making the personality of Rikki is of the mentor, Mrs. Bridie who showers her motherly affection on Rikki. For him, she becomes such a woman as possesses "the key to locked, mysterious boxes that he barely knew existed except for the barest outlines that were showing up hazily in the distance" (*The Pleasure City* 6). She always advises him: "If a thing is worth, it is worth doing well. You must always aim to be immaculate" (*The Pleasure City* 16). She takes care of him well and sees the image of her son in him. Even after her death she is present on the screen of his mind. At the end of the novel, he repeats the words of Mrs. Bridie: "There was a time and a season, for everything. A time to sow and a time to reap" (*The Pleasure City* 341). In spite of her infertility, she is fertile as she considers others' children as her own. She presents the image of mother—Universal Mother.

Human relationship can be seen in Amma who becomes the foster mother of Rikki after the death of his parents and relatives. "Call me Amma, if you like, she said, busy with the bellows and charcoal so as not it embarrass the child. I am your mother now, and lucky to be" (*The Pleasure City* 9). Mrs. Pearl, though a Western, loves Indian spiritualism. She takes the responsibility of the infant found at the cave. Valli is helpful to her parents and brothers—Muthu and Rikki. She is more co-operative to her foster brother Rikki than her real one Muthu. Rikki saves Corinna from the currents of water but while saving her, Rikki is hurt. In the end, Corinna realises her mistake and repents for it. "I am sorry, Toby. About Rikki, I mean. It was unforgivable. I must have been mad" (*The Pleasure City* 317). She fails to go into the depth and peep into the hearts of Indians. "She would never know Rikki, or perhaps the country he was bound up with, were equally outside her reach" (*The Pleasure City* 318). She fails to find out the key to the heart that leads to human relationship. She presents a weak image of the relationship. She is self- satisfied and wishes to live in her own world without caring for others. Mrs. Contractor is very practical lady who advises her guests what to do, where to go and what to eat. She is very polite in her treatment when the guests thank her for her precious advice and care, she tells them: "Would you not do the same for me if I were a stranger in your country? No, no it is nothing it is simply do unto others" (*The Pleasure City* 151). Mrs. Lovat wishes to write a book about India. She says: "It is just that your country fascinates me. I'd like to find out as much as I can, that's all" (*The Pleasure City* 154). She feels more comfortable in Rikki's company. She is indebted to him for his active co-operation. When she goes away, she does not forget to wish good health for Rikki. "I want to finish my book. And don't be surprised; she said archly. If you find yourself in it" (*The Pleasure City* 333). Hence, human relationship is breathed almost by every character in the novel *Pleasure City*.

But this human relationship has the Janus faces—one that is optimistic and co-operative while the other face is darkened—darkened with deep desire that has a glimpse of the possession. Now the ghost of the Occident once again has appeared in the pleasing shape of a gentleman with the new brand that can be named 'Neo-colonialism' as M.K. Bhatnagar writes: "Pleasure City seems a more sustained and simple study of the historical process of neo-colonialism through the coming together of a sensitive Britisher and an ingenious Indian villager" (4). These imperialists once possessed the land, now they have come with the intention of colonising the mind so that the Orient may become slave mentally. "The same old imperialists at it again only this time disguised as technocrats. And they saw their case proved by the balance sheets" (*The Pleasure City* 22). The multinational companies like AIDCORP are exploiting in the name of 'White man's burden'. In adjusting himself to the local custom, Tully reflects the mentality of the Occident of exploiting the Orient emotionally. The disguise of gentleman is for the benefit of the Occident, not for the natives. "Empires, on the whole, are not won or run for the benefit of the original inhabitants" but these empires, "like any commercial enterprise, operate for the benefit of the shareholders" and aborigines are "shunted off into second place" (*The Pleasure City* 22).

The Occident is aware of the magical power of English language, which is the only way to colonise the mind. If the natives are taught in English language, they will be uprooted from their own indigenous culture. The English language will make them realise of their inferiority and with this concealed intention, Benjamin and Mrs. Bridie guide the fisher boy Rikki through the Western education that makes him see with the world with the Occident lenses. Cultural hegemony through the English language becomes the objective of the Occident and herein lies their conspiracy of alienating the Orient from its culture in order to acknowledge the supremacy of the Occident.

In the post-Independence era, the permission of the Indian Government to AIDCORP to build a pleasure resort 'Shalimar' proves to be a curse as it becomes responsible for the displacement and the poverty of the natives of the village close to the coastline of the sea. Rikki, the protagonist is "a fisherman's son" who "lived by the sea with a fisherman's family" (*The Pleasure City* 41). The natives here live by the fishing; they feel happy and eat well when there is good season but they remain hungry when the fishing is bad. At the advent of the AIDCORP, they are lured to pledge their services and the free fishermen line up to turn into coolies in order to save themselves from hunger. The novelist presents the poignant picture of the fishermen saying: "Day after day the catch burned out poor. They ate so meagerly; the cramps were beginning. These were not unknown, but good seasons made them forget. The suicidal mackerel had spoilt them all" (*The Pleasure City* 56). When Rikki expresses his desire: "Wish there was more to eat,' Muthu very tartly replies to him, "Who doesn't?" (*The Pleasure City* 56). After hot talks, they quarrel. Their sister Valli knew the reason: "when the boats came back empty it could happen that men flew at each other like fighting cocks" (*The Pleasure City* 57). When there is skimpy catches as "The sea is in no mood to give anything" (*The Pleasure City* 61), the poor state of the natives forces them to join the Shalimar as labourers. Very pathetically and realistically, the novelist presents the scenario:

> Rikki hummed. He did not wish to reveal the extent of their dilapidations, which were going from bad to worse, and were now spectacular. With prices shooting up every day it was inevitable—unless one had opted into Shalimar. Those who were in could afford far above what they were used to. Those who baulked, like Apu, could not afford even the minimum they had been accustomed to buy (*The Pleasure City* 65).

The poor natives were leading their lives without stir sharing among themselves their joys and sorrows but Shalimar polluted not merely the environment responsible for the poor catches but also their joys and made them slaves. The infant that is found in the cave is the result of the ill effect of the so-called progress and it shows the trade of the flesh alluring the victims with the power of money.

To think of synthesis leads one to utopia, which displays impracticability of the concept. No doubt the text focuses the friendship of the Rikki and Tully, i.e., of the Orient and the Occident but there are many instances that prove it to be a myth. Tully tells Rikki the reason of taking over the country: "Why we took over your country, to impose our order on what seemed to us your confusion" (*The Pleasure City* 79). Tully is not in favour of staying too much in the country as there is, he says, "That ever-present danger, or temptation. It alters people" (*The Pleasure City* 79). Though Tully is inspired by the spiritual remarks of Rikki who makes him see the whole ocean in spite of the cactus and lets him see two sides of the same face that look "serenely on creation, preservation, and destruction" (*The Pleasure City* 83), Tully finally admits before Rikki that there is an ocean between them. Rikki himself feels the division:

> between them, between one man and another, their minds, their reach and sway, the reality of the distance between himself and Tully. Distance? Notes of incredulity sounded as well. Distance between them, chipping at marble in the pool room together, sharing the light, and emotions? Where was the reality, what was vapour? Presently he had to lay down the chisel and simply sit, wondering, looking full face at Tully. (*The Pleasure City* 147)

But the myth is demythologised soon when in spite of admitting an ocean between them, Tully wonders: "For was there an ocean? Really? Actually? His incredulity echoes Rikki's". He becomes aware of the feelings—touching feelings in the inner conscience and these feelings were not to subject to corruption. Now his vision is quite clear and he feels something that "washed over them like water or light, and merged them into the one landscape" (*The Pleasure City* 147).

Pleasure City becomes the bible of assimilation of the Orient and the Occident on the basis co-operation and mutual understanding without losing their identity. No doubt there is an ocean between them but it is the touch of the water that makes the two shores realise their unity. Kamala Markandaya has presented the mantra saying: "A two-way deal, getting to know one's fellow. Advancing beyond language to contemplation. Contemplating another human, most complex of beings, each engaged in a voyage of discovery no less strenuous, or ravishing, than a physical adventure" (*The Pleasure City* 81). Synthesising on the basis of the concept of discovering each other's affirmative virtues and without being prejudiced, their assimilation is the only solution that will lead them to the path of progress, peace and prosperity without affecting the roots of each other's culture. The myth of cultural hegemony of the Occident over the Orient is only a myth and will never translate into reality.

Works Cited

Bhatnagar, Anil Kumar. "East-West Encounter." *Kamala Markandaya A Thematic Study*. New Delhi: Sarup and Sons, 1995: 49. Print.

Bhatnagar, M. K., ed. *Kamala Markandaya: A Critical Spectrum*. New Delhi: Atlantic, 2002. Print.

Lakshmi Kumari, "A Pleasure City: The New Frontier." *Kamala Markandaya: A Critical Spectrum*. Ed. M. K. Bhatnagar. New Delhi: Atlantic, 2002: 116. Print.

Maya, D. "The Discourse of Resistance: A Reading of kamala Markandaya's *Pleasure City*." *Kamala Markandaya: A Critical Spectrum*. Ed. M. K. Bhatnagar. New Delhi: Atlantic, 2002: 108-115. Print.

Markandaya, Kamala. *Pleasure City*. London: Chatto and Windus, 1982. Print.

8

Bombay Tiger: A Posthumous Feast

Kamala Markandaya, after the publication of *Pleasure City* in 1982, was thought to have said goodbye to Indian Novel in English, to which she gave a new dimension at the time when it was quite new to the Indians, particularly women. But, a lover of literature can never be silent. It happened with Markandaya who continued writing even after *Pleasure City*. Thanks to her daughter Kim who "discovered the finished typescript of a new unpublished novel *The Catalyst* alias *Bombay Tiger*." Charles R. Larson's "The introduction", replete with personal touches, offers the life-story of Kamala Markandaya right from the beginning to the end in flashes. "Reading *Bombay Tiger*", Larson believes, "twenty years after Kamala Markandaya began writing the novel is a kind of revelation—especially for what it says about contemporary India." He further adds: "Her sense of India was always extraordinarily vivid, filled with rich vitality, and imaginative in the way of all great writers (and especially novelists) who have been connected to place. Ganguli, the main character and the inventive force of her narrative, is emblematic of so much of his country's economic transformation that began in the mid-1980s" (xvi).

The Bombay Tiger is based on Ganguli (earlier known as Gokhale) alias the Bombay Tiger who displays his superiority to all, including Narahari Rao. Rao's family includes his father Thata (Shankar), Mrs Rao, son Seshu, daughter Nalini, daughter-in-law Shakuntala (Sakku), grandson Pompom, the cook Kesav and tutor Miss Teresa Pinto. Ganguli's family includes his wife, daughter Chandralekha and son Rajiv (named after Dr Rajiv Pandey). Kothari, the lawyer is the common friend to both the families. Kothari's daughter Manjula is the friend of Chandralekha, Ganguli's daughter. The novel is divided into five parts: 'Leaves from a Family Album', 'Power Game', 'The Film, 'Landscape with People and Passion' and 'Duel'. It begins with Seshu's request to his father Rao for giving the car to bring his friend Rajiv from airport. Rao, though in the beginning reluctant, allows him to take it. Seshu asks Butalia, the driver to go to the airport from where he receives Rajiv. Rao welcomes him though asks him to take the family as it is. Mr Rao and Mrs Rao think of Rajiv as a right match for Nalini, "a remarkably plain girl" with "somewhat bottom heavy" (16).

Rao comes to Bombay first, Ganguli later. Ganguli belongs to a village which is "on the outskirts of Srirangapatnam, once the capital of Sultans" (17). Both get education under the guidance of Pandit Pandey who teaches Mathematics, Sanskrit and History. While teaching History, he tells how and why the subcontinent of India was empowered by the Britishers. He tells them citing greed and stupidity saying: "Their greed, Our stupidity" (17). Ganguli, "a roughneck water buffalo" does not like it and so reverses it in future. Rao who is like a "sleek, slender dolphin" (17) is proud of himself and his knowledge but later on it is Ganguli who gets upperhand on him. Both differ in their approach and method. Rao whose method is "fine scale and judicious" reserves "his paeans for Dalhousie" (19) while Ganguli who pounds away "like a battering ram" (19) appreciates "the peerless Robert Clive" (19). Rao thinks "miniature and manageably" while Ganguli thinks "big" and takes the world to be the cake like Alexander. He is indeed "the bulldozer" (19) to the extent that he does not take sentiments into consideration and also neglects the advice of the school master who used to say: "If the means are bad, lad, rest assured it will end up badly" (20). Rao develops jealousy and comes to Bombay in the hope that he will be "the big fish in a big pond" (20) and leave Ganguli "behind to play the minnow" (20).

Ganguli's parents are no more and the ancestral house is burned down. He comes to Bombay with "one monumental slab of Cuddapah stone" (21). He begins with zero and soon overshadows Rao by virtue of reversing his teacher's adage from "*Their* greed, *our* stupidity" to "*Our* greed, *their* stupidity" (22). He proves to be "a trenchant, witty, barnstorming jeering performer" (22). Words like 'Purity', 'Morality', etc., are not in his dictionary. He knows that it is commerce that brings power. He becomes a 'Tiger' and roars commercially in the human jungle of Bombay. He keeps an eye open because of his "rogue brilliance" which is a product of "sophisticated market rigging" and power politics. Moreover, commercial considerations overpower the humanitarian ones. Krishna is his accountant and personal aide. When he sees that Bombay needs bricks, steel, cement and glass, he provides them and earns the title of being "cement Sardar" (25). Mathur, the cerebral and Marchandani, the first rate fixer are his partners working for him. He knows life fully because of his clear thinking that all these things are "Maya: totally enjoyable but totally unreal, the stuff of a passing dream" (26). Business and emotions are anti-poles to each other. He develops his own style and feels comfortable. He marries very late and has one daughter from his wife whom he treats savagely and possessively in the beginning but later on cares for her and develops spiritual as well as erotic love for her. When she dies, he wants to die. He realises his love for her and feels that no man can take her place. His rival Rao feels satisfied as he feels that Ganguli is "a spent force, not a river to fear" (31). But, quite contrary, Ganguli lives for his daughter and is ambitious for her.

Mrs Rao, who is less urbane, is religious by nature. She is worried about her feeble daughter Nalini. The family plans for a picnic with Dr Rajiv Pandey. The astrologer Joshi is consulted for the auspicious time to leave for their outing. Thata, Dr. Pandey, Dr Jinwala, Seshu, Pompom, Shakuntala, Nalini and Miss Pinto leave for an excursion to Elephanta. Ganguli becomes powerful because of the theory "*our* greed *their* stupidity" (52). He faces problems concerning the loan from the foreign bank that demands the application of the human rights properly. They (the foreigners) now take morality while considering business and strictly wish to have global social condition. The reality is that little girls work in factories and earn money for the family. If they do not work, the family will not have enough to eat. Mr Platt who is a good practice businessman from London likes to work with Ganguli. Greed is an essential thing for a big businessman who satisfies it through power. Ganguli gives good money to the labour and provides essential facilities including government dispensary. The foreigners fear of losing trading edge because of the cheap Indian labour. Ganguli cares for his daughter Lekha, "a skinny, cheerful and pretty child, an extraordinarily sensible creature" (62). She takes part in firm's annual theatricals and plays the role of Radha. All the workers consider Lekha as "the firm's child, not just the boss's" (63). When she is eight years old, she gets Omega bicycle, kittens, a dog and a donkey. She wishes for the doll's house at the age of ten and gets it. At the age of twelve, a voice coach teaches her how to play on sitar. A maestro comes to teach her classical dance. Her heart is in cinema. She remains at St Philomena's convent till age fifteen. In the convent, she plays the role of Mary Magdalen, the whore and this part shocked other parents. No doubt, she is "a very likeable child" and "gifted in so many ways" but scholastically she is not so.

Now, the story moves to Shakuntala whose son Pompom is ill. Sundari, the maid goes to call Dr Pandey who manages to admit the child to the hospital considering it a serious case. His timely help saves the child suffering from meningococcal infection as he is admitted to the hospital where it is treated by Dr Anwar, a senior medical officer. Dr Pandey has soft corner for Shakuntala and dreams of her being with him. But, he is surprised that Seshu is always absent at the critical time. He thinks why he should care when Seshu does not. He leaves everything to time. When he is ready to go to Pune at the invitation of Ganguli, Shakuntala who feels much obliged because of saving the life of her baby gives Pompom for the last hug.

Dr Pandey thinks that success is a result of greed—greed for power which Ganguli has in store. Ganguli admits that he is "renowned for all sorts of terrible qualities" (93) but does not have squeamishness. He has a project—the project of providing fridges to everyone. It is his dream that even a rickshaw-wala should have his fridge. Dr Pandey busies himself with his health programmes and employee welfare. The clinic is named Mahatma Gandhi Clinic which has now first rate staff, equipment and facilities. Ganguli admits that he has no conscience which is reserved for Rao and Dr Pandey's father. The festival Holi makes everyone happy and fresh. Lekha looks "fresh and lovely, absolutely radiant" (113) while Miss Pinto looks "luscious". Everyone enjoys the festival and especially the maddening dance of a gypsy girl called Zingari. Dr Rajeev Pandey becomes the centre of attraction because of his unavailability to all.

The buyer-seller friendship is between Ganguli and Mr Pratt. Manjula who went to America for space programme returns without completing it. Now, she shares Lekha's apartment. Lekha is interested in the film which she gets when Seshu introduces her to Sebastian Price who selects her after rejecting the twelve girls earlier. She is the lucky thirteen girl for Polypictures company owned by Anglo-American Film cooperative. Plat gets Ganguli interested in the film for finance. The film will be based on the life of Benjamin. Seshu works there as an assistant for the problems arising out of language in dealing with the local men.

The Dwight-Sebastian crew becomes busy in shooting the film. Lekha is supposed to do the role of a whore. Sebastian takes her to be one. He considers her to be a high class tart and out of passion she becomes one. It is Sebastian who enjoys sex with Lekha and makes her pregnant. Lekha and Sebastian decide to terminate the pregnancy. Jinji comes to Dr Pandey and shares his fear that Ganguli will come to him regarding the case of Lekha but he does not want to take it in his hand. Out of fear, he leaves Bombay for Dunkeld with his Great Aunt Nargiz. As expected, Ganguli comes to Dr Pandey and asks him to take Lekha's case but he denies. Rao feels happy when he thinks that no doubt his daughter wishes to embrace a foreign cult but has not done anything shameful like Ganguli's daughter Lekha who has brought disgrace to her father by losing her virginity. Teresa Pinto comes to visit Dr Rajeev

Pandey and somehow becomes affected out of her passion for him but both become conscious and remain as they are. As Dr Pandey refuses to abort, the case is taken by another, the result of which is that Lekha dies. The death of Lekha brings disaster to Polypictures and the people associated with it. Ganguli with his men attacks them and shoots Sebastian but unfortunately the bullet hits Seshu. Inspector Akbar Ahmed saves all the foreigners and is praised for his action. Mahatma Gandhi Clinic is also closed at the order of Ganguli who faces the trial in the court and is sentenced for five years.

During the second year of imprisonment, Mr Platt visits Ganguli. Mr Platt meets Dr Pandey and asks him to talk to Ganguli. Dr Pandey meets Ganguli whom he tells that he has a son—a son from Zingari girl who shared the secret with him. Kothari, the lawyer searches for the Zingari girl and finally succeeds in finding her and the child Rajiv who is named after Dr Rajiv Pandey. He brings the boy with him and puts him at his house where he is taught the civilised way of life. Ganguli is released at the end of the third year of his imprisonment for his good action. He, though happy, has some doubts regarding the boy Rajiv who shows some similarities with Dr Pandey. Dr Pandey when he was driving loses the balance of the car which strikes the debris on the way. Sister Chatterjee lifts him in her lap where he dies. Ganguli has doubts concerning the existence of the boy. He goes to meet Dr Jinwala for confirmation about the veracity of Dr Pandey's statement. Dr Jinwala advises him for DNA testing if he doubts. Rao becomes a shrunken man because of the death of Seshu while his wife becomes a stoic and thinks that all have to die one day. Ganguli wishes to sell the land of clinic to Ajoy Chakravarthy but decides to talk to the boy Rajiv first. To his surprise, the boy Rajiv refuses to sell it and requests Ganguli to reopen the Mahatma Gandhi Clinic. Hence, Ganguli acknowledges that he never backs away from battle and so is mentally prepared for the fight against the boy Rajiv as he used to fight with Dr Pandey.

Kamala Markandaya is aware of young men's infatuation for the foreign countries. The young men, who go there for studies, think of settling there. For the sake of materialism, they do not hesitate even in bartering their souls. Rao thinks the same about Rajiv Pandey. He says:

> Our young people go abroad, they become so enamoured of what they see that they lose their *souls*. No, it's no exaggeration to say they barter even their souls for whatever trinkets Western society dangles in front of them—and I've no reason to suppose Rajiv is an exception. (5)

Later, quite contrary to Rao's opinion, Rajiv settles in India and serves the poor people. Rao is not happy when he finds his son reacting to what he says. He thinks that denigration of the uppercastes or opposition to someone's views is the modern fashion which the young generation follows without caring for the sentiments of the elders. He is pained to see that the old men are not respected in the modern society. Though he talks to Seshu in a complaining manner, he generalises the case stating:

> ...it's the modern fashion to denigrate the uppercastes and classes. But is it wrong to cherish certain values? I'm sorry but it is a fact that we have high standards. Rightly or wrongly we believe in upholding them. Naturally it is upsetting when the younger generation—I don't speak for myself, I am a man of the world—but for our elders ...white hair...Show them some respect. (7-8)

In India, it is believed that the male member will light the pyre of his father. A man without a son thinks himself unlucky and cures the life that he leads. Pandit whose wife died without leaving a son thinks of marriage for the second time only because of his consideration: "who would light his pyre..." (5). Rao who has a son feels proud of himself for having "the male fruit of his loins" (32) while his competitor Ganguli, who is blessed with a daughter, wonders: "who was going to light *his* pyre, when the time came" (244). Manjula also feels that in this male-dominated society, the male organ is the only thing that is wished for. When Lekha becomes pregnant, Ganguli,

Manjula thinks, wishes to take a chance of delivery. For him, life is a gambling. Out of this gambling, he flourishes his business. That is why "a sonless man like him would have jumped at the chance of a male heir" that will be "virtually his salvation" (212). Kamala Markandaya knows the fact that in India the birth of a son is a good sign and an occasion for celebration while the birth of a daughter becomes a matter of sorrow.

The Bombay Tiger Ganguli, Charles R. Larson observes, "is often bigger than life, almost unbelievable in his mercantile obsession" (xvi). The tiger roars commercially without the sentiment of morality. Morality and commerce are poles apart for him. He needs power, which comes from money. Money can never be got with morality which, he thinks, is changeable. He declares:

> Morality, he declared, was in any case mutable. Power dictated where the boundaries lay, and power shifted them as expedient. And where was power rotted? Why, in commerce of course! That was plain even to a one-eyed fool. (23)

This tiger eats the flesh in the form of money. For him, money is "the only yardstick to measure up people" (24). He knows that it is shameful when the foreigners comment on the poverty of Indian people. But, he cannot blend emotion with business. He is a capitalist to the core and feels proud of himself to be such. He is a man without conscience, which for him is a "rich man's bane" (100). He is so selfish that he does not hesitate even to pollute the planet if it is a question of profit for him. He asks Dr Rajiv Pandey to look around him in order to see that "to live is to exploit—it can't be helped" (111). He does not mind to employ the unskilled labour particularly women and children for his benefit. He knows their poverty which is to the extent that if they do not work, they will die from hunger. The white fellows fail to compete before the Indians because of the availability of the cheap labour. Hence, regarding the loan case they always put the condition of not employing the child labour so that the Indians may not get cheaper labour. Ganguli tells about the real fear of the white people:

> Then they're all bothered and righteous and they've more or less accusing us of running a sweat factory, sweated labour etcetera; though what bothers them actually is unfair competition, meaning they're dead scared of losing the trading edge to our cheap labour. (57)

People are poor and, hence, all the members—men, women and children—work. With the help of the acronyms like EMU, ECU, GATT, etc., the rich and powerful imposed tariffs which resulted in the decline of the cottage industries. It resulted in the employment of the poor people in the factories. Neela, a girl, who was injured, also worked in Ganguli's factory. "The family would go hungry if she did not work—in a factory that employed child labour because it was cheaper" (137).

Ganguli does not believe in Gandhian ideals which will give him nothing except showing the way to the jungle leaving everything to the people like Platt. It is not proper to copy the white men. It is only trade that can give the opportunities. He shares with Dr Rajiv Pandey the secrets of his success in the business:

> You see, I'm not like some fools, I'm a self-made man—made in India, not like you posh fellows half finished off abroad. But that doesn't mean I'm one of those donkeys we seem to breed in this country who say foreign is bad and home-made always good, under every conceivable circumstance. (152)

He dreams of providing "fridges for everyone" (153). It is not only his dream but his ambition also. He believes in himself and so promotes the home-made things. The West does not wish to see the East as prosperous and peaceful. What is best for the West becomes the worst for the East. Technology has come first to the West and, then, to the East. How can the same technology be harmful to the East? How can the East be responsible for the pollution? The West has the right but when the East uses the same technology, it is held responsible criminal. What is banned in the West is declared fit for the third world. Ganguli makes Dr Pandey aware of the conspiracy of the West:

> Each one: each one of those millions packed with technology that had been declared unsafe in the West because it spewed out fluorocarbons that punched a hole in the ozone ceiling. Technology that was bad for the First World, but okay for the Third. (155)

Ganguli also shares with Dr Rajiv Pandey that the demand of the white men will keep the fridge away from the reach of the poor:

> Let me tell you what price they want, Raj. They demand royalties or every friendly CFC we use, which will put fridges forever out of reach of our rickshaw-walas, even our scooter and moped-walas if we don't watch out. (159)

Rajiv Pandey, who got education in the foreign country, believes in the White man's burden. He is thankful to the priest who taught him "decent English" (200). He has also learnt "how to act by conscience" (200). He is indebted to Father Benjamin for teaching the values and making him what he is. No doubt, colonialism is over but, he believes, "there's a spiritual colonialism going on here" (201).

Bombay Tiger is masculine in spirit and, hence, dominates all including women. No doubt, the tiger Ganguli is influenced by his wife first and then by his daughter. The canvas of the novel is decorated by women like Chandralekha, Manjula, Miss Teresa Pinto, Shakuntala, Zingari, Radha, (Kothari's wife), Sundari (Shakuntala's maid), Amrit (wife of the Mayor Chetty), Mother Josephine, Vedavalli (maidservant of Mrs Rao), Neela (patient), Miss Chatterjee, Miss Mehta, Nargiz etc. But, out of them, only Chandralekha, Manjula, Shakuntala, Miss Pinto and Mrs Rao impress while others are not so vividly sketched. The Bombay Tiger is not sentimental because of his business that never allows him to be a man with heart.

Mrs Rao is quite philosophical. She makes her husband Mr Rao understand about the theory of karma. When he thinks that he is responsible for the condition of his son, she says: "Nobody can do that, why torment yourself? Only Fate. It is our karma, that is all" (256). She believes that a man always remains in the world though he may die physically. She convinces Teresa that Dr Raj is dead physically but he is everywhere. It is her Indian faith that makes her say:

> 'But he is not gone,' said Mrs Rao gently. 'We all have to die, which of us won't? But why do you think Raj has gone? He is everywhere. In the earth and the air around us. We are never bereft, you know. Rao sahib says Seshu is gone from us, we have lost him, but I tell him that is only an illusion.' (314)

It is Radha, Kothari's wife who, in spite of being "artless, ill-educated girl" reads "countless virtues into virtual illiteracy" because for her "the domestic arts of thrift and housekeeping" are proper to a woman. She is traditional not modern like her daughter Manjula.

Kamala Markandaya is an expert in the presentation of the forbidden landscape. While presenting such scene, she keeps in her mind the Western readers who enjoy the Indian spice and Indian beauty. *Bombay Tiger* is no exception in matter of sex. It also portrays the forbidden landscapes which is dotted with red colours. It is man who shows his masculinity to his wife at the first night. It may be because of his nature of proving his superiority over her. She seems to be only possession or commodity which is just a means of enjoyment and releasing lust. Ganguli when he meets his wife for the first time does not waste time in talking or any other thing. What he does is that he pounces upon her like tiger to eat her flesh. He is on the verge of a brute in his treatment with his wife. He becomes violent in copulation to the extent that it seems to be a rape.

> On their wedding night, out to prove himself, possessed, still, by brute ambition, he had taken his wife savagely.

> And continued to do so, throwing the doll of a girl on the bed without wasting time on preliminaries and more or less raping her; he was set on demonstrating something—masculinity, or power, he wasn't sure. Sometimes his violence bewildered him.
>
> The girl bore it all remarkably, without a word of protest, going to her family for help only after weeks of enduring her husband. (29)

The body becomes a commodity which he exploits to the full. Later on, he discovers that masculinity is "a two–edged sword" that incorporates "feminine and creative" (30) force. He coaxes his "shy girl-wife out of her shyness" and makes her learn "the refinements as well as the boisterous carnal diversions of marriage". This results in "a spiritual and erotic love, liberally dusted with tenderness and divine comedy" (30). His wife becomes a part of him but alas she dies leaving a daughter behind. Her death shatters Ganguli to the extent that he thinks of making an end of his life. This Bombay Tiger, who, for Manjula, is "a bit frightening, perhaps even a bit overpowering" (121) is tamed by his wife and later by his daughter Lekha.

The most sexual scene is between Lekha and Sebastian who out of passion enjoy sex which results in pregnancy. In the film, Lekha is supposed to play the role of a whore. She is natural in her acting. She is the thirteenth girl, the last one who was selected for the role. She combines "all the elements" that he wished for. When she performs before Sebastian, he takes her to be a tart. When she is selected, she feels elated. Happiness turns into sorrow when the reel life becomes real life. Manjula presents the scene when Lekha becomes a victim of a victimiser.

> It was inevitable, given that overheated pit Sebastian ran…And the man himself was compulsive, he was the complete package, burning eyes, thick skin, black hair all over the place, and whenever the picture started sticking, tense like wire. He gave you the impression of a grenade primed to go off. Only a single pin held it together, take it out and he would explode.

> You could say he virtually exploded into Lekha.
>
> In the name of checking out the performance he wanted out of her and that she was already giving and it was pretty hot stuff, sizzling—I mean I was *there*! A lot of it was alfresco so I *saw*! (211)

Kamala Markandaya becomes bold enough to declare virginity as syndrome created by man out of fear. The virginity syndrome is a part of sex-politics played on the fair sex in the name of purity and faithfulness. All the restrictions are on women so that they may not go astray and men remain free to go where he likes. Even, Mother Josephine, a nun becomes rebellious in her opinion regarding the chastity belt given by man to woman for her restriction.

> Well, chastity belts, one can be fairly confident men invented them on behalf of women, to preserve them from harm...Ill-conceived, possibly, But so—one must give credit—so poignant, when you think about it. (65)

This is virginity which is considered pious by men. Ganguli's competitor Mr Rao feels happy that his daughter, though not beautiful, is pious as she has not brought disgrace to the family by losing her virginity. Virginity is the pearl that is lost by Ganguli's daughter Lekha. Once a girl loses her virginity becomes impious to the extent that a man does not think of marriage with her. Rao states:

> But at least there was one blessing. His daughter, unlike Ganguli's had not sunk so low, had not so utterly disgrace her family, by losing what he would call that pearl beyond price, her virginity. That remained intact. It was more than Ganguli could boast. What man now, thought Rao with a mountainous relish, would marry the great man's daughter? (225)

Manjula also believes in independence for women. The battle for the independence that is begun by the city matrons should be seen in wider perspectives. She boldly supports women's independence:

> Nevertheless, all the city matrons fussing like hens—over that basic bottom line, our independence. Which surely must be seen as a microcosm of the larger, world concept. (103)

It is surprising that men are free to choose any girl from anywhere for his enjoyment or for sex. He is not interrogated. Ganguli is a man with power. He can pick a girl from anywhere. She may be a gypsy or any. Girls are always restricted and given no choice. Women are considered to have saintly characteristics. They are programmed to without their choice of making programme. Mark the excerpt for the revolutionary spirit that comes out of the unequal treatment to sex:

> What we meant was he could access if he felt like it: kerb-crawl, to be crude. Granted, it was unthinkable that a man of his class would seriously tangle with a girl off the streets, a gypsy- come-lightly. Whereas where was the harm if he picked that little Zingari or Lambani or whatever nosegay on the side? Men have always felt free and girls have always tagged along totally forgiving, like saints, they're programmed to. And anyhow, wasn't he a professional, with every kind of prophylactic answer tucked under his belt? It was entirely understandable, we nodded knowingly, we were very—streetwise. Though actually how little we knew! I for one, *Miles* off, and in a totally different direction.
>
> As for that girl—Burst out of nowhere and back into who can tell what and where. Story of human life in a nutshell. (125)

Kamala Markandaya surprises the reader when she declares like Shaw that it is woman, not man who takes initiative. She thinks that men are controlled because of a kind of moral taboo that they feel. Rajiv Pandey is persuaded by many women but he remains as he is. She makes Manjula think what she herself thinks:

> My thinking is that men are generally a bit too inhibited. There's some kind of a moral taboo that holds them back, they're not brave enough yet to tamper with that, and besides, they'd have the mamas to reckon with. (209)

Mark the excerpt for Manjula's love for Lekha that tells a different story that offers a clue to lesbianism:

> But naturally it made her popular. There was a lot of good feeling going for her, real fondness. Including form me, actually. But I wasn't just fond of the girl, I guess I loved her, and people may smile—I mean a more hetero pair that the two of us you can scarcely imagine—but that's how strongly I felt. (208)

Again, here is an excerpt that shows the love of the Bombay Tiger Ganguli for Dr Rajiv Pandey despite their quarrels. For the tiger Ganguli, Rajiv Pandey is his better-half. Such remark again smells of homosexuality.

> Much of this Ganguli sensed. His instincts were active; the tycoon had never given up citizenship of the commons, it was his wealth base and he knew it. Only, knowing more than most, he had a sneaky suspicion that truth to tell it wasn't him alone, he and the doctor *both* had a hand. They were rolled into one, and Raj had been his better half: which nobody sensible or rational would ever credit, and neither did he, in his robust moments.
>
> Now there came a feeling. Not to take on this better half. A bone warning. (322)

Kamala Markandaya is not as fresh as she is in *Nectar in a Sieve* that makes the reader spellbound with its narration. Her syntax is not correct as it is in her earlier novels. It seems that she does not wish to be chained in grammatical ifs and buts. She crosses the boundary and runs in the open field. Now her sentences may be of one word or two words or many words. It can be of one line or of many lines. Here are two excerpts that display her structural patterns:

> But there was an air. He continued to feel these youths were less jokey. Got in the way. Were unhelpful. Were rude. There were incidents. Just when things were moving, and this difficult priest was working out, felt Sebastian viciously, the bloody country had started playing up. (248)

> ...
>
> And yet, and yet...everything in him still yearned for her, she was everything he wanted in a woman. Everything about her confirmed it, spoke of a wealth of loving and giving. Everything he perceived in her contributed to a precise definition of womanhood, with all its riches and distinctions made flesh in her simplicity and freshness, her soft flesh and its fragrance, her clear eyes and tender mouth and nape revealed by the brief, low-cut cholis she often wore and the way she always did her hair, twisting and piling the heavy coils up with hairpins and combs to hold these riches. He could tell it would descend precipitately, like a lovely waterfall, dark and glistening, when the tortoiseshell props were taken out at night. He had even, once, seen it come tumbling down, flowing like heavy silk over his burning hands. (204-5)

These excerpts display the sensuous words which are on the verge of poetic expression. Sometimes, she also packs her lines with images and symbols that make the idea clear and easily understood. The use of prisoners and gecko make the text rich with symbols that offer meanings other than the surface ones.

> The car stood steaming in the portico, and soon its two prisoners emerged. (12)
>
> Rao stared glassily at the ceiling where a gross gecko was guzzling off his houseflies. Its stomach was black with corpses, bodies were visible piling up under the hideous yellow skin, but still it kept on snapping. (16)

She has used a new technique often used by the playwright through the chorus. She seems to offer commentary either on what has happened or what is to happen. Here are the three excerpts that become almost chorus like and the reader makes himself mentally prepared for the story.

> It is clear from the foregoing that Ganguli at this period had problems. But so had Rao, because his agent provocateur, alias Dr Pandey, had vanished. (74)
>
> ...

> At this point, clearly, the two men, Rao and Ganguli, both for their own reasons, badly wanted to get hold of Dr Pandey, who being holed up in Pune had no inkling. (84)
>
> ...
>
> Both men, Ganguli and Pandey, were at this time immersed, Ganguli with his grant project, Pandey with his clinic, which in his view was coming along very nicely indeed. (134)

Kamala Markandaya has also used Indian words like 'Chalo! Airport, jaldi!' (8), 'Arre Rao-ji!' (39), 'ek dum' (56), 'Jaane do, Sister' (300), 'Arrey, these film-walas' (171), 'jhopad-patti-walas' (176), 'badam halwa', 'masal dosai', 'paisa', 'feringhees' (57), 'thai-thakka-thati-thai' (70), 'chutney', 'puris' (105), 'chup' (151), 'bhai' (154), 'tola' (156), 'topi' (158), 'samosas' (162), 'tamasha' (174), 'huh' (177), 'pulau'(196), 'pyjamas' (199), 'salaam' (208), 'swastika' (226), 'puja' (227), 'dhobi' (227), 'ayah' (240), 'dupatta' (244), '*Bas*' (278), 'lunch dabba' (311), 'chillarh' (34), 'paan-supari' (35), 'nimbu pani' (42), 'brahmachari' (56) etc., which make the reader feel the Indian atmosphere. But, the abusive words also enter her world though such words are not expected and particularly when a woman is writing.

She makes Lekha say "Behenchod" (69). Dr Rajiv Pandey declares: "Why should *he* fucking care if Seshu didn't" (80)? The Zingari girl says: "the police behenchods are never satisfied" (285). Kothari when he hears the Zingari girl replies: "I am not police behenchod" (285). In her world, the officer state frankly: "The maaderchod would have boarded the next plane—they can't take the punishment—before he could lay one finger on the girl" (276).

Bombay Tiger is a posthumous feast for Kamala Markandaya's readers who are not disappointed because of the magical feats that are shown by Ganguli, the tiger whose roaring does not frighten, rather makes them spellbound. Charles R. Larson tells the secret of Ganguli, the Bombay Tiger stating that he "dominates the novel by his sheer audacity whether as business mogul, lover, parent or barely domesticated animal on the prowl. In its narrative force, its kaleidoscopic vitality, even its dazzling comic tone, *Bombay Tiger* becomes Markandaya's sometimes disturbing summation of late-twentieth-century India" (xvi).

WORKS CITED

Markandaya, Kamala. *Bombay Tiger*. New Delhi: Penguin/Viking, 2008. Print.

Larson, Charles R. "Introduction." *Bombay Tiger*. New Delhi: Penguin/Viking, 2008: v-xviii. Print.

9

Social Consciousness through Postcolonial Lenses

The recurrent material that makes literature a true representative of the society is reality. It is reality that determines a work relevant or irrelevant to the present-day scenario. Great literature expresses not merely the external landscapes that are apparent but the inner landscapes that reveal longings, aspirations and motives of the people of the time. It is not the representation merely for the betterment of the people living in the society but for the evolvement of the culture that gives a meaning and way of life for explorations of their personalities. Literature which does not reflect this tendency is not serious one. Socio-realism is the foundation on which the building of life is built. Social consciousness as a tool is employed in the domain of creation and criticism. Creation is mixed with realism. The very first question raised by most of the critics is that how far the creative work is socially relevant and what contribution it will make in the field of social realism. The controversy over the aim of art—for art's sake or for life's sake—is still in fashion. Art for life's sake gets the upperhand. Hence, to study any work of literature in the context of social realism is in vogue. In India, after the independence, critics put a postcolonial mirror before a literary text in order to see its image.

Before tracing out the image of social consciousness through the postcolonial lenses, it is mandatory to comprehend the concept of postcolonialism. Historically, postcolonialism, as the term suggests, is the period after the independence from the colonial rule. It is "a set of theoretical approaches which focus on the direct effects and aftermaths of colonisation" (www.altivasta.com). It refers to ""different forms of representations, reading practices and values" (Rai 1). G. Rai states: "Postcolonialism is an enterprise which seeks emancipation from all types of subjugation defined in terms of gender, race and class. It does not introduce a new world which is free from the ills of colonialism; it rather suggests both continuity and change" (Rai 2). Hence, postcolonialism studies the aftereffects of response and resistance to the legacy of colonialism in the field of philosophy and literature and presents the identity of the colonised and its culture representing the un-represented and voicing the un-voiced with a post not available in colonialism (Arora 30).

India got freedom from the British rule in 1947 and the post-independence era, better known in the imported brand as postcolonialism, provided a milieu for the people to be free from all kinds of subjugation—be it personal, financial, intellectual or social. *Swadeshi* culture was promoted resulting in the expulsion of *videshi* one. The earlier colonised who suffered a lot now explore their identity with a feeling of belongingness with native culture. Native culture depends on various factors which have their own particular marks. Postcolonial lenses offer them an image from different angles. The British went away from India but left memory—memory of exploitation, memory of superiority and memory of a way of life—that has entered the mind of the Indians who find it deposited to the extent that it cannot be wiped out in spite of their wish. Somewhere, it has become a part of latent tradition that is imprinted in the name of modernity and forwardness. In *Two Virgins*, the boys show the image of social transformation when they remark: "Society generally but especially Western society, which is a spreading thing, one cannot escape it" (*Two Virgins* 67).

The landscape of social consciousness becomes well-defined when it is taken into focus through the lens of postcolonialism. Personal, financial and psychoanalytical are interfused to make the fabric of social consciousness. All the things that make the person aware of the society enter the domain of social realism. People care for the society as they live in it and explore themselves while living in it and outside it, they cannot think of their existence. The very statement "What other people will say?" haunts them day and night and makes them social conscious to the core. The psychoanalytic theory of Freud has the seed of social responsiveness as it represents the struggle of the individual between the two extremes—the family and the society. An individual has the instinct and impulses that he wishes to translate but the family and the society react to his wish and ultimately he has to mould himself in accordance with the norms. Social Darwinism leads a man on the path of progress with the hope that one day he will be superior to others in status in the society. The wish to show himself superior to others makes him so arrogant that he thinks himself superior socially and others inferior. He applies the theory of "otherness" and places himself on the top of social hierarchy. The postcolonial lenses focus the scenario and display it in the true light. "Transference, displacement, and alienation constitute the postcolonial experience of not only of the Indians settled or born abroad, but also of the Indians in India due to the Western impact" (Ramakrishna 116). The Western impact that has gone into the psyche of the natives makes them alienated and displaced even in the postcolonial era. This is the colonial legacy that has entered the spaces of memory never to wipe out and, hence, comes to work consciously or unconsciously.

Kamala Markandaya's graph that begins from rural India in *Nectar in a Sieve* shoots up to make up 'Shalimar Complex' in *Pleasure City*. Her career from 1954 (*Nectar in a Sieve*) to 1982 (*Pleasure City*) demonstrates a linear progress that can be traced not only in the structure but also in the texture of the novels. It is she who makes her protagonists socially aware and also develops social Darwinism in them so that they may vie with the male counterparts in the male-oriented society. Struggle which may be of body or of mind makes her protagonists move on the safe path—the path which leads to the society where certain norms are followed and where they can explore themselves to reach the peak of social status. It is she who makes them socially alive by virtue of offering them certain qualities that help them in order to fight for the right of being person and not merely possession. It is she who has depicted her love for India particularly rural India even while living out of India. Dr. A.V. Krishna Rao observes: "Kamala Markandaya's novels, in comparison with those of her contemporary women writers, seem to be more fully reflective of the awakened feminine sensibility in modern India as she attempts to project the image of the changing traditional society" (55). It is she who, with her realistic touch, female-identity stance, the diasporic feelings isolation and rootlessness and wonderful knack to adjust in the changing scenario, makes her novels a vehicle for presentation of social realism. Though sometimes she becomes partial in presentation because of the Western readers in her mind, she has done her job in making her characters not only socially conscious but also socially constructive. Let us see through postcolonial lenses how far her novels depict social consciousness.

Kamala Markandaya's *Nectar in a Sieve* mirrors social consciousness in true colour as it reflects the Indian patterns of life. In Indian society, a woman is supposed not to call her husband by his name. Rukmani calls her husband only husband because of the social code that applies in the Indian society. Mark the narration for her awareness for the social conduct that is expected from her: "It was my husband who woke me—my husband, whom I will call here Nathan, for that was his name, although in all the years of our marriage I never called him that, for it is not meet for a woman to address her husband except as 'husband' " (*Nectar in a Sieve* 9-10). Her father chooses a man like Nathan because he is not so rich to get a rich and handsome husband for her. Her mother is not happy with this below match.

Beauty and dowry play a significant role in the choice of a husband. Rukmani does not have these two things as she admits frankly: "I was without beauty and without dowry and it was the best she could do" (*Nectar in a Sieve* 8). When she hears the talks of the people about her own and Kunthi's marriages, she does not react too much and considers that the two differ as Kunthi is undoubtedly beautiful while she admits frankly that she is not so pretty. She is glad because she considers that Nathan, who is beneath her, loves her but Kunthi is not so lucky in this sense. Mark the passage for the reflection of difference that Rukmani makes between her and Kunthi: "She had, everybody said, married beneath her. Perhaps they said that of me too but I was plain and she was pretty, so it didn't make sense in her case. For myself, I am glad I married 'beneath me,' for a finer man no one could have had; but possibly she was not so lucky" (*Nectar in a Sieve* 13-14).

In male-dominated society, a woman who bears children particularly male ones is respected. Girls are not welcomed as people think that it is a male baby that makes a family tree grow. When Rukmani bears the female child, tears come to her eyes as every woman dreams of a boy for her first issue. "I turned away and, despite myself, the tears came, tears of weakness and disappointment; for what woman wants a girl for her first born" (*Nectar in a Sieve* 19)? Later she goes to Kenney so that she may bear a son. She states to him: "I have no sons," I said at last, heavily. "Only one child a girl" (*Nectar in a Sieve* 24). The birth of a male child brings happiness to the family and even her own father comes to bless the child. Rukmani is conscious of these social realities. She says: "My husband was overjoyed at the arrival of a son; no less so, my father. He came, an old man, all those miles by cart from our village, to hold his grandson" (*Nectar in a Sieve* 24).

An Indian is always conscious of his or her status and, hence, keeps in mind some functions like birth, marriage, home etc. that display the social status. Rukmani, who is aware of the way of the society, begins to save some money from the point of view of Ira's marriage so that she may spend it in keeping view of her status. Dowry, though an evil is taken into consideration. Mark the excerpt for saving money for Ira's marriage: "Every month I put away a rupee or two against the time Ira would be married. So we still could not grumble" (*Nectar in a Sieve* 28). Beauty is the endowment that is always considered from marriage viewpoint and is helpful for the less amount of the dowry. Old Granny convinces Rukmani that Ira is "endowed with beauty," and "It will make up for a small dowry—in this case" (*Nectar in a Sieve* 40). After marriage, if a woman who does not bear children is not respected and declared 'barren'. Ira, despite "a good wife and a comely one" (*Nectar in a Sieve* 65) is returned to the family because "She is a barren woman" (*Nectar in a Sieve* 54). Her husband tells Rukmani that he has waited for five years and states: "She has not borne in her first blooming, who can say she will conceive later? I need sons" (*Nectar in a Sieve* 54). Even Nathan, Rukmani's husband does not blame Ira's husband as he is socially conscious of the fact of having children. "I do not blame him," Nathan said. "He is justified for a man needs children. He has been patient" (*Nectar in a Sieve* 54). When Ira is cured of barrenness, Rukmani goes to Ira's husband but it is too late. He says: "I have waited long and now I have taken another woman" (*Nectar in a Sieve* 65). Barrenness becomes a curse in case of a woman and makes her socially insecure and inferior.

A girl when she comes to puberty is not allowed to go freely out of home as she becomes the centre of many young men who eye her with lust. Freedom is given to the boys but girls if they go outside go with their brothers. Mark the words of Rukmani: "I think the end of my daughter's carefree days began with the tannery. She had been used to come and go with her brothers, and they went whither they wished" (*Nectar in a Sieve* 33). When Rukmani is warned by Kali who comes to her to tell that it was the right time to look to Ira, she shares with her husband: "She is maturing fast." "Do you not see the eyes of the young men lighting on her? If you are careful you will not find it easy to get her a husband." But Nathan does not listen to such pleas and believes that his daughter is beautiful but not wanton. "My daughter is no wanton," Nathan replied. "Not only men but women look at her, for she is beautiful" (*Nectar in a Sieve* 34). But the same Nathan scolds her and calls her a strumpet the moment he comes to know that she parades every night (it does not matter that she does only to keep away hunger from home) as he fears what people will say. Mark the heated conversation that takes place between daughter and

> "I will not have it said—I will not have you parading at night—"
>
> "Tonight and tomorrow and every night, so long as there is need. I will not hunger any more."
>
> "Like a harlot," he said. "A common strumpet."
>
> (*Nectar in a Sieve* 103)

Due to hunger that intends to take the life of her younger brother, Ira is compelled to sell her body. The change comes in the form of tannery that takes away the peace not only of Rukmani but also of the village as it is turned into town. For Kunthi, tannery is a boon as it makes her socially conscious that she is not now a village woman. She states: "The tannery is a boon to us, Have I not said so since it began? We are no longer a village either, but a growing town. Does it not do you good just to think of it?" (*Nectar in a Sieve* 50) But, to Rukmani, tannery is not a boon as it has snatched away peace from her life. She states: " As for living in a town—if town this is—why, there is nothing I would fly from sooner if I could go back to the sweet quiet of village life. Now it is all noise and crowds everywhere, and rude young hooligans idling in the street and dirty bazaars and uncouth behaviour, and no man thinks of another but schemes only for his money" (*Nectar in a Sieve* 50). Hearing it, Kunthi does not feel good and calls Rukmani "senseless peasant woman." A villager has to live less in hope and more in fear. Hope and fear are the "twin forces that tugged at us first in one direction and then in another" but it is fear that embraces a villager as his life totally depends on vagaries of nature. "Fear" is the "constant companion of the peasant" (*Nectar in a Sieve* 83). She tells: "Hunger, ever at hand to jog his elbow should he relax. ...Fear; fear of the dark future; fear of the sharpness of hunger; fear of the blackness of death" (*Nectar in a Sieve* 83). It is Nathan who accepts the upper hand of Rukmani: "You are a good wife," he murmured. "I would not have any other" (*Nectar in a Sieve* 84).

It is not binding that a man who lives in a foreign land feels the diasporic feelings. A man while living in one's country may experience the diasporic feelings when he or she is uprooted from home. Rukmani and Nathan feels uprooted and displaced when they are asked to vacate the hut and land. Sample the excerpt for the diasporic feelings of alienation and displacement:

> This home my husband had built for me with his own hands in the time he was waiting for; brought me to it with a pride which I used to better living, had so very nearly crushed. In it, we had lain together and our children had been born. This hut with all its memories was to be taken from us for it stood on land that belonged to another. And the land itself by which we lived. It is a cruel thing, I thought. They do not know what they do to us. (*Nectar in a Sieve* 137).

Kamala Markandaya's *Some Inner Fury* is the fury of Mira's inner heart that feels for the lover Richard but takes the side of Indian people. It is Mira, the protagonist who joins the club-culture as she is socially aware that she has to marry a man of her class. She says:

> I went because I was taken; and to learn to mix with Europeans. This last was part of my training, for one day-soon – I would marry, a man of my own class who, like my brother, would have been educated abroad and who would expect his wife to move as freely in European circles as he himself did. (*Some Inner Fury* 24)

No doubt, she is forward, yet somewhere she is Indian at heart and, hence, this training of club culture does not help her from feeling shy when she presents a garland to him: "And yet the first time we meet I was so shy I hardly looked up until someone prodded me and I stumbled forward and garlanded him" (*Some Inner Fury* 8). The postcolonial lens focuses her mind that reflects the different inner patterns that display that one has to return to the society of which he or she is a part. She knows that one can explore only in the society in which one lives.

> And it was our life, by our own choice, by being born when we were, even, if one were so minded by destiny. We

> created it, as much as it created us; belonged to it as much ... To keep our peace we would have to go back then to the world from which we come, to which we would always return because it was a part of us even as the earth was of these others who stayed, we could no more renounce it than a bird the air, or fish the sea, or any other creature its element.... (*Some Inner Fury* 192)

Social consciousness is awakened in her and in the end, she leaves Richard, her lover for her country. Mark the narration for the conflict and her decision to be with her people:

> Go? Leave the man I loved to go with these people? What did they mean to me, what could they mean, more than the man I loved? They were my people those others were his. ... and I know I would go, even as I know Richard must stay. For us, there was no other way, the forces that pulled us apart were too strong. (*Some Inner Fury* 285)

In India, one has to think again and again while leaving or divorcing husband but it does not apply in the West. Roshan, who has "dual citizenship" because of her birth "in one world, educated in another", divorces her husband and can remain on friendly terms with him. She never follows the destructive path of Govind as she believes that "There is no power in violence ...only destruction" (*Some Inner Fury* 126). In spite of her nurture in Western set-up, she is social in her nature and connects political freedom with social one. She lets Govind know that "Everybody is interested in freedom ... only, we do not all agree on the means to the end, as I think you know too" (*Some Inner Fury*126). The postcolonial lens shows the hidden nature of Mira's mind that works under the influence of Roshan. Freedom over body is realised when one leaves the right over it. Finally, she succeeds in establishing her identity. "She gave me chance to go and I took it; and though I left my home. I discovered at least the gateway to the freedoms of the mind and gazed entranced upon the vista of endless extensions of which the spirit is capable" (*Some Inner Fury* 71). Premala, "gentle and unassuming" is conscious of her social status and when she is married to Kit, a man socially superior in status, she attempts to cope with him in following his ways. She, who never wore shorts, wears for the sake of her husband. She feels shy even when someone including her husband looks at her naked part. Mark the passage for Premela's modesty:

> ... for she would have done anything for him- Premala came to borrow my shorts, put them in' blushing: blushed again, furiously, when Kit looked at her bare legs, for she had never worn anything but a sari. But this modesty, which is supposed to grace a woman, found little favour in Kit's eyes. (*Some Inner Fury* 53)

It is postcolonialism that has given a voice to the repressed woman, "twice colonised." Kit symbolises the image of a man who exploits woman sexually and mentally. It is he who wishes to colonise the mind of Premala by not telling anything at all:

> Kit was equally incommunicative: there is a tradition, perhaps not only in India, that the best way to ensure this is to keep them as far as possible in ignorance and so now Kit insisted, blandly, that there was nothing to tell. (*Some Inner Fury* 117)

The postcolonial lens highlights the exploiter's face of Kit who talks of certain domains in which women are not allowed to encroach and hence, considers them socially inferior. "Certain domains belong to men alone, and Indian women learn early not to encroach. Kit knew he would not have to remind Premela a second time" (*Some Inner Fury* 117). It is Kit who considers woman 'Other' and always thinks of showing his domination and over-possession over his wife whom he gives nothing. Govind puts a mirror before him to show the real image of relationship with Premala.

> "She loved you," he said, "You never loved her—you do not even know the meaning of love. You gave nothing—not even a home. You drove her to the village—you drove her to her death." (*Some Inner Fury* 240)

Kamala Markandaya's *A Silence of Desire* offers centre-periphery issue of woman. In Indian society, it is woman who is the centre as she runs the family and turns a house into a home. The proverb—"Where women are worshipped, gods reside there"— reflects her role in the family. But, she is put to periphery whenever there is a question of her identity. When a man hides something from his wife, nothing happens. If a woman like Sarojini hides something, many question marks rise against her character. The postcolonial lens reveals the policy of dual dealing in case of woman. A man like Dandekar differs in conception and execution regarding woman. It is he who believes that Indian women are different from the western ones. "Our women are not like that. They do not flaunt themselves in front of men either before marriage or after. They are brought up differently" (*A Silence of Desire* 24). She is expected not to have any male friends without the knowledge of her husband.

One day when he misses her at home, his suspicious mind starts working and it results in making conclusion that "all women are the same" after hearing the remark of Joseph that "Women are sly cats, you never know what they're going to be up to next" (*A Silence of Desire* 37). He expects only traditional qualities in a woman and so praises Sarojini for having them. She is "a good wife, good with children, an excellent cook, an efficient manager of his household, a woman who still gave him pleasure after fifteen years of marriage, less from the warmth of her response than from her unfailing acquiescence to his demands" (*A Silence of Desire* 7). But, an action taken without husband's consent brings an earthquake of suspicion which ruins the confidence and faith between them. He feels isolated and is not confident now as he used to be. He makes a shower of questions and claims for being husband. This questioning spirit is not only of Dandekar but of many Dandekars in the society. Kamala Markandaya is socially conscious when she makes Dandekar ask questions:

> What were you doing? You say you, a married woman, were with this man in his house but you do not say why or what for. Am I not your husband, entitled to know? Or am I some kind of hireling gigolo to be told only as much as is good for him? (*A Silence of Desire* 85)

Kamala Markandaya uses postcolonialism as a means to voice her female protagonists. It is she who instills courage in the spirit of Sarojini who ultimately interrogates her husband and shows that she is not merely a possession as he thinks of but a person who has her own individuality. "You listened to the office gossip and you spied on me" (*A Silence of Desire* 72) and further she rebukes him stating: "But you have eyes. If you wish to see you can. See for yourself—there is nothing to stop you" (*A Silence of Desire* 73). Sarojini is aware of Dandekar who never believes in the healing faith theory. Hence, she does not let him know about the treatment of her growth through the healing technique of the Swamy. She does not confide in the Westernised hospital that seems to her only monster who will take her life.

When the Swamy puts courage in her, she gets the inner force to face the knives and doctors. "I'm not afraid now of knives or doctors; or what they may do? All will be well. He said so. Her face was confident" (*A Silence of Desire* 218). Finally Dandekar, who earlier remarked "a soiled woman is no good to anyone, not even to her children" (*A Silence of Desire* 71), has to accept Sarojini's importance in the family. He states: "My wife is part of me now—I did not realise it in all the years it has been happening, but I know now that without her I'm not whole" (*A Silence of Desire* 140).

Kamala Markandaya's *Possession* Caroline's possession over the mind of Val and through mind over his body. It is she who on the name of Whiteman's burden exploits Val intellectually and physically. When she buys the boy from his parents, she puts her hands round him to show that he was her possession. "Caroline must have known at once she had won for she put her arm round the boy, as it were taking possession of him in full view of his family" (*Possession* 20). She feels proud in introducing Val to the public with the words: "I discovered him in a cave. Oh yes, a real one. In India. Hideously bare and uncomfortable, except for those superb walls. And Val of course" (*Possession* 125). She belongs to those people who "do not easily give up what they think are their possessions" (*Possession* 198) and hence, frankly says to the Swamy:

"Valmiki is yours now, but he has been mine. One day he will want to be mine again. I shall take care to make him want me again: and on that day I shall come back to claim him" (*Possession* 232). Ellie, a twenty-year Jewish girl bleeds within as she has been "a victim of European crime in European confine" (*Possession* 73). As she is orphan, she knows that she has no social status: "She had no parents, no state, no passport, no papers none of those hollow stacking blocks on which the acceptable social being is built. Her one asset was that she was trained and fully experienced domestic help" (*Possession* 72).

The novel *Possession* is different from other novels of Kamala Markandaya in this respect that it is not a man who exploits a woman but a dominating woman who exploits a man. Once again the issue of central and periphery becomes alive and Caroline's superiority is traced everywhere. Even Val accepts her exploiting nature: "She does not care for me. She cares only for what I can do, and if I do it well it is like one more diamond she can put on the necklace round her throat for her friends to admire: but when I do nothing I am nothing to her, no more than a small insect in a small crack in the ground. It was not a slip of the tongue, a manner of speaking: it is what she thinks of me when I am as I am now" (*Possession* 55). Val is put to periphery as a design of Caroline's conspiracy.

Kamala Markandaya's *A Handful of Rice* depicts the genuine picture of the society as the postcolonial camera through its lens shoots life covering its dimensions—love, hunger, lust and social reputation in the tradition set-up. In India, a strict watch is kept on the girls and if they wish to go anywhere, they are not allowed to go. If allowed, a male member goes with them. In the Western society, girls are free not only to move anywhere but to take decision also. Such behaviour becomes shameless if any traditional girl imitates the modern Western girl. Ravi knows such social customs and is aware of the way of the society. There is reference to social consciousness regarding the strict control on the unmarried girls. Mark the excerpt: "Ravi had sisters and so he knew the strict watch that was kept on young unmarried girls in their community, in all communities except shameless ones like the Europeans" (*A Handful of Rice* 40).

Ravi dreams of Nalini and feels that he will be socially secure if he makes her his wife. He thinks of buying a house that will be turned into home by her and, then, he will get socially reputation: "If I had a wife, he thought as he ate, she would cook for me, it would like this every day—but what had he to offer to get himself a wife?—I'll buy her a little house, small but nice" (*A Handful of Rice* 11). The novel exposes the social concerns of Ravi who comes from village to the town but remains hungry and unemployed and finally comes in touch of Nalini who provides him a social status by turning him from a ruffian to a gentleman. It is the magic of her personality that Ravi becomes "a respectable house holder, a decent citizen with a decent job and a wife to support" (*A Handful of Rice* 25). It is Nalini who makes him realise that they are poor and hence, should not think of high class. She makes him socially conscious of their own class and asks him to be satisfied with what they have. Mark the excerpt: "You are getting high and mighty; putting yourself on a level with high-class folk. How can we ever be like them? Why can't you be content with what we have?" (*A Handful of Rice* 75) Further she speaks to him in a realistic tone: "Such ideas. Do you think we are grand people? Is not this good enough for us?" (*A Handful of Rice* 77) She cannot tolerate the insult of her husband and does not like anyone to call him a vagabond. "I just don't want to hear them calling you vagabond again, that's all" (*A Handful of Rice* 77). The novel also highlights Jayamma who does not care for being raped by her son-in-law when he asks for pardon. It shows that she is not morally sound but is socially manipulator as she succeeds in marrying her daughters without giving any dowry. Her meanness concerning her moral degradation is traced here in this excerpt: "What for last night? Do you think I care about that? Who cares what goes on between four walls?" (*A Handful of Rice* 223)

Kamala Markandaya's *The Coffer Dams* offers many interpretations that may be social or political or cultural or economical ones. Postcolonial lenses when are centred on it uncover many covered things. Clinton, who has come to India to build a dam, is more a builder than a human being. It is he who thinks himself superior to the natives and hence, suffers from social arrogance. He does not allow his wife to mix up with the tribals but she explores her 'Self' through them connecting her with them in a bond of relationship. She states: "It's nothing to do with age. I just think of them as human being, that's all. You've got to get beyond their skies, darling. It's a bit of hurdle, but it is an essential one" (*The Coffer Dams* 12). It is she who scolds her husband for the indifferent attitude towards the non-white. She does not suffer from white man's superiority syndrome. She lectures her husband: "Don't human beings matter anything to you? Do they have to be a special kind of flesh before they do" (*The Coffer Dams* 105).

The postcolonial lens goes deeper in her heart and displays the thought process of her mind that does not have any yardstick to differentiate people. "These people aren't different class, they're like me, like people like me. What is for me, is for them, there's no other kind of yard stick that's worth anything" (*The Coffer Dams* 49). She makes Bashiam realise that she is an ordinary lady and asks him not to call her a memsahib as she has never been a memsahib. She does her best to make Bashiam and others secure regarding the social status and in this way, never lets them feel inferior before an English lady or man. "Look at me, I've never been a memsahib. You're not some kind of freak to me. We're alike, we're freaks only to the caste. We come from not to each other" (*The Coffer Dams* 136). She believes that the tribals are themselves responsible for their condition as they do not protest. She incites Bashiam stating that he is called 'Jungly wallah' an uncivilised man. She blames him because he belongs to the tribals and has done nothing for them. What is about their social status when they do not have their own residences? They do not raise voice even when they are asked to go away to the other place. It seems that the 'other' attitude has deeply gone to their mind. That's why they behave like animals and move away like them.

> "There used to be a village where the bungalows are...where our bungalow is. A tribal village."
>
> A small settlement, yes.

> When they were told to go, they went.
>
> Yes.
>
> Without protest. Just got up and walked away, like animals.
>
> I suppose you could put it like that. (*The Coffer Dams* 48)

She rebukes Bashiam for not protesting those who encroached their lands in the name of white man's burden. She states: "You were—you are—a member of that tribe. It was their land. They didn't want to leave it, they were persuaded. What did they allow themselves to be? Why did you? Without even protesting?" Bashiam takes it coolly and connects it with the history of colonisation stating: "It was past history….When one is building a dam" but instantly she corrects him saying: "'It wasn't a dam they were building. It was bungalows with a view" (*The Coffer Dams* 49). She holds the tribals responsible for their condition and if they are being exploited, it is their fault. The other Indian Krishnan is not happy with the 'other' attitude of Clinton. In spite of having all the abilities and capabilities, he is considered inferior to the English counterparts. His anger regarding social consciousness in the technical field can be traced here:

> Brush us off like flies, hurt and insult like splinters under his skin: despise us because they are experts and we are just beginning. Beginners, he repeated bitterly, barred from knowledge and power as from the secrets of a mister guild; and the memory of those neglectful years lay in deep accusing pools in his mind. But it's over now, he said to himself. Our day is coming. The day when they will listen to us. (*The Coffer Dams* 19)

The postcolonial lens discovers the revolutionary nature of Krishnan who suffers at the hand of white engineers. Rawlings considers Indians to be "an excitable breed, a quality that diminished rational behaviour" (*The Coffer Dams* 18). In male-dominated society, a woman is considered only as a possession. Clinton, though educated, thinks Helen a possession as it clear from the excerpt:

> She is mine, he said, stubbornly; why should I let her go? What I have I hold. But knew this to be an illusion, having touched the emptiness where she had fled him, so that the bolsters began to sag under the weight of knowledge. (*The Coffer Dams* 126)

Kamala Markandaya's *The Nowhere Man* is a diasporic text of alienation, isolation and displacement. It relates the story of Srinivas and his wife Vasantha who have to leave India under unfavourable circumstances. It is they who feel socially insecure and socially isolated in an alien land. 'Bread, clothes and house' are the three basic necessities that are required by a man. Absence of any one results in insecurity. A house gives a sense of belongingness to the persons who live under its roof. It is woman who turns it into home by her emotional attachment. Vasantha when she comes to an alien land feels nomadic and longs for a house that will provide her social security and the sense of owning something concrete. She states:

> There is no nomadic strain in us, that forces us to wander. Although it may well manifest in our children if we continue this vagabond existence." "...We will buy a house. "We", she said, "my family, have for generations been accustomed to living in a house." (*The Nowhere Man* 17)

She feels satisfied when she owns a house No. 5 Ashcroft Avenue which, she knows, will give her and her children a sense of belongingness.

In Indian society, the ashes of a dead person are considered sacred but in the Western set-up, only rubbish. When Srinivas throws the ashes of his wife into the river, the policeman asks him not to throw the rubbish. Mark the poignancy: "It was not rubbish," "It was my wife" (*The Nowhere Man* 41). When Laxman enquires of the identity of Mrs. Pickering, Srinivas introduces her that she is a friend who shares with him in his loneliness and manages his house well. By introducing her so, he provides her a social reputation.

Srinivas becomes a victim of racial antagonism in spite of his attempts to show his relation to the country. He is harassed and sometimes socially boycotted by men (like Fred) who think that a man (like Srinivas) has no right to live in their country. But, there are some persons who console Srinivas and make him feel comfortable assuring him that he belongs to this place as much as they belong. It is Mrs. Fletcher who consoles Srinivas stating:

> You don't want to pay any attention to Fred. He doesn't know what he's talking about. You've got as much right to live here as he has. More. Even if you weren't born in this country, Mr. Srinivas, you belong here, and don't let anyone convince you different. (*The Nowhere Man* 174)

Kamala Markandaya's *Two Virgins* is replete with social touches that affect the course of the two sisters Lalitha and Saroja. Lalitha, who thinks that "it is barbaric, not having a fridge", is indeed conscious of her beauty. She believes that it is beauty that gives a status in the society. She is very particular about her beauty. She is afraid of none except the spoiling of beauty. It is she who "would rather have died than have her beauty spoiled" (*Two Virgins* 37). She is appreciated everywhere for her beauty and her parents are so conscious of her beauty that they get her vaccinated not on her arms as it will spoil her beauty but on her thigh. When she is asked to show her marks, she lifts her skirts to show them. She blushes not on account of shyness but because of the compliments that she gets from the nurse and others.

The lens brings into light one more aspect that rich women are conscious of their breast which they do not wish to spoil because of the feeding the children. They hire poor women like Manikkam's wife for feeding their children. Mark the excerpt for breast consciousness of the rich women:

> The women, she told Saroja, used her because they did not want to spoil the shape of their breasts, which suckling did. They wanted to keep them firm and round for their husbands. (*Two Virgins* 6)

City, which adds "a certain luster" is Lalitha's passion as she wishes to explore herself only there and village where she feels suffocated becomes hell for her. She rushes to the city where she enjoys the luxury and when she returns to the village, she thinks herself superior as she has tasted the pleasure. She feels socially superior to others when she depicts the joys of the city life. For her, city is the place which will give everything. She cannot think of going back to the village which has "stifled her, her talents, her ambition" and hence, intends "to stay in the city where she belonged" (*Two Virgins* 236). Quite contrary to Lalitha is Saroja who loves village where she wishes to have roots that make her identity.

The feeling of 'Other' has been deep rooted in man and woman so much that even after independence from the British rule, they apply it in life though unconsciously. Appa always prefers Lalitha to Saroja. No doubt, Lalitha is more beautiful than Saroja but he is expected to treat both in an equal manner. He is partial to the extent that he sends Lalitha to the school of Miss Mendoza while Saroja is sent to an ordinary school. Saroja is aware of this partiality of Appa for Lalitha. Mark the excerpt for the preference: "She knew Lalitha was borne in Appa's mind more frequently than Saroja, from the number of times he brought home presents for her but forgot about Saroja" (*Two Virgins* 26). Dual treatment from Appa is painful to Saroja who wishes to be "active and vivacious and smart like her" but finds herself wanting and thinks that she is a peasant with wooden limbs. Somewhere the seed of jealousy is growing in her mind.

> Saroja had to envy her, had to admit by comparison she was a peasant, with stiff wooden limbs. She wondered if it was going to Miss Mendoza's school that made the difference, or if it all came naturally to Lalitha, who was so gifted; she concluded it must be a bit of both. (*Two Virgins* 64).

But the same Saroja is bold enough to resist the temptation of Devraj and Chingleput. Lalitha proves to be inferior to Saroja on the moral ground as she is tempted and becomes a victim of Mr. Gupta who makes her pregnant.

To have sons is the status symbol in the society. Amma goes to Varanasi to take a bath to keep a vow to have boys. A widow has no status in the society. Aunt Alamelu who is Amma's widowed sister knows the fact as she states: "I am only a widow, less than the dust, so do not torment yourself about my fate" (*Two Virgins* 29). She is shocked when she hears about Nalini's mother who is wronged because of the false news of her pregnancy, she becomes serious and tells Saroja and Lalitha: "A woman's good name is her most precious possession" (*Two Virgins* 53). Pregnancy is a good sign and is celebrated in Indian society provided that it is from socially sealed relationship, i.e., marriage. But, if it is the result of illicit relations, it becomes a sin. Lalitha is socially conscious on this issue and hence, wishes to commit suicide as she does not wish to give birth to the child. She tells Saroja: "It's sin to bring an unwanted child into this world, cracked or otherwise. It's a sin to cause suffering to an unborn child, but what alternative" (*Two Virgins* 178). Saroja speaks over pregnancy in detail concerning the social aspects related to this issue. She states:

> Pregnancy could be one thing, it could be quite another. ...If you were married and got pregnant everyone was pleased except those unfortunate women who were barren. There were little ceremonies to call down blessings on you and when the baby was born everyone came round smiling bringing little presents.... If you were not married and became pregnant that picture was quite different, it was altogether grim. You hushed it up as best you could and your baby, if ever it got born, had no future at all. (*Two Virgins* 201)

In Kamala Markandaya's *The Golden Honeycomb*, the focus is more on the political aspect than the social one. But the political aspects have their seed in the social consciousness of the people who feel rebellious when they are made aware of the present in which they are and the glorious past which they have lost by remaining as they are. Manjula, Mohini and Usha are the female characters who instill patriotism in the veins of Rabi who awakes the social consciousness in the masses that become against the British who are forced to make India free. Every woman wishes to be socially and financially secure by marrying a man. If the man is King himself, any woman will compromise for anything. Every woman wishes to be the Queen of the King. But, it is Mohini who does not marry in spite of temptations that are offered to her by the King. She is satisfied with her position of being a concubine. As she has to take care of the child, she refuses to marry. She frankly states: "I don't want to be your queen. I want to be free" (*The Golden Honeycomb* 32). Usha participates in the Non-Cooperation Movement and attends the procession and meetings in order to make the masses socially aware. She shares her feelings of the Movement with her father stating:

> It was like a revelation. We did not believe, you know never really believed how much force there could be, if you trust yourself. But there is I've never felt like that before. So powerful. All of us. All the fright gone. They couldn't have touched us whatever they did. I think they knew. (*The Golden Honeycomb* 383)

Here, in the Movement, people gather, become one social unit, recognise the power of the unit and march with the political motive. A kind of social consciousness among people leads to political consciousness. In the forthcoming excerpt, Jaya seems to be socially conscious and knows before hand what the people think about her. Hence, she asks Rabi not to feel guilty for having sex with her as none expects from her to be a nun. She does not care for the society that already expects from her to be loose in character because of her living alone. "You do not have to worry about that either....I'm not a nun, no one expects me to live like one either, not around here. I find for myself, I have to. Do you understand?" (*The Golden Honeycomb* 283) This is the negative knowledge of the society that she has beforehand and is quite conscious about it that it will have no objection regarding her personal life. It differs from person to person. She is like Jayamma (*A Handful of Rice*) who also believes that the society does not care what happens amidst the four walls. Sometimes, it happens that a person is quite awake to the improper behaviour but does nothing on account of the circumstances he is placed in. What a king does is right and no one has courage to register protest. Shanta Devi is the legal Queen of Bawajiraj III but is helpless when he asks for the summer palace for his concubine Mohini. She has no other option but to obey him. In spite of being conscious socially and morally, she remains helpless and gives what he likes.

> A love nest for her and her son in which you will be welcomed. That's what you want. That's what you're asking me for. Why do you ask? I do not want to know. Take what you want. You will anyway. You always do. (*The Golden Honeycomb* 43)

Kamala Markandaya's *Pleasure City* seems to be a "dream world in which there are no barriers of caste, colour and creed and in which human values are supreme" (Bhatnagar: 15). Here in this novel, the postcolonial lens has more power to detect and so, traces some new things which remained yet unobserved. The layers of globalisation wrap social consciousness to present it in a new brand. The knowledge of English, money power, pleasure palace and job-orientation are now associated with status in the society leading to the social understanding among people on these issues. It is Mrs. Bridie who teaches Rikki her own language English. When he learns it, he becomes quite conscious of his superiority among his own group and feels inferior among the English. The very knowledge of English becomes a means to awake in him a sense of superiority among his people and inferiority among the foreigners. What Bridie wishes to develop in him is a sense of perfection in a work. "If a thing is worth, it is worth doing well. You must always aim to be immaculate" (*Pleasure City* 16). It is Rikki who forgets neither her nor her valuable sayings like "There was a time and a season, for everything. A time to sow and a time to reap" (*Pleasure City* 341). In a society, an orphan like a widow has no place until or unless he or she is adopted. In *Nectar in a Sieve*, it is Puli who is adopted by Rukmani. In *Two Virgins*, it is Chingleput who is orphan and being orphan, he is named after the platform where he was found. In *Pleasure City*, it is Rikki whose parents die but soon is adopted by Amma who cares him like her own children Muthu and Valli. "Call me Amma, if you like, she said, busy with the bellows and charcoal so as not it embarrass the child. I am your mother now, and lucky to be" (*Pleasure City* 9). The adoption is a boon to the child as he feels secure and socially alive. Valli is in transitional phase as she is on the verge of being modern though not modern wholly. She is capable of appreciating beauty and feels herself superior to Muthu who has no aesthetic sense. She is not beautiful, simply passable and is aware of this but she improves her personality and looks divine while dancing. She serves as a sales assistant in the Shalimar Gift Shop and Emporium and it develops in her confidence to feel herself conscious of her social status. Mrs. Contractor has a professional attitude which makes her aware of her place that she has on account of her skill. It is her skill to tackle the people who come to Shalimar. She provides entertainment. Here social consciousness merges with the skill of making one's profession better than others and this feeling differentiates Shalimar from others. Social etiquettes with social feelings create a sense of pleasure among people who feel socially reputed to come there for entertainment. Her behaviour to the guest is praiseworthy. She behaves in informal manner to make them feel comfortable.

Kamala Markandaya's novels illustrate the fact of social consciousness among her characters who make a linear progress. They never behave in the same manner as they were first introduced and, hence, a kind of change is felt by the characters as well as by the reader as the novel comes to an end. The change makes them aware of a certain growth in their thought process. One thing is sure that her characters grow because of social consciousness which is the consequence of two factors—the traditional set up which they follow as they are quite socially conscious to it and the other global set-up which attracts more as it makes them more conscious than ever.

Some characters stick to the traditional set-up though they smell change while others welcome change and shake hands under the influence of the new breeze of globalisation. Rukmani, Mira, Sarojini, Nalini, Helen, Saroja, Lalitha and Valli, etc., are the characters who while oscillating between these two factors of social transformation, adjust themselves. Hence, a close focus of her novels through postcolonial lenses obviously confirms that Kamala Markandaya is socially aware to the core.

She has made her characters charged with extra energy that alerts them and motivates them to climb the social ladder with the intention of contributing something constructive to the society. It is she who has filled her women characters with enthusiasm so much that they are ready to cope with the male counterpart as they believe that it is not the man only who can contribute but the woman also and so, she makes Usha assert: "This is a revolution. Who ever heard of a revolution for men only? No, it's everyone. Men and women. They do belong to the same species" (*The Golden Honeycomb* 432).

But, sometimes, Kamala Markandaya comes out of the boundary of social confinements and depicts the forbidden landscape which is not expected from her particularly from Indian viewpoint. In doing so, she applies psychoanalytic approach and her postcolonial lens displays the naked reality which must be hidden for the sake of the sacredness of the Indian society. She may be right and may be favourite to her Western readers but not to the Indian readers who though inwardly taste the forbidden fruit, criticise it and forbid even to see, not to talk of taste. Every author has his or her lacunas, so is Kamala Markandaya. But, her presentation of the Indian society, notwithstanding her living on the alien land, is true to a great extent. It is her truthfulness to social realism that makes her a novelist of a high order.

Works Cited

http://www.Altavista.com>on "Post-colonialism Today: Theoretical Challenges and Pragmatic Issues" based on a Multidisciplinary Conference held in Toronto from September26-28, 2002. Web.

Arora, Sudhir K. "Postcolonialism: Theory, Issues and Applications." *Presentations of Postcolonialism in English New Orientations*. Ed. Jaydeep Sarangi. New Delhi: Authorspress, 2007: 29-42. Print.

Bhatnagar, Anil Kumar. *Kamala Markandaya: A Thematic Study*. New Delhi: Sarup and Sons, 1995. Print.

Markandaya, Kamala. *Nectar in a Sieve*. New York: Signet Books, 1954. Print.

____ . Some *Inner Fury*. London: Putnam & Co., 1955. Print.

____ . *A Silence of Desire*. London: Putnam & Co., 1960. Print.

____ . *Possession*. London: Putnam & Co., 1963. Print.

____ . *A Handful of Rice*. New Delhi: Orient Paper backs, 1966. Print.

____ . *The Coffer Dams*. Delhi: Hind Pocket Books, 1969. Print.

____ . *The Nowhere Man*. 1972. Bombay: Orient Longman (Sangam Books), 1975. Print.

____ . *Two Virgins*. 1973. Vikas Publishing House, 1975. Print.

____ . *The Golden Honeycomb*. New Delhi: B. I. Publication, 1977. Print.

____ . *Pleasure City*. London: Chatto and Windus, 1982. Print.

Rai, G. "Post Colonialism: Its Meaning and Significance." *The SPIEL Journal of English Studies*. Vol. 1, No. 2, 2005: 2. Print.

Ramakrishna, D. "Bhabani Bhattacharya's *A Dream in Hawali*: A Study in Postcolonial Spirituality." *Indian Writings in English*. Vol. 7. Ed. Manmohan K. Bhatnagar and M. Rajeshwar. New Delhi: Atlantic 2000: 112-119. Print.

Rao, A.V. Krishna. *The Indo-Anglian Novel and the Changing Tradition*. Mysore: Rao and Raghvan, 1972. Print.

10

Kamala Markandaya in the Postcolonial Space

Exploration of Indian Writing in English, particularly fiction, from the postcolonial angle is an obsession with the critics in the post-independence era that has provided them an environment for the critical release of their intelligence. Independence from the colonial rule in 1947 gave a death blow to the *angrazi babu sahib* image in India and to wipe out the memory of the colonial experience that touched the psyche of the Indians, the crucial movement for the promotion of *desi* (native) culture was accelerated.

The colonial period wounded the Indian consciousness and the postcolonial period provided the ointment for the wounds. The hyphenated 'Post-colonialism', though simply a historical period associated with the switching over of the power from the colonialists to the natives, became unhyphenated 'Postcolonialism', a term for the recuperation of the indigenous ethos and the awakening of the Indians to be conscious of their identity. Hence, the postcolonial writings, as Prof.D. Ramakrishna believes, echo the "relocation of the self and retrieval of the native culture from foreign dominance" (112). No doubt, the trio—Mulk Raj Anand, R. K. Narayan and Raja Rao—dominated the post-independence Indian fictional panorama but the ingenious fecundity of the women novelists could not be underrated as it gave birth to the novelists of repute like Kamala Markandaya, Anita Desai, Ruth Prawar Jhabvala, Nayantara Sahagal, Shashi Despande, Arundhati Roy etc., who portrayed the inner and outer Indian landscape with multifarious colours, the colours which were not provided to them in the colonial era with such free will.

Chronologically, Kamala Markandaya is the first major woman novelist who with her fictional spacecraft—well equipped with the postcolonial lenses viz. *Nectar in a Sieve* (1954); *Some Inner Fury* (1955*); A Silence of Desire* (1960); *Possession* (1963); *A Handful of Rice* (1966); *The Coffer Dams* (1969*); The Nowhere Man* (1972); *Two Virgins* (1973); *The Golden Honeycomb* (1977); *Pleasure City* (1982) and the posthumous *Bombay Tiger* (2008) entered the postcolonial space to explore the unexplored.

The postcolonial space allured the novelists to survey the identified as well as unidentified areas that remained unexplored because of the colonial rule that did not allow the colonised to prove the talent in any field and if the talent was made known, it was exploited for the maximum benefit of the colonialists. Kamala Markandaya exposed herself to this infinite postcolonial space and succeeded in registering her name in the list as a novelist with uncanny gift of giving expression to the woman who by virtue of her gender was considered a lifelong 'satellite' that moves round the 'planet' man. The credit goes to her for voicing against this myth and for providing an authentic place—the place of the planet—in the male oriented society. Her female protagonists show that they are not weaker in any way than their male counterparts. But when she does so, she never crosses the limit, as she is aware of the particular space where she has to work. She has lived both lives—the life of being a native due to her birth and bringing up in Indian tradition and the life of a disaporic writer as she settled in England after her marriage with Taylor. In both lives there is one thing that is common. That is her deep rootedness in Indian ethos and culture. No doubt, she lives in England she never forgets India and her people and so pens the Indian feelings with Western words. While exhibiting the Indian traditions and customs she keeps the Western readers in her mind. She becomes the Indian juggler in the land of the colonialists exhibiting her Indian feats before the Western spectators. Here lies her weakness as a novelist who fails to justify her postcolonial flight as an idea.

A close reading of her fictional texts reveals that she has done her homework to enter the postcolonial space. The homework shows her trainings of locating her identity and place, of experiencing the alienation due to displacement, of exposing the contemporary life, of voicing feelings erstwhile repressed in the colonial era, of reacting the East-West encounter and finally of assimilating the best of both East and West without losing the basic native touch. On account of this homework she launches her spacecraft towards the postcolonial space but she is not bold enough to cross her boundary and, hence, wishes to maintain her purity of 'Home' with her regards for 'Heaven.'

Kamala Markandaya's female protagonists explore their identity in the postcolonial space. Usha in *The Golden Honeycomb* echoes her points of view when she says: "Who ever heard of a revolution for man only? No, it's everyone. Men and women. They do belong to the same species" (*The Golden Honeycomb* 432). The other female characters venture the same explorations. Rukmani in *Nectar in Sieve* is the protagonist who though experiences the blasts of misfortunes discovers her own identity and makes the male world realise of her 'Self.' She locates her 'Self' in the society and searches for the values in living. She crosses the threshold in order to work for the family. Her daughter Ira searches for her ground and takes the bold step of selling her body for the sake of saving her brother Kuti from death. After the cure of barrenness, she conceives a baby (sickly albino) in one of the encounters with men and suffers the spiritual anguish from the male world. Believing in life for living, she defines and sets her own parameters of life without considering the dual code of morality of the society. *Some Inner Fury* is the fury of Mira, the narrator who is so bold that she takes her own decision whether it is of her marriage with Richard or of leaving Richard for the country, of Roshan, the firebrand freedom fighter who thinks that each one has to grapple with circumstances and has to find one's own via media to arrive at a definition of self and of Premala, a complete housewife who proves to be a misfit in the world of her husband Kitsamy. It is Premala who brings up an orphan girl to make her husband realise that she is not mere property or possession at his disposal but a woman who has her own identity. In *A Silence of Desire*, the protagonist Sarojini feels angry with her husband Dandekar who spies on her. She states her identity when she opposes him boldly: "You listened to the office gossip and you spied on me" (*A Silence of Desire* 72). And further she states: "But you have eyes. If you wish to see you can. See for yourself—there is nothing to stop you" (*A Silence of Desire* 73). Nalini in *A Handful of Rice*, though she is traditional supports her husband to come out from the immoral world through her love and care, checks his wild flights of imagination and thus with the passage of time, becomes the voice of realism and sanity. Not only Indian protagonists but the English characters also declare their identity. Helen in *The Coffer Dams* scolds her husband Clinton for showing the cruelty to the tribal people. She says: "Don't human beings matter anything to you? Do they have to be a special kind of flesh before they do" (*The Coffer Dams* 105)? Mrs. Pickering in *The Nowhere Man* also belongs to this category. In *Two Virgins*, Lalitha explores her identity in the glamour of the city life but fails miserably. Her character is a warning to the young girls not to be misguided by their beauty. Usha in *The Golden Honeycomb* has fire in herself, and with it she inspires the hearts of those who come in her touch. She reveals her anger saying that freedom struggle is not meant only for men. In her attitude, she asserts the spirit of independence. *Pleasure City* becomes a pleasure city that offers jobs to the women who experience independence and a will to do what they wish. Hence, Kamala Markandaya's female protagonists like Rukmani, Ira, Mira, Roshan, Nalini, Helen, Lalitha, Mohini, Usha, Valli etc., explore their identity and place in the postcolonial era.

"Transference, displacement, and alienation constitute the postcolonial experience of not only of the Indians settled or born abroad, but also of the Indians in India due to the Western impact" (Ramakrishna 116). Kamala Markandaya's experience as an expatriate enabled her to acquire a first-hand knowledge of the British policy of colonialism and imperialism. In order to have a first-hand knowledge of rural life, she lived in a South Indian village and observed minutely the life of villagers. Thus, her life is an epitome of the experiences of displacement resulting in alienation and rootlessness. Her protagonists reflect her own rootlessness. As she is well-versed in the depiction of both kinds of displacement—displacement due to shifting from rural to urban life and from natives land to foreign land. The displaced protagonists search for the place in imagination. But when they awake, they face the reality of displacement that is never translated into placement.

In her married life, Kamala Markandaya led a diasporic life feeling rootlessness in the foreign land and making futile search for the roots in alien culture. She hangs between the two cultures—native and foreign. She lives in 'House' but longs for 'Home'. Rootlessness becomes an outcome of this bicultural paradigm. This is clearly reflected in her novels, which present "a real slice of life as long as a man has roots, he lives and dies if he is uprooted" (Bhatnagar 58). Rukmani, the protagonist in *Nectar in a Sieve* feels uprootedness when the tannery, a villain of industrialisation, swallows up the land ensuing in the displacement of her family. She with her husband Nathan moves to the city in the hope that she will lead a better life with her son Murugan but quite contrary, she has to lead a beggarly life finally resulting in her shift from city to village after the death of her husband. In *Possession*, it is Caroline who uproots the talented artist Val from his soil for the material possessions. Val feels uncomfortable and fails to adjust in the new environment. The plant is uprooted for its native place and is planted in the alien soil. Finally, he survives in securing his soil with the spiritual self-awakened by Swamy.

A Handful of Rice exposes the failure and frustration of a youth named Ravi who uproots from his village to lead a respectable life. But as soon as he comes, his dream is over as he faces the reality of city life that compels him to be criminal. *The Nowhere Man* is said to be the poetics of displacement as it reveals the cry of Srinivas, a man of 70 who settles in England uprooting himself from India with his wife Vasantha, an ideal Indian typical wife. It is Vasantha who searches for her India, her culture but fails and, hence, remains restless and rootless. Srinivas forgets India as he takes England to be his country. "My country: I feel at home in it, more so than I would in my own" (*The Nowhere Man* 61). But he is disillusioned when Fred makes him realise that he is a foreigner. "You got no right to be living in this country" (*The Nowhere Man* 172). At last, his life in a foreign land becomes a life of "a nowhere man looking for nowhere city" (*The Nowhere Man* 174). His endeavour to realise his identity results in utter failure. *Two Virgins* represents a modern misguided girl in Lalitha who, on account of the allurement of the glamour of city life, leaves the place of her roots and suffers the tragic consequence by losing her virginity while her sister Saroja is deep rooted in her soil and, hence, is not displaced. *The Golden Honeycomb* offers the displacement of the English without their roots in India and their displacement on account of their failure in identifying themselves with the Indian soil.

As Kamala Markandaya is a postcolonial novelist, she holds the mirror and shows the social face from diverse angles. Postcolonial space provides freedom to soar, as it has set no limit. The novelist is free to articulate the silence if she wishes so. She presents commentary on the Indian scenes boldly and unhesitatingly. She feels no hesitation in showing the ugly face of the society. She sees hunger and degradation of human values. In *Nectar in a Sieve*, Rukmani and Nathan have to work as stonebreaker to keep the soul and flesh together. It is Ira who has to sell her body to save the life of her brother. It is Old Granny who dies of starvation. Nature decides the life of the peasants who ever live in fear either of draught or of flood. Ravi in *A Handful of Rice* enters the house of Jayamma as a thief to steal food. On account of this poverty he degrades himself so much that he often beats his wife Nalini. For the want of money he fails to arrange a doctor for his son who dies. Out of the greed of money the father of Val in *Possession* sells his son to Caroline for just merely five thousand rupees. *Two Virgins* is the realistic presentation of the degradation but not on account of hunger of food but hunger of leading a comfortable and glamorous life. Desire for such life leads Lalitha to the mud of immoral world where she loses her virginity. The impact of modernisation can be seen on the fishing colony where the people were still poor and to save themselves they have to work in the Shalimar Complex.

From the postcolonial space the view of the colonial rocks is clear. Nothing is hidden. Kamala Markandaya shoots the peak named 'East-West encounter' from her postcolonial camera. She shoots it from various angles—the political, the social, the human, the technological, the cultural and the artistic. The conflict in her novels is the consequence of her familiarity with the bicultural world—the native land where she was born as well as England, the foreign land where she led her married life. While presenting these two worlds she remains neutral. Anil Bhatnagar opines: "She does not show favour either to the East or the West. Rather she brings to light the various points of weakness and strength of both the cultures. Through the eyes of the East she looks at the West and through the eyes of the West she looks at the East" (29).

Nectar in a Sieve presents the East-West argument through Rukmani and Nathan symbolising the East and Industrialisation and Dr. Kenny symbolising the West. It is the West that feels disgusted with follies, poverty and silent humility of the East. Dr. Kenny scolds Rukmani: "You will suffer and die, you meek suffering fools. Why do you keep this ghastly silence? ... There is nothing in this country. Oh God, there is nothing" (*Nectar in Sieve* 48). He never likes the purification of the body through fasting. He fails to understand Rukmani and, hence, says: "Oh God! I do not understand you. I never will. Go, before I too am entangled in your philosophies" (*Nectar in a Sieve* 116). Marriage is a sacrament in Indian culture while it is a contract in the West. Dr. Kenny states: "My wife has left me. My sons have been taught to forget me" (Nectar 111). Feelings of hatred between the ruler and the ruled are sown in the *terra firma* of *Some Inner Fury*. Kitsamy is immersed in the Western culture while his wife Premala fails to imbibe the West as her roots are in the soil of the East. Govind adopts the path of violence to drive the rulers out of the country. Kit and Govind demonstrate the conflict of the East and the West. Though Richard does his best to imbibe Indian culture in him, he has to accept the concept of 'your people' and 'my people' as the fire of national movement proves to be stronger before the fire of love. The clash between Indian spiritualism and Western modernism is seen in *A Silence of Desire* that reflects the influence of the West on Dandekar. He suspects his wife Saroja who goes to Swami for the cure of the tumour. She has complete faith in the healing power of the Swamy while her husband Dandekar who has faith in the Western modernism wishes to get it cure through an operation by a qualified surgeon. The Western materialism in Caroline Bell in *Possession* possesses Val but the spiritual values of the Indian culture are so deep rooted in him that he succeeds in liberating himself from the clutches. She has a sort of love-hate relationship with Indians. In *A Handful of Rice* Ravi and memsahib reflect difference in cultural values. Kamala Markandaya exposes the shamelessness of the Europeans; she also chides Indians for not appreciating the value of time. Ravi is lured by the modern world of city life and is caught in its net. He struggles to survive but fails despite the support and love of Nalini. *The Coffer Dams* displays the encounter on the technological and human values. *The Nowhere Man* is the cry of Srinivas who has to encounter the reality that he is a foreigner in the foreign land and finally accepts that he is "an outsider in England" and in actual fact he is "of course, an Indian" (*The Nowhere Man* 243). Srinivas and Vasantha are left alone in the foreign land. It is quite an alien element as in Indian culture parents in old age are respected. *Two Virgins* is the saga of the two sisters Saroja, who leads traditional simple village life and Lalitha who embraces modern life and is deceived by Mr. Gupta. East-West encounter in *The Golden Honeycomb* is on the political level. There is cultural diversity in *Pleasure City* that is more a novel of harmonious relations than an encounter between the East and the West.

With her 'Indian soul', Kamala Markandaya sows the seed with her 'Body' in an alien soil towards the end of her life. Like Shakespeare who talks of forgiveness and reconciliation in the last stage of his life, she also offers her formula of assimilation of the East with the West that will help in understanding each other. Dr. Kenny who sympathises with the villagers, Richard who indianises himself in order to get his Indian beloved Mira, Helen who favours Indians and ties her emotional thread with Bashiam, Mrs. Fletcher who soothes Srinivas in his tragic situation are the characters who try to develop their relations with Indians sharing with them in their predicament. But the novel *Pleasure City* is a glaring instance of assimilation of the East and the West as it provides an environment to the natives and the foreigners who come together and reciprocate the best. The friendship of Rikki and Tully is the ideal one in the changed independent atmosphere. Tully, the English officer is the representative of the transcontinental consortium with the touch of modern technology. He comes to a fishing village in South India with the intention of transforming its face by building a holiday complex 'Shalimar'. The imperialists cross the threshold in the disguise of technocrats in the name of modernity and progress. Kamala Markandaya has presented them with the promise of fresh areas of understanding and co-operation and it is the only approach that can bring the East and the West together resulting in the development and prosperity of each other. It is Tully, the representative of the West who acknowledges Rikki's perception of beauty, his honesty and the sense of spiritualism that characterise Indian culture. Knowing that there is an ocean between the East and the West, Kamala Markandaya suggests the mantra of love and understanding that will be helpful in crossing the cultural barriers and developing universal brotherhood.

From the postcolonial space she uses the telescope to see the reality of alluring things wrapped in globalisation. The telescope reveals the heinous face that intends to mutilate the face of the Eastern culture. In the name of progress the West has created an elite class that would hate its own countrymen. The Britishers want to brain drain Indian so that they may forget the roots and start hating their own culture. But Rabi in *The Golden Honeycomb* makes their intention futile and with Usha and the natives he plans for future. The postcolonial lens reveals a different image of the West in the *Pleasure City*. The novel requires a careful postcolonial reading. It can be treated as a postcolonial text as the West in the guise of technocrat enters the Indian soil with the intention to wipe out the effect of native culture and to make the East totally dependent on the West. The fishing village is transformed and given a modern look by building a holiday complex Shalimar. The modern Tully makes friendship with the traditional Rikki who is provided the English education by Mrs. Bridie. Cultural imperialism is on the way. Somewhere in Tully there is the feeling of possession to possess Caliban's mind in order to make him realise of his 'otherness' and 'inferiority'. Now this Caliban is modern enough to see the reality and decide what is best for him. Now option is left to him to opt the 'other' image designated by other than him or he is to be the author of this other image. The Western serpent has entered the Eastern garden and is alluring the natives to eat the forbidden fruits in the name of the knowledge of globalisation. Now the need is to come out of this 'other image' to recognise the 'mother image' of the East.

A few words about her techniques will be indispensable to come to a final estimate of Kamala Markandaya's postcolonial flight. "Her divided loyalty", Ramesh K. Srivastava believes, "to the places of her birth and her stay is reflected in her non-committal language, which has the fusion of an ounce of East and many pounds of West, of an occasional sprinkling of an Indian in a huge heap of English words" (71). Her language becomes poetic with Indian words, sometimes reflective, sometimes figurative but it is not an Indian English like Raja Rao and Mulk Raj Anand. It caters the taste of the English, as it is purely English, such language as is used by the intelligentsia. Though she uses Indian words like *chowkidar, dhoti, ghee, jutka, bania, arák, baksheesh, pakora, shamiana, namaste, chup, tamasha, thali, nak-ke-vaste* etc., she explains them at the end of the novels. It is quite surprising that she makes her illiterate characters speak—sometimes in correct English and sometimes in incorrect English—and this mars the realistic touch in her novels. She is miraculous in her narrative techniques that make her a storyteller *par excellence*. Her effective and forceful narrative techniques that include 'First Person Technique', 'Third Person Omniscient Technique', 'Stream of Consciousness', 'Interior Monologues' and others make her narration authentic and innovative.

A close scrutiny of the fictional world of Kamala Markandaya proves that she is postcolonial in her approach and very safely she makes her spacecraft enter the postcolonial space in search of a place for her. But she crosses the limit when she offers the Eastern food mixed with the western spicy nudity before the Western readers who relish the spicy dishes with pleasure and contentment. Almost all her novels are the presentation of sex and sensuality and she takes interest in depicting the first night scene as she shows the blood, the blood of virginity.

It seems that she does so in order to please the Western readers who wish to see the Eastern beauty naked. But it does not mean that her contribution is negligible. Though she is no more today as she breathed her last on May 18, 2004, she is still alive through her novels. Her place in the postcolonial space remains uncontested even today. Her fictional spacecraft in the postcolonial space is secure and safe.

Works Cited

Bhatnagar, Anil Kumar. *Kamala Markandaya: A Thematic Study*. New Delhi: Sarup and Sons, 1995. Print.

Markandaya, Kamala. *Nectar in a Sieve*. New York: Signet Books, 1954. Print.

____ . Some *Inner Fury*. London: Putnam & Co., 1955. Print.

____ . *A Silence of Desire*. London: Putnam & Co., 1960. Print.

____ . *Possession*. London: Putnam & Co., 1963. Print.

____ . *A Handful of Rice*. New Delhi: Orient Paper backs, 1966. Print.

____ . *The Coffer Dams*. Delhi: Hind Pocket Books, 1969. Print.

____ . *The Nowhere Man*. 1972. Bombay: Orient Longman (Sangam Books), 1975. Print.

____ . *Two Virgins*. 1973. Vikas Publishing House, 1975. Print.

____ . *The Golden Honeycomb*. New Delhi: B. I. Publication, 1977. Print.

____ . *Pleasure City*. London: Chatto and Windus, 1982. Print.

Ramakrishna, D. "Bhabani Bhattacharya's A Dream in Hawali: A Study in Postcolonial Spirituality." *Indian Writings in English*. Vol. 7. Ed. Manmohan K. Bhatnagar and M. Rajeshwar. New Delhi: Atlantic, 2000: 112-119. Print.

Srivastava, Ramesh. "Kamala Markanadaya's Style." *Perspectives on Kamala Markandaya*. Ed. Madhusudan Prasad. Ghaziabad: Vimal Prakashan, 1984: 71- 92. Print.

Bibliography

Novels by Kamala Markandaya

Nectar in a Sieve. New York: Signet Books, 1954.

Some Inner Fury. London: Putnam & Co., 1955.

A Silence of Desire. London: Putnam & Co., 1960.

Possession. London: Putnam & Co., 1963.

A Handful of Rice. New Delhi: Orient Paper backs, 1966.

The Coffer Dams. Delhi: Hind Pocket Books, 1969.

The Nowhere Man. (Originally published in 1972), reprinted, Bombay: Orient Longman (Sangam Books), 1975.

Two Virgins. (Originally published in 1973), reprinted, Vikas Publishing House, 1975.

The Golden Honeycomb. New Delhi: B. I. Publication, 1977.

Pleasure City. London: Chatto & Windus, 1982.

Bombay Tiger. New Delhi: Penguin/ Viking, 2008.

All these novels except *The Golden Honeycomb*, *Pleasure City* and *Bombay Tiger* were first published by New York: John Day.

The Golden Honeycomb was published by New York: Thomas Y. Crowell. 1977. *Pleasure City* was published by London: Chatto and Windus. It was also published by New York: Harper and Row in 1983 under the title *Shalimar*.

Books on Kamala Markandaya

Abidi, S.Z.H. *Nectar in a Sieve*. Bareilly: PBD.

Almeida, Rochelle. *Originality and Imitation: Indianness in the Novels of Kamala Markandaya*. Jaipur: *Rawat* Publications, 2000.

Arora, Sudhir Kumar. *A Study of Kamala Markandaya's Women*. New Delhi: Atlantic, 2006.

Bhatnagar, Anil Kumar. *Kamala Markandaya: A Thematic Study*. New Delhi: Sarup, 1995.

Bhatnagar, M. K., ed. *Kamala Markandaya: A Critical Spectrum*. New Delhi: Atlantic Publishers, 1995.

Das, B. K. *Kamala Markandaya: A Handful of Rice*. Bareilly: PBD, 1994.

Garg, Neerja. *Kamala Markandaya's Vision of Life*. New Delhi: Sarup and Sons, 2003.

Jha, Rekha. *The Novels of Kamala Markandaya and Ruth Jhabvala: A Study in East West Encounter*. New Delhi: Prestige. 1990.

Joseph, Margaret P. *Kamala Markandaya*. New Delhi: Arnold Heinemann, 1980.

Misra, Pravati. *Class Consciousness in the Novels of Kamala Markandaya*. New Delhi: Atlantic, 2001.

Parameswaran, Uma. *Kamala Markandaya*. Jaipur: Rawat Publication, 2000.

Prasad, Madhusudan, ed. *Perspectives on Kamala Markandaya*. Ghaziabad: Vimal, 1984.

Rao, Krishna A. V. and Madhavi Menon. *Kamala Markandaya: A Critical Study of Her Novels 1954-1982*. New Delhi: BR Publishing Corporation, 1997.

Sharma, Urmila. *Women Characters in the Novels of Kamala Markandaya*. Meerut: Shalabh Publishing House, 2005.

Singh, Nagendra Kumar. *Society and Self in the Novels of Ruth Prawer Jhabvala and Kamala Markandaya*. New Delhi: Sarup and Sons, 2005.

Singh, R. A. *The Novels of Kamala Markandaya: A Study*. Bareilly: P.B.D., 2005.

Sinha, Ravi Nandan and Sujit Bose. *Three Women Novelists: Essays in criticism (Anita Desai, Kamala Markandaya and Arundhati Roy)*. Jaipur: Book Enclave, 2004.

Tilak, Raghukul. *Nectar in a Sieve*. New Delhi: Rama Brothers, 1997.

Wali, Sham Kumari. *Kamala Markandaya, Nectar in a Sieve: A Stylistic Study*. Jaipur: Printwell Publishers, 1987.

Some Selected Critical Articles on Kamala Markandaya in Journal and Anthologies

Appaswamy, S. P. "The Golden Honeycomb: A Saga of Princely India by Kamala Markandaya." *The Journal of Indian writing in English*. Vol. 6, No. 2. July 1978.

Arora, Sudhir K. "Decoding the Forbidden Erotic Landscape: A Study of Kamala Markandaya's Novels." *Indian Fiction in English Roots and*

Blossoms. Vol. Two. Eds. Amar Nath Prasad and Nagendra Kumar Singh. New Delhi: Sarup and Sons, 2007: 127-140.

____ . "Synthesizing the Orient and the Occident." *SBJES*, Vol. 4, 2008. 46-55.

____ . "Kamala Markandaya in the Postcolonial Space." *Indian Women's Writings in English*. Eds. T. Sai Chandra Mouli and Jaydeep Sarangi, Delhi: Gnosis 2008.

____ . "Social Consciousness through Postcolonial Lenses: A Study of Kamala Markandaya's Novels." *Social Consciousness in Postcolonial Indian English Fiction*. Ed. P. K. Mukhopadhyaya. New Delhi: Sarup, 2009.

____ . "Kamala Markandaya's Women through Male Narration." *Poetcrit*. Vol. XXIII January 2010. No. 1. 54-63.

Baliga, Jaya. "Being and Becoming: The Quest of Three Women in *Some Inner Fury*." *Indian Women Novelists*. Set II, Ed. R. K. Dhawan. New Delhi: Prestige, 1993.

Chandrasekharan, K. R. "East and West in the Novels of Kamala Markandaya." *Critical Essays on Indian writing in English*. Eds. M. K. Naik, et. al. Dharwar: Karnataka University Publications, 1967. (Also published by Macmillan, Madras in 1977)

Chauhan, P.S. "Kamala Markandaya: Sense and Sensibility." *The Literary Criterion*. Vol. XII, Nos. 2-3, 1976.

Ezekiel, Nissim. (Review of Kamala Markandaya's *Possession*), *Imprint*, February 1964:188-193. "Puppet Show." (review of Kamala Markandaya's *Two Virgins), The Illustrated Weekly of India*. June 15, 1975: 32.

Geetha, P. "Feminism in the Novels of Kamala Markandaya." *Indian Women Novelists*. Set II, Vol. II Ed. R. K. Dhawan. New Delhi: Prestige, 1993.

Ghosal, Madhumita, and Mehru M. Major. "The Indian Scenario in the Novels of Kamala Markandaya: An Assessment of Popular Indian Superstitions and Beliefs." *Indian Women Novelists*. Set II, Vol. II, Ed. R. K. Dhawan. New Delhi: Prestige, 1993.

Harrex, S. C. "A Sense of Identity: The Novels of Kamala Markandaya." *The Journal of Commonwealth Literature*. No. 1, June 1971.

Jain, Jasbir. "The Novels of Kamala Markandaya." *Indian Literature*. 18, No. 2, April-June, 1975.

Kumar, Shiv K. "Tradition and Change in the Novels of Kamala Markandaya." *Osmania Journal of English studies*. Vol. VII, No. 1, 1969.

Mennon, Madhavi. "Review of *Pleasure City.*" *The Journal of Indian* Writing *in English.* 11, No.2, July, 1983.

Nayar, Promod K. "Towards a Feminist Proxemics: Kamala Markandaya's *Possession.*" *Remarkings*. Vol. 1 No. 1 March 2002: 7- 17.

Parameswaran, Uma. "India for the Western Reader: A Study of Kamala Markandaya's Novels." *Texas Quarterly*. 11:2 (1968).

Parasad, Hari Mohan. "The Quintessence of Kamala Markandaya's Art." *Commonwealth Quarterly*. Vol. 3, No. 9, December 1978.

Rajeshwar, M. *Indian women Novelists and Psychoanalysis*. New Delhi. Atlantic, 1998.

Srivastava, Ramesh K. *Six Indian Novelists in English*. Guru Nanak Dev University, Amritsar, 1987.

Sudipta B. "A Feminist Perspective of Women Characters in the Novels of Virginia Woolf and Kamala Markandaya."*Indian Women Novelists*. Set II, Vol. II, Ed. R. K. Dhawan. New Delhi: Prestige, 1993.

Taneja G. R. "Deconstructing Feminism: *Nectar in a Sieve*-The Phenomenon of Change." *Indian Women Novelists*. Set II, (Ed.) R. K. Dhawan. New Delhi: Prestige, 1993.

Venkateswarn, Shymala. "The Language of Kamala Markandaya's Novels." *The Literary Criterion*. IX: 3, 1970: 57-87.

Vishwakarma, K. K. "Humanism in Kamala Markandaya's *The Golden Honeycomb:* An Evaluation." *Literary Perspectives*. Vol. 2, No. 1, July, 2007.

Williams, Haydn M. "Victims and Virgins: Some Characters in Markandaya's Novels." *Indian Women Novelists*. Set II, Vol. II. Ed. R. K. Dhawan. New Delhi: Prestige, 1993.

General Books on Indian English Literature

Barche, G. D. *Interpreting Literature A Myth and A Reality*. Bareilly: PBD, 2008.

Dass, Nobel Veena, ed. *Feminism and Literature*. New Delhi: Prestige Books.

Gandhi, Leela. *Postcolonial Theory*. New Delhi: Oxford University Press, 1998.

Iyengar, K. R. Srinivasa. *Indian Writing in English*. New Delhi: Sterling Publishers Pvt. Ltd. 1993.

Kalinnikova, Elena J. *Indian English Literature: A Survey*. Ghaziabad: Vimal Prakashan, 1982.

Khatri, Chhote Lal. *Indian Novels in English*. Jaipur: Book Enclave, 2004.

____. *Indian Fiction in English: Recent Criticism*. New Delhi: Adhyayan, 2010.

Krishnaswamy and Archna S. Burde. *The Politics of Indians' English*. New Delhi: Oxford University Press, 1998.

Mehta, P. P. *Indo-Anglian Fiction* (Second Revised). Bareilly: Prakash Book Depot, 1979.

____. and P. N. Bhatt. *The Novel: A Study in Form*. Bareilly: PBD, 1987.

Mishra, Binod, and P. J. Paul Dhanasekaran, eds. *Inventing Ties and Bonds in English: Diasporic Literary Consciousness*. New Delhi: Authorspress, 2008.

Mukherjee, Meenakshi, *The Perishable Empire*. New Delhi: Oxford University Press, 2000.

____. *The Twice Born Fiction: Themes and Techniques of the Indian Novel in English*. New Delhi: Pencraft International, 2005.

Naik M. K. *Critical Essays on Indian Writing in English*. Madras: The Macmillan Company of India, 1977.

____. *Aspects of Indian Writing in English*. Madras: The Macmillan Company of India. 1979.

____. *A History of Indian English Literature*. New Delhi: Sahitya Akademi, 1982.

Nicholson, Kai. *A Presentation of Social Problems in the Indo-Anglian and the Anglo Indian Novel*. Bombay. Jaico, 1972.

Paramashwaran, Uma. *A study of Representative Indo-English Novelists*. New Delhi: Vikas Publishing House, 1976.

Prasad, Amar Nath, ed. *New Lights on Indian Novelists in English Part 1*. New Delhi: Sarup and Sons, 2003.

____. *New Lights on Indian Novelists in English Part II*, New Delhi: Sarup and Sons, 2004.

____. *New Lights on Indian Novelists in English Part III*, New Delhi: Sarup and Sons, 2005.

____. and S. K. Paul, eds. *Feminism in Indian Writing in English*, New Delhi: Sarup and Sons, 2006.

____. and Rajiv K. Malik, eds. *Indian English Poetry and Fiction: Critical Elucidations Vol. One*. New Delhi: Sarup and Sons, 2007.

____. *Indian English Poetry and Fiction: Critical Elucidations Vol. Two*. New Delhi: Sarup and Sons, 2007.

Rao, A. V. Krishna. *The Indo-Anglian Novel and The Changing Tradition*. Mysore : Rao and Raghvan, 1972.

Sanyal, Samares C. *Indianness in Major Indo-English Novels.* Prakash Book Depot, Bareilly, 1984.

Sengupta S. P. and S. C. Mundra. *The Novel: Its Forms and Techniques.* Bareilly: PBD, 1998.

Shantha, Krshnaswamy. *The Woman in Indian Fiction in English.* New Delhi: Ashish Publishing House, 1984.

Shirwadkar, Meena. *Image of Woman in the Indo-Anglian Novel.* New Delhi: Sterling Publisher Private Ltd., 1979.

Singh, Arunima. *Persecuted Women in Indo-Anglian Novels*, Bareilly: PBD, 2005.

Singh, M. D. *Problem of Alienation in Post-Independence Indo-Anglian Fiction*, Bareilly: PBD, 2003.

Singh, Sushila, ed. *Feminism and Recent Fiction in English.* New Delhi: Prestige Books, 1991.

Srivastava, Sharad. *The New Woman in Indian English Fiction.* New Delhi: Creative Books. 1996.

Williams, H. M. *Indo Anglian Literature 1800-1970 (A Survey).* Madras: Orient Longman, 1976.

Index